# Practice of Mediation in Civil Court
## And in the Commonwealth of Virginia

### Introduction to Mediation, Process, Skills and Problem Solving
3rd Edition

Pamela K. Struss, Ph.D.
Adjunct Professor, George Mason University

Alexander B. Pais, B.S.
School of Conflict Analysis and Resolution, George Mason University

Mason Publishing

**Practice of Mediation in Civil Court and in the Commonwealth of Virginia**
by Pamela K. Struss, Ph.D., and Alexander B. Pais, B.S.
Copyeditor: Pamela D. Okosun, MLIS, San José State University

ISBN: 978-1-942695-10-3 (Print)

Book design: Aditi Priyamvara
Cover images: "Blue Winter texture," Rachael Towne, used under Creative commons License (CCBY 2.0). "Hands" photo used under Creative Commons Zero license.

**Mason Publishing**

Mason Publishing provides support and resources to the George Mason University community for creating, curating, and disseminating scholarly, creative, and educational works.

George Mason University Libraries
4400 University Drive, MS 2FL
Fairfax, VA 22030
www.publishing.gmu.edu
Printed in the United States of America

*This course is certified by the Office of the Executive Secretary of the Supreme Court of Virginia. However, please note that mere attendance at this training does not guarantee successful completion of the course for mediation certification purposes. Recommendations by the certified trainer that a participant receive additional training before continuing in the certification process will be given great consideration by the Office of the Executive Secretary in evaluating a candidate for certification. (Commonwealth of Virginia, 2011a)*

# Table of Contents

## Chapter 8: The Mediator's Character

## Chapter 9: Problem Solving ....................................................................83

## Chapter 10: Document Writing.................................................................95

# List of Tables

# List of Figures

# Preface

Conflict and disputes are inevitable because we are human. Theorists in the past viewed conflict as bad and to be avoided; it was seen as a threat to a functioning society. However we know now conflict and disputes can bring much needed change so should not be viewed as bad or detrimental to society. We are not discussing violent conflict here, which is always destructive.

The body of knowledge about dispute resolution is growing and there are many good books that discuss the process at length. This particular textbook offers one perspective of mediation in the context of practice within a civil court system and intended as an introduction to that type of practice. The civil court system provides a robust venue for practice by offering a plethora of cases and is a great place to gain experience. Some may wish you to expand your practice into family matters or into specific arenas, and this text offers a great place to launch into court mediation.

Practicing in the courts provides some insulation from concerns you would have in a new private practice; the rules and guidelines are both instructive and helpful. You will build experience and knowledge about mediation tactics in a more familiar culture and environment. Some may wish to practice internationally and are encouraged to do so, however developing a personal set of tools is easier when the culture, language and societal norms are the same as yours. Depending on the geographical location a mediator will be exposed to many different cultures and can begin building understanding of how they handle disputes and most importantly how to navigate cross-cultural civil disputes.

The 3rd edition has been revised with the addition of a chapter discussing the attributes one needs to be an effective mediator. Additionally, the role-plays have been enhanced and a few new ones added. The formatting is changed to comply with a textbook format and may be used in training or classroom settings. While some of the materials are specific to meet the Supreme Court of Virginia's mediation certification requirements it largely meets the knowledge base required of a mediator-to-be in training.

# Chapter 1:

# Mediation Introduction

# Mediation Introduction

**Objectives**

- Understand basic conflict terminology;
- Understand causes of conflict;
- Become familiar with your conflict and mediation style;
- Know the difference between dispute and conflict.

This course is designed to acquaint the student with a basic knowledge of the anatomy of disputes, conflict, and mediation. The participant will understand conflict, its sources, nature, conflict styles, mediation and its styles, and appropriate resolution methods. By the end of the course, students will:

- Understand their personal conflict style;
- Understand their personal mediation style;
- Recognize the styles of conflicting parties;
- Prepare and conduct a mediation session;
- Provide an orientation to mediation for the parties;
- Facilitate a meaningful exchange between the parties;
- Help the parties recognize their positions;
- Facilitate the parties in finding their best alternatives to a court rendered judgment;
- Act as a scribe for the parties when they reach an agreement.

Each student will also become familiar with basic cultural knowledge and recognize how it interacts during the conflict process. There are numerous ethnicities and cultures living in close proximity, particularly in the Northern Virginia area, so it is important to be familiar with its impact. Because of cultural illiteracy, people operating from their own cultural lens often misunderstand others' cultural norms; thus, it is critical for mediators to build cultural awareness.

**What is Conflict?**

Conflict is a perception by two or more parties that each has incompatible goals with the other party or parties; in other words, one must lose something they desire for the other to gain what they desire—akin to a zero-sum game. It also can be described as an "expressed struggle in which two or more independent people are experiencing strong emotion resulting from a perceived difference in needs or values" (Katz, Lawyer, & Sweedler, 2011, p. 81). Coser provides another useful definition: "conflict is a struggle over values or claims to status, power, and scarce resources, in which the aims of the conflicting parties are not only to gain the desired values but also to neutralize, injure, or eliminate their rivals" (as cited in Picard, 2002, p. 3). In yet another perspective, conflict is described as a divergence of thought, feelings, or actions between individuals, groups, organizations, communities, or nations who must interact.

Conflict and disputes are part of human nature and have happened since the dawn of time. People usually come into conflict with others for several reasons such as to gain something that is perceived as scarce or because needs are incompatible (Picard, 2002, p. 3). Christopher Moore identified the following five reasons why people come in conflict with one another:

- Relationship issues
- Value conflicts
- Conflicts over interests
- Discrepancy over data issues
- Structural inequality (as cited in Picard, 2002, p. 3)

Resources are believed to be another source of conflict; resources can be physical, economic, or social commodities (Picard, 2002, p. 3). Resources can be things such as land, money, jobs, and social position, or they can be things that cannot be seen such as love, esteem, recognition, and respect (p. 3).

### Structure of Interpersonal Conflict

As a general rule people tend to avoid conflict and disputes. They feel that if they become engaged in a conflict then somehow they have failed. People may feel overwhelmed, confused, and not in control (Schrock-Shenk, 2000, p. 71). It may also cause people to feel hopeless. Conflict need not always be seen as negative because it has some real benefits such as:

- Opportunity
- Change
- Clear understanding

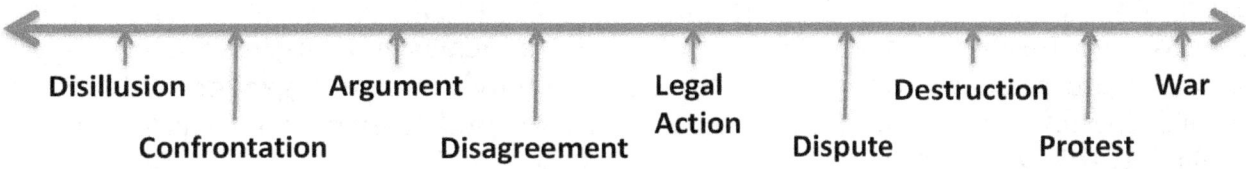

**Figure 1: Continuum of Conflict**

The Mennonites offer a positive way to reframe conflict by viewing the conflict with three distinct parts: people, process, and problems. Either separately or in combination, any of these sources can cause disputes, and therefore, need to be included when developing a resolution and outcome (Schrock-Shenk, 2000, p. 71). Each source is explained as follows.

- People are part of the relational and psychological dimensions of conflict. Their point of view is framed by their emotions, feelings, and self-esteem; their life lens (composed of experience, education, and aspirations), the way they frame problems/disputes; and how they view others. Typically people experience the outcome of the resolution process on a psychological and interpersonal level, which culminates in closure.

- Process is defined as a way decisions are reached and how people feel about it. Many times people ignore this aspect of the dispute. This is shortsighted because resentment, feelings of unfairness, and feelings of powerlessness begin here. People who believe they were excluded or were not part of the decision making process—which impacts their life directly—are not likely to be cooperative and support the decisions and outcomes.

- Problems are specific issues and differences people believe they have with each other. Some examples of perceived differences are values, the approach to decision making, incompatible needs or interests, as well as how to use, distribute, or access scarce resources (such as land, money, time). These examples are often viewed as the root cause of conflict and cause people to become entrenched in their position (Schrock-Shenk, 2000, p. 71).

## Historical Context

Great thinkers such as Plato, Aristotle, Hobbes, and Locke viewed conflict as a threat to the well-being of society (Picard, 2002, p. 2). Their beliefs led people to view conflict as bad; and if present, should be kept to a minimum. In the seventeenth century, Hobbes and Locke believed social contract theory was critical for a functioning society, so systems must be put in place to assure a healthy community (p. 2). Current thinkers underwent a paradigm shift, resulting in the acceptance of conflict as inherent in humans, groups, organizations, and government. In fact, conflict is embraced as positive and can lead to positive change in every entity, and is no longer dreaded.

Today, the conflict field is evolving and includes a multi-disciplinary approach including anthropology, history, political science, psychology, and sociology. It has developed into a discipline similar to psychology and sociology and is following a similar path of recognition. Within the conflict field a number of subspecialties have emerged such as interpersonal, organizational, international, development, environmental, gender, and religion. In each specialty and subspecialty there is a need for conflict analysis tools and resolution skills, regardless of its nature.

Many of the early theorists of the conflict analysis and resolution field established the conflict analysis and resolution program at George Mason University, now a school known as the School of Conflict Analysis and Resolution (SCAR). SCAR currently offers degrees at the undergraduate, graduate, and doctoral levels plus offers a certificate program as well.

Many of its graduates have gone on to found programs at other higher education institutions here in the U.S. and throughout the world (Burton, 1990).

### Are There Differences between Disputes and Conflict?

Is there a difference between conflict and disputes? According to John Burton, yes, there is a difference. Disputes are considered a natural outgrowth of normal and often collaborative and creative relationships common in all social interactions-relationships (Burton, 1990, p. 1). He also asserted that they are an integral part of a competitive system. Furthermore, conflicts are often deeply rooted in human needs and require major restructuring in policies and the environment in order to be resolved (p. 1).

Yet another distinction between disputes and conflict is made. Disputes are situations having issues that can be negotiated, are subject to compromise, and do not involve altered institutions or structures (Burton, 1990, p. 2). Conflict, in contrast, concerns behavior of people, groups, or nations that are beyond disagreement or confrontation over social, economic, and competitive issues in societal life (p. 2).

For the purpose of this course we mainly will be discussing disputes and their resolution using mediation, but the term conflict will be used interchangeably. However, we will also touch upon protracted violent conflict and mediation.

### Activities

1. Name a few disputes you are aware of:

    a.

    b.

    c.

2. Name a few conflicts involving groups:

    a.

    b.

    c.

3. Name a few conflicts between nations:

    a.

    b.

    c.

# Chapter 2:

# The Anatomy of Conflict

# The Anatomy of Conflict

## Objectives

- Understand sources of conflict and possible intervention tactics;

- Understand types of disputes;

- Understand conflict styles and recognize your own style;

- Understand culture's influence on conflict and resolution and the broad types of culture

The types of disputes this course discusses are of an interpersonal nature, for example, personal loans or property, but disputes can also involve business relationships such as consumer, contract, fee for service, or landlord/tenant issues. There are a number of components contributing to disputes, which will be covered in this chapter. First, the sources of disputes and possible interventions will be explored.

## Disputants: Sources of Disputes and Possible Interventions

- Data – people will often disagree over information presented, i.e. facts, figures, etc. They challenge how the information was gathered or the results presented. The presentation will either uphold their position or argue against it. Data is subject to negotiation. Clearly, explaining the data's origination or how the information conclusions were arrived at can help calm disagreements.

- Interests – "refers to occupational, social, political and economic aspirations of the individual" (Burton, 1990, p. 38). Interests can change over time or with circumstances, and they often relate to materiality or roles (p. 38). Interests are subject to negotiation and may be traded (p. 39). (Note you will encounter numerous discussions about interest throughout this book).

- Goals – people generally pursue four types of goals: topic, relationship, identity/face work, and process. These goals often overlap and change in significance compared to the others.

  - Topic goals – specifically relate to what a person wants, for example, what to do, what decisions to make, where to go, how to allocate resources, and other external, objectifiable issues (Hocker & Wilmot, 2014, p. 75).

  - Relationshipss goals – how are the parties related to each other; how do they want to be treated by the other; is there an interdependence (Hocker & Wilmot, 2014, p. 77).

  - Identity/face work goals – related to who the parties believe they are; how they feel they are in an interaction; concerned with protecting or repairing the self-identity within the conflict (Hocker & Wilmot, 2014, pp. 80-81)

- Process goals – the communication style can use formal speech or may use casual/conversational language; people often use different communication styles to resolve the conflict differently (Hocker & Wilmot, 2014, p. 85).

- Prospective goals – relates to people's intentions before they engage in conflict (Hocker & Wilmot, 2014, p. 93).

- Transactive goals – takes place during the conflict episodes in contrast to before or after the conflict episode (Hocker & Wilmot, 2014, p. 94).

- Retrospective goals – this type of goal presents itself after the conflict is over; the parties spend time trying to justify the decisions they made in the past (Hocker & Wilmot, 2014, p. 97).

The advantages of goal clarification are:

1. Solutions may go unrecognized if the party does not know what they want.

2. Only goals that are clear can be shared.

3. Parties can alter their clear goals while vague goals are difficult to change.

4. Most of time clear goals can be achieved whereas unclear goals are difficult to fulfill (Hocker & Wilmot, 2014, pp. 98-99).

*Collaborative goals* are clear, help promote cooperation between the parties, and are belived to be good goals. The characteristics of collaborative goals are:

- A ranges of issues will be addressed – short, medium, and long term.

- Goals state specific and desired behavior.

- Statements are made in the present or future time frame.

- Interdependence is recognized in the stated goal.

- Goals are an ongoing process which is recognized (Hocker & Wilmot, 2014, pp. 101-102).

- *Structural*: Such conflicts often relate to resources, timelines, communication delivery, setting locality, and power-decision making. Within the situation, issues of objective resources along with legal and political realities are sources of conflict. It also involves the party's formal authority and objective choices (Mayer, 2012, p. 72).

- *Values*: Refers to beliefs, which are intangible and are held in high esteem by people. It is the basis upon which people differentiate between right and wrong, good from evil, and the principles people use to govern their lives. Value conflicts can be intractable and often more emotionally charged. Values are part of people's identity, so when values are under attack, people feel directly and personally attacked. In short, value conflicts are difficult to resolve. Once differences in values and beliefs are articulated positively, then the parties can focus on what they believe rather than what they don't believe in, allowing resolution to move forward. However, compromise or problem-solving resolution methods will not be effective in resolving value differences. Solutions will be discovered only when parties find a way to move forward by setting value differences aside, and when circumstances change along with a larger value intervention (Mayer, 2012, p. 14).

- *Relationships:* Parties can be harmed by one another through hurtful verbal messages, actions, prior unresolved conflict, money, alcohol or drug use/abuse, tragedy and loss, and time spent at work or with family and friends. This is not meant to be an exhaustive list. The harm can range from "regrettable and hurtful messages to psychological and physical violence" (Hocker & Wilmot, 2014, p. 305). The types of messages leading to harm include:
  - Accusatory
  - Judgmental/evaluative
  - Commands/orders
  - Advisory
  - Preference/comparison
  - Information disclosure
  - Veiled opinion posed as a question
  - Threats
  - Lies
  - Gaffes
  - Stereotypical remarks (Hocker & Wilmot, 2014, p. 305)

Bernard Mayer designed a pictorial model called the "Wheel of Conflict" which combines a majority of the facets involved in conflict. It shows all of the influences upon the conflict dynamics usually in play. The figure follows:

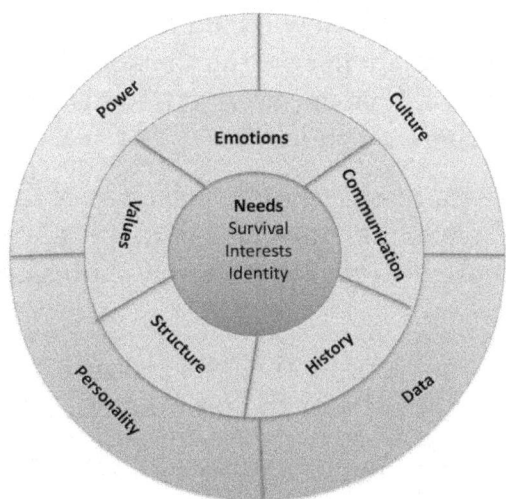

**Figure 2: Interpretation of Wheel of Conflict by Bernard Mayer**

## Types of Disputes

Disputes occur when two or more people have differences of opinion regarding how to achieve a goal. In a domestic relationship it can be as simple as, for example, the menu for the evening meal, how to manage the family-spending plan, what activities the children will engage in, or where to go on the next vacation. Sometimes there are deep-rooted philosophical differences about how to engage in social relationships, how to manage money for long-term growth, how important work life is, and how to raise children. Many times these differences are not discovered until there is a commitment to the relationship.

Work is another place where disputes may occur. Work offers a plethora of dispute opportunities. Differences can center on work hours or breaks, and ways to accomplish a given task or priorities for the workload. Because people in a given work environment are from a variety of places, cultural or personality differences may be present. People speak and listen through a filter (sometime called their lens) that has been shaped by their history, education, experience, and aspirations. Their lens accompanies them in all their interactions with others. It requires effort for a person to alter this lens; mediation can precipitate such an alteration. Other situations in which disputes can occur are: consumer, landlord/tenant, contract, personal loans, and employment, fee for service, property and accidents.

Consumer disputes may involve merchandise or products. Either the product has failed to meet the consumer's expectations, or it is faulty in its function causing dissatisfaction. Retail establishments often have a return policy (liberal or not), specifying the time returns are accepted or conditions under which a consumer may return the products. The consumer expects that the retailer will accept the returned item; however, if the retail establishment feels it is outside the parameters of their return policy, a dispute begins. So, what is the root cause of most conflicts?

---

The disputes commonly encountered in mediation include:

1. Personal loans — an individual will lend money to another. Often there is no written contract or agreement so either a cancelled check or something similar will be offered as proof. If cash was given, then it is verbal arrangement so both parties must agree there was a loan.

2. Landlord/tenant — there are several variations of landlord/tenant disputes such as late rental payments, property damage, and unreturned security deposits, or lease terminated early. Roommate disputes are typically under this category.

3. Consumer — when a person purchases a product or service and is unhappy or the company was never paid for the product or service delivered.

4. Employment wages — employees will seek compensation for time and service performed but not paid.

5. Personal property — property is either borrowed or not returned, and the owner is seeking its return.

6. Home improvement/repairs — homeowners will contract for home repair and then the work is not completed, but the homeowner paid the money up front or the contractor has not been paid for work performed and completed.

7. Automobile repair — car owners will have cars repaired and are unhappy with the outcome or the repair shop is seeking compensation for work completed.

8. Contract — two people contract for products, services, etc., and one of the parties does not perform so the other seeks enforcement or a refund.

9. Broken relationships — unmarried couples or friends will seek property or compensation stemming from the past relationship.

**Human Needs**

Throughout this manual human needs will be discussed in the context of the subject matter being discussed. While there may seemingly be contradictions, when taken as a whole, it makes sense. Most people are familiar with Maslow's Hierarchy of Needs. However, there is a lesser-known social theorist, Johannes Antonious Ponsioen, whose writings are relevant to this discussion; he discussed human needs in terms of social change. Both human needs theories will be briefly discussed.

Abraham Maslow, a proponent of human needs, developed a Hierarchy of Needs through a series of articles and books that articulate what motivates humans regardless of culture, geographic location, socioeconomic status, or religious traditions. He expounded that humans have a variety of needs, and once a categorical need is fulfilled then humans will "move up" and seek to fulfill the next categorical need until at last they achieve self-actualization. The following figure represents Maslow's hierarchy in the form of a pyramid; to the right are brief explanations/examples of those types of needs. As one level is attained, a person moves to the next level.

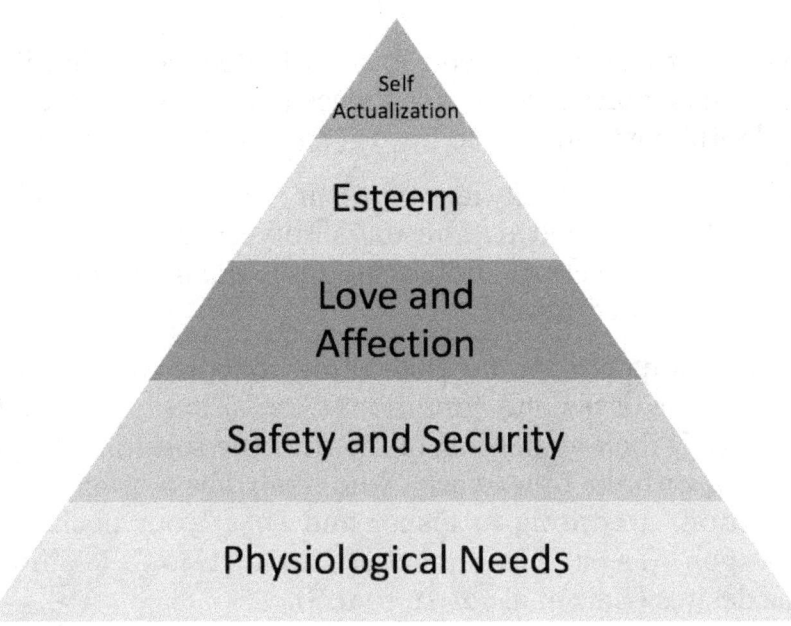

**Figure 3: Human Needs Theory By Maslow**

Ponscioen believed that a society's duty is first to meet basic survival needs of its citizens "including biological, social, emotional and spiritual needs" (Kettner, Moroney, & Martin, 2013, p. 61). He acknowledged these needs may be defined differently over time, but an important addition to the discussion is "each society or community will identify a level below which no one should fall" (p. 61). His theory holds that social needs exists when some members/groups do not have access to the "necessary" goods or services while others do (p. 61). The concept of need is relative to the situation, place, and time. A graphic representation of Ponsioen's Needs Theory follows.

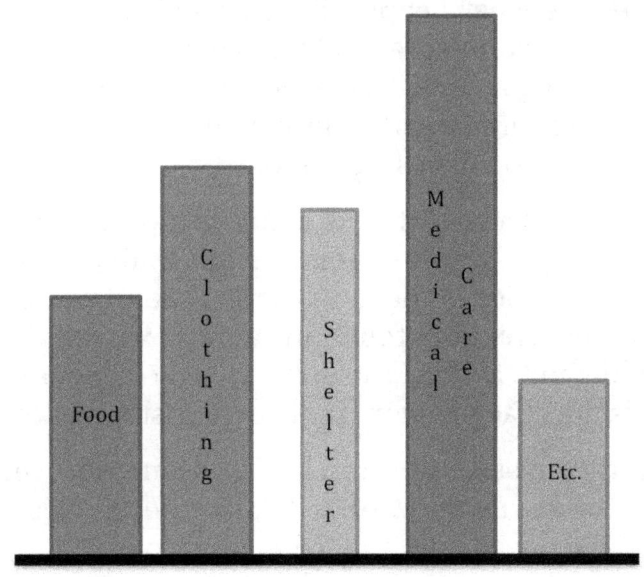

**Figure 4: Ponsioen's Needs Theory**

When looking for solutions to meet the needs, it is most effective to identify shared needs between the parties. Focusing on shared needs moves parties away from their own point of view and story to identifying their shared needs (Katz et al., 2011, p. 108).

Often people are not able to immediately identify their needs; instead their needs may be expressed as positions. Those attuned are able to identify their interests. To assist people in naming their needs it helps to clearly define their positions and underlying interests. Katz et al. offers the following definitions:

- *Positions* — positions are the tangible things people say they want; it can be related to money or terms and conditions. A position is the solution the party believes will satisfy their goal. Most of the time the solution sought is not based on collaboration with the other party, who likely has a different opinion on the optimum solution. According to Fisher and Ury, "your position is something you decided upon" (as cited in Katz et al., 2011, p. 105). Positions can also be expressed as desires (Katz et al., 2011, p. 108).

- *Interest* — often underlying a person's positions is their interest, also known as human needs (Katz et al., 2011, p. 108). The interests are intangible and motivate the party to advocate for a particular position. When finding a solution, identification of the parties' interests will point the way to a mutually satisfying agreement (p. 108).

### Different Approaches to Needs

**Normative.** Normative need suggests a standard or norm understood by the community (Kettner et al., 2013, p. 67). Customs, authority, or general consensus may establish the level against which the quality and quantity of a situation, condition, or resource is measured. When the resulting measure falls short, there is a need. However, as knowledge, technology, and values change, the minimum level may increase or decrease.

**Perceived.** Perceived need is what people think or feel their needs are or should be (Kettner et al., 2013, p. 67). A felt need can be unbalanced. People's perceptions of their needs are changing and evolving as well. The economically affluent may feel their needs are a higher standard of living compared to those living in poverty. The challenged with perceived needs is that there is no normative standard.

**Expressed.** Expressed needs can be stated as either met or unmet (Kettner et al., 2013, p. 68). A question of whether the goods or services are available should be considered; further, even if the good or service is made available, the question of "will it be used" should also be addressed. The strength of thinking about expressed needs is the focus on people translating "a feeling into action" the unmet need or demand becomes the target for complaint (p. 68). This approach is more individual instead of community focused.

**Relative.** Relative needs do not assume a standard or desirable level that should be met, or already exists (Kettner et al., 2013, p. 68). Relative needs exist in the gap between current standards or levels in one community compared to another community. It could be extended to one person looking at the gap of their resources as compared to another. Relative needs are focused on equity, for example 'do I have the same opportunities living in the blighted, southern section of town versus living in the well-manicured, northern section of town?'

## Conflict Styles

Patterns of behavior or responses people use in conflict constitute their style. A person's preferred style of conflict is developed throughout a lifetime based on "personal characteristics, life experience and family background" (Hocker & Wilmot, 2014, p. 143).

- *Accomodating style* — people typically prefer to help the other even at their own expense. They prefer cooperation and harmony and will do what is necessary to achieve that. Accomodation is pleasing others (Hocker & Wilmot, 2014, p. 163).

- *Avoiding style* — characterized by denying the conflict exists, changing topics of conversation or refusing to talk about certain subjects, and using inappropriate humor. A person using this style may also sidestep the topic or just withdraw from the conversation. Using this style can lead to lower satisfaction (Hocker & Wilmot, 2014, p. 151).

- *Compromising style* — results in some wins and some losses. It is moderately assertive and cooperative. Parties engaging in this style will give up some goals to gain others, and power is typically shared (Hocker & Wilmot, 2014, p. 161).

- *Collaborating style* — is the most engaged style compared to the others and is characterized by a high level of concern for self goals and other's goals, as well as finding a successful resolution for both parties and enriching their relationship (Hocker & Wilmot, 2014, p. 165).

- *Competing style* — characterized by "power over" and aggressive or uncooperative behavior (Hocker & Wilmot, 2014, p. 156). Parties using this style are more concerned for themselves and their goals, often at the expense of the other party. Also, they often engage in direct confrontation. Winning is the goal, and it is akin to a zero-sum game (Hocker & Wilmot, 2014, pp. 156-157).

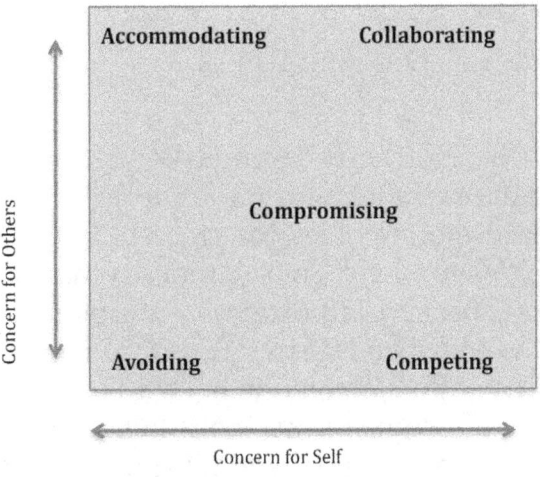

**Figure 5: Conflict Styles**

The above model illustrates conflict styles in a graph and explains how some styles are more self-focused versus other-focused, while an optimum conflict style is balanced between the two.

## Culture

How is culture related to conflict? Culture is a system of meanings — dentity, beliefs, traditions, customs, language, and faith — that influence people and their organizations. Culture can also involve age, gender, socioeconomic status, sexual orientation, educational level, and physical ability (Picard, 2002, p. 15). A society's customs and traditions create a "pool of habits" encouraging its members to conform and share the norms (Augsburger, 1992, p. 22). While culture does not directly affect individual behavior, it can, however, influence it and shape how it is viewed and managed. Within each culture, there are a wide variety of habits, personality types, and behavioral patterns related to conflict (p. 22). John Burton poses the following question with regard to culture:

> If culture refers to behaviors that can be acquired by societies or communities it becomes difficult to know where to draw the line between on the one hand, different ethnic or major community behaviors, which are continuing behaviors and, on the other hand, behaviors associated with a particular groups at particular points of time. (Burton, 1990, p. 212)

When there are cultural differences it is often centered on ethnic differences related to religion, language, food, and other phenomena related to ethnicity (Burton, 1990, p. 213). Simultaneously, ethnic identity can be closely associated with safety and security, one of the basic human needs (p. 213).

"Conflict is universal yet distinct in every culture; it is common to all persons yet experienced uniquely by every individual" (Augsburger, 1992, p. 18). Culture is part of the lens or filter which people view and interpret life through. Cultural behavior is difficult to predict if one focuses strictly on country of origin. For example, consider all of the different culture norms between the North and South in the United States. Thus, there are more accurate predictions of cultural behavior if one focuses on two types of culture: individualistic and collectivistic. Another way to classify culture is using communication styles: high and low context. Religion may also be used to classify culture. These will be discussed in detail below.

The U.S. and particularly the Northern Virginia-DC Metro area become increasingly diverse. Each person experiences their culture in some aspect of their life (Hocker & Wilmot, 2014, p. 67). A major stumbling block to understanding culture is the tendency to view everything through a Western lens. So a significant task is to "de-Westernize" communication research; this is especially important in interpersonal conflict (Hocker & Wilmot, 2014, p. 67). We need to go beyond simply acknowledging other cultures; we need to respect and appreciate all they offer. When one belongs to the dominant group it is difficult to know the experiences of people in the "non-dominant cultures without authentic dialogue and de-westernized research" (Hocker & Wilmot, 2014, p. 67). It is important a trained mediator or conflict resolver understands culture's influence on individuals and how to handle the conflict.

Generally, cultures can be divided into several groups. Below are the categories and characteristics of each in a side-by-side format for easy comparison and contrast.

| INDIVIDUALIST /LOW CONTEXT | COLLECTIVIST /HIGH CONTEXT |
| --- | --- |
| Tend to be direct | Tend to be indirect |
| Are straightforward in making demands | Are ambiguous when expressing their preferences |
| Confrontational | Non-confrontational |
| Open self-disclosure | Subtle in communication, indirect speeh |
| *Conflict Management* | *Conflict Management* |
| Conflict is one on one | Conflict interaction unfolds within cultural and social norms |

**Figure 6: Culural Styles Comparison**

## Conflict Intervention System

When a practitioner is invited to intervene in a conflict, they must build an intervention system upon the partie's needs, goals, and culture. Bernard Mayer provides an intervention system graphic showing the interrelatedness of the components in building an effective intervention system.

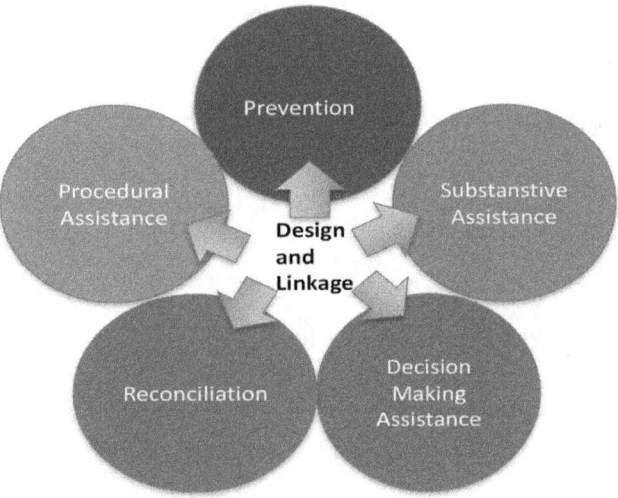

**Figure 7: Interpretation of Conflict Intervention of System by Bernard Mayer**

## Activities

1. When you think of conflict what comes to mind? How do you describe conflict?

2. Name a few disputes you have been involved in:

   a.

   b.

   c.

3. Identify your conflict style:

4. Needs, Interests, and Positions Role-Play

Read the story in Appendix B5 and as you do so think about the following questions:

- What is the relationship of the parties?
- What are the issues?
- Can intervention help?

- What are their needs, positions and interests?

Identify each of the following types of human needs involved with both parties:

| Hierarchy of Human Needs | Party 1 | Party 2 |
|---|---|---|
| Physiological | | |
| Safety/Security | | |
| Love/Affection/ Belongingness | | |
| Esteem | | |
| Self-Actualization | | |

*Adapted from Katz et al., 2011, p. 111*

5. Using the same story name the parties' interests.

| Interests | Party 1 | Party 2 |
|---|---|---|
| | | |
| | | |
| | | |
| | | |

6. Now name the parties positions.

| Positions | Party 1 | Party 2 |
|---|---|---|
|  |  |  |
|  |  |  |
|  |  |  |
|  |  |  |

What type of dispute is it? Is it a conflict over data, goals, structural issues, values, or relationships?

Identify the culture of each.

| Culture | Party 1 | Party 2 |
|---|---|---|
| Direct | | |
| Indirect | | |
| Low/Individualist | | |
| High/Collectivist | | |

# Chapter 3:

# Understanding Alternatives for Resolution

# Understanding Alternatives for Resolution

**Objectives**

- Know the different methods and what their characteristics are to resolve conflict;

- Understand how negotiation and mediation work together

Parties may seek to resolve their differences in a variety of ways. Among the resolution methods are: negotiation, mediation, arbitration, and litigation. For those involved in conflict, each technique allows a range of control in determining both the process and the outcome of the resolution. If placed on a continuum, negotiation empowers the parties in both aspects with litigation doing so the least.

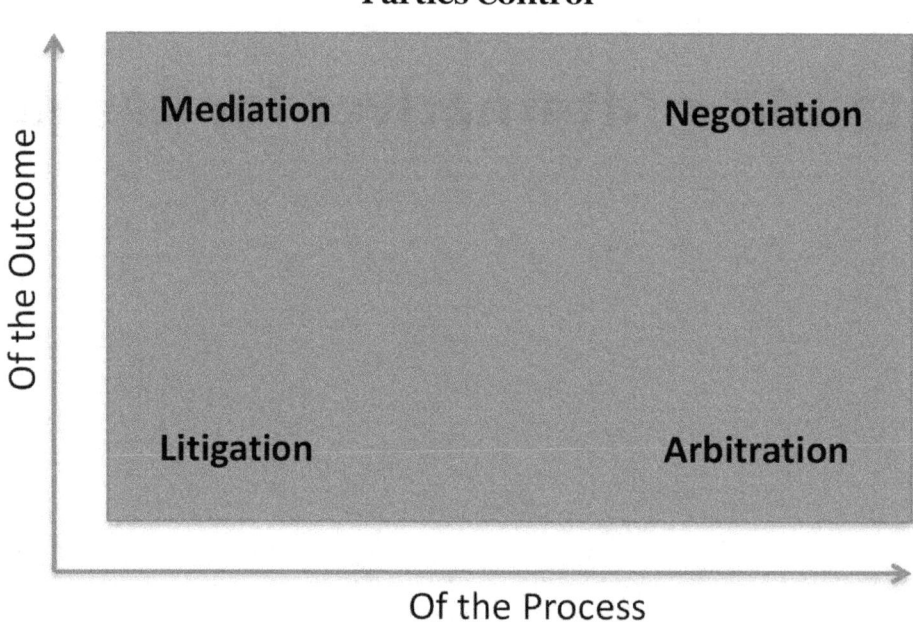

**Figure 8: Conflict Resolution Tools Outcomes and Process**

Alternative Dispute Resolution includes programs that are sponsored by the courts, industry groups, private agencies, or volunteer-based community centers (Schrock-Shenk, 2000, p. 157). Below is a linear continuum that depicts various resolution types ranging from less control to more control.

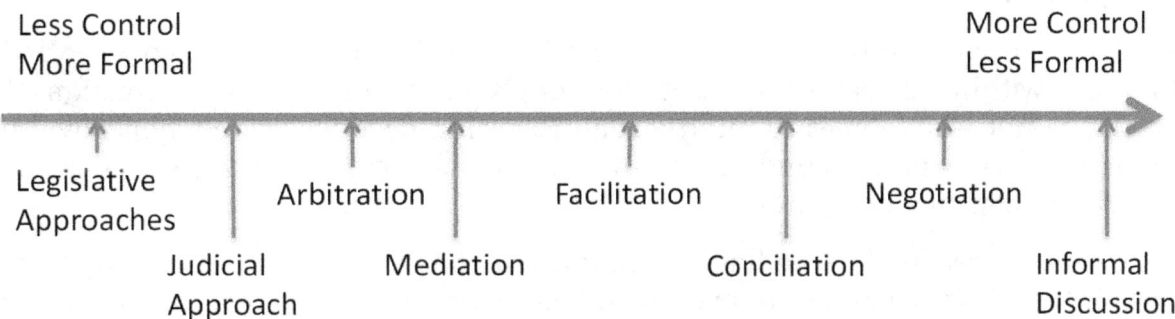

**Figure 9: Interpretation of Dispute Resolution**

## Arbitration

Arbitration is a process whereby parties in conflict seek the assistance of a neutral third party; however, in this process the third party has decision-making power (Mayer, 2012, p. 326; Moore, 2003, p. 9). Generally, the parties in conflict present their respective cases before an arbitrator pseudo-judge. After, the case is heard the arbitrator makes a decision, and depending upon the circumstance, the decision may be binding.

Mayer (2012) discusses two types of decision-making processes an arbitrator may adopt. First is an interest-based approach. Using this approach an arbitrator sifts through the various concerns of each party and seeks to address their needs within a framework of the law (p. 326). The second approach is a rights-based approach whereby the arbitrator determines the outcome similar to a litigated case. They review the issues and apply legal doctrine to guide their decision-making. As such, parties' interests are a secondary concern (p. 326).

## Litigation

Phillips (2001) states that "Litigation is not a trial, it is the preparation for the trial that, 95 percent of the time, will not happen" (p. 6). In essence, litigation is the advocacy of one's issues by another. In the legal context, parties seek representation from lawyers to argue their case with the intention of winning.

Generally, this is an adversarial approach. Parties cease communication and posture themselves for the courtroom. While the parties may gain excellent and forceful advocacy of their position, they lose the ability to control both the process and the outcome.

Furthermore, parties generally do not find the catharsis they seek. The litigation process is impartial and does not necessarily address needs. The parties seek a win/lose decision from the court that will state rightness of one party and wrongdoing by the other (Moore, 2003, p. 10).

## Negotiation

Everyone negotiates (Mayer, 2012, p. 213). Daily we participate in a series of negotiations with others within our realm of contact. It is simply a function of social interaction. However, this is not what comes to mind when discussing negotiation. We typically understand it as a formal process undertaken by professionals or organizations such as during labor and management disputes.

For a more concrete understanding, negotiation can be defined as a relationship between parties in which they bargain to overcome real or perceived differences. Moore (2003) states that:

The parties voluntarily join in a temporary relationship designed to educate each other about needs and interests, to exchange specific resources, or to resolve less tangible issues such as the form their relationship will take in the future or the procedure, which problems are to be solved. (p. 8)

Since negotiation is a mutual process, both parties have issues, needs, and interests they hope to address, and both parties are attempting to do so simultaneously. It is difficult to juggle one's own concerns while recognizing the legitimacy of the concerns of others – a dilemma known as the "Negotiator' Dilemma" (Mayer, 2012, p. 218). Essentially, the question is how can one address their personal needs, and also allow space for the other party to address their needs without compromising one's own interests (p. 218)? After all, true resolution or agreement requires a mutually beneficial outcome such that all parties involved are sufficiently satisfied.

Achieving mutual satisfaction with an outcome depends how the parties view the negotiation process. Each brings certain assumptions to a negotiation, which can be fluid and shift depending on the relationship with the other party. Negotiation can be thought of as a game, a collaborative endeavor, a win-win or win-lose process, or a necessity to be either mean or nice (Mayer, 2012, p. 213). These assumptions are integral to how the negotiation will proceed and what its central focus will be.

Mayer (2012) asserts that a negotiator may adopt two separate focuses: distributive or integrative (pp. 221, 228). Distributive negotiations are characterized by approaches that:

- Frame issues with a focus on how to compromise amongst conflicting needs or between exclusive outcomes (p. 222).

- Use power to achieve concessions from the other party (p. 222).

- Leverage alternatives to persuade the other parties to concede or give up potential benefits (p. 222).

- Achieve agreement when involved parties believe they have achieved better alternatives or at least alternatives as good as other options (p. 223).

- Control information. Information may be used or viewed as currency (p. 223).

Distributive negotiations are most concerned with achieving a share of the pie. Parties seek to maximize success and achieve agreement based upon what is desirable to them.

However, it is important to understand that distributive negotiators should not be viewed as negative per se. Mayer asserts that distributive negotiations need not be adversarial since parties may work and communicate well with one another throughout the process (2012, p. 224).

The integrative approach seeks to expand the pie. Parties discuss issues and seek to maximize outcomes for all parties involved (p. 224). In doing so, integrative negotiation lessens the negotiator's dilemma. It focuses heavily on building and maintaining relationships, as well as effective communication to help drive an interest-based process to the negotiations (p. 227).

Neither a distributive nor integrative negotiation is a panacea. Each approach possesses benefits and drawbacks. Moore (2012) asserts that the challenge is to ensure "that the integrative potential is maximized, to find a way of approaching the distributive elements without escalating a conflict, and to be effective partners at the same time" (p. 229).

### What is Mediation?

"Mediation is an art form, incorporating intuition, subtlety, and vision."

*(Smith & Smock, 2008, p.5)*

Mediation may be understood in a variety of ways. It is one of the conflict resolution tools used to intervene in social conflict with many believing it is the central tool used by conflict resolution professionals. Mediation is an intervention as well as a role, a skill, an approach, and a practice specialty, which has been utilized for many years, and is often used by clergy, political leaders, elders, and community leaders (Mayer, 2012, pp. 270-272). Also, like negotiation, it is a life skill that individuals may often use (p. 270).

At its core, mediation occurs when a third party in tervenes in a dispute and helps the parties involved communicate about how to resolve their respective issues (Mayor, 2012, p. 271). Participating in mediation is typically voluntary. Price (1995) defines mediation as "A process, facilitated by a third party, by which disputants discuss their concerns and issues and explore possible options for mutually satisfactory solutions to differences" (as cited in Mayor, 2012, p. 157). In mediation, the parties in conflict maintain power over the outcome and potential agreement; however, they allow the third party to guide them through a more effective communication process. As an alternative to litigation, it is less costly and time consuming. Like litigation, mediation brings an end to the dispute and helps the parties find a mutually acceptable resolution to their dispute.

Mayer (2012) states "In a serious conflict, it is not the absence of an effective solution that perpetuates a destructive interaction, but the lack of an effective process or structure for communication and engagement" (p. 281). This is the job of the third party in mediation. The mediator must creatively find a way to open space in a conflict through dialogue, as well as aid the parties in exploring their respective needs and interests. For mediation the parties in conflict must first recognize a need for outside help. Moore (2012) outlines the following premises of mediation.

- The disputants need help and perceive they would benefit from such help.

---

- As disputants voluntarily enter the process, they view the process as advantageous.

- The mediator helps facilitate a communication process and assists disputants in dealing with their conflict more constructively.

- The parties maintain power over the outcome and agreements created through mediation(s); the mediator does not have the power to impose or enforce outcomes or agreements.

- Process is important. (p. 284)

In mediation (and conflict in general) parties arrive with distinct and often contentious narratives of what brought them to this point. For example, they may view their adversary's past as littered with wrongdoing and injustice, while they have personally acted justly and rightly. As Moore (2003) states, ,We [interveners] never deal with reality per se, but rather with images of reality—that is, with interpretations" (p. 235).

To deal with the "images of reality" mediators are tasked with bringing closure to the past and promoting a focus on the future (Moore, 2003, p. 235). Mediators must explore the past with parties to identify issues, positions, and interests in order to aid parties in discovering solutions. More on this matter will be discussed in the problem-solving chapter.

## Synergy between Negotiation and Mediation

Up to this point, we have discussed negotiation and mediation as separate resolution techniques. There are nuances and differences between the two; however, they are best understood as parts of a whole. They are interrelated in both process and potential, and aid one another in the overall resolution of a conflict. Furthermore, this synergistic understanding of negotiation and mediation will provide better insight into the mediation practiced in court, which is, of course, the purpose of this class.

We defined negotiation as a bargaining relationship between parties. It may be official in a boardroom or unofficial such as when friends try to determine which movie to see. In either case, the negotiation process may break down. There may be a divergence, whether real or perceived, over what outcome is most desirable to each respective party.

When negotiations fail and the parties are unable to sort it out alone, a third party can be helpful. The third party's sole purpose is to aid the disputants through dialogue to allow them to identify mutually agreeable solutions. This is precisely the role a court mediator fills.

Many scholars identify mediation as an extension or alteration of a negotiation process. Piccard (2002) defines mediation as a form of assisted negotiation (p. 21). Moore (2003) asserts that "Without negotiation, there would be no mediation" and that the mediator's role is to introduce a more effective negotiation process in order to settle contested issues (p. 16).

**Activities**

1. Name a couple of times when you intervened in a dispute.

2. What are some examples when you used negotiation?

# Chapter 4:

# Structure of Negotiation

# Structure of Negotiation

## Objectives

- Understand negotiation approaches;
- Be able to guide disputants from a destructive resolution system to a constructive system;
- Understand culture's impact on negotiation styles

There are three fundamental negotiation approaches to resolving disputes: interests, rights, and power. Analyzing the costs of the three approaches is informative; however, reconciling interests is usually the least costly and produces more satisfactory results instead of determining who are right (Ury, Brett, & Goldberg, 2010, p. 1). The most costly and least satisfactory approach determines who is more powerful (p. 1). Mediation uses interest-based negotiation with a goal of reconciling those interests. A brief description of rights and power-based negotiation will be discussed followed by an expanded discussion on interest-based negotiation.

## Rights Based

Rights based negotiation uses an independent standard of measurement (synonymous with rights) to determine fairness or perceived legitimacy to decide who is right (Ury et al., 2010, p. 3). Rights are codified in a number of places, for example, the U.S. Constitution, as well as federal, state and local laws. In addition, organizations typically have rules and regulations protecting or affecting people's rights. There are also unwritten laws guiding social interaction dictated by a person's family, education, and culture. So people's rights are affected by a number of sources.

Unfortunately, rights often exist in the gray portion of life, so rights are not clear, can be contradictory, and standards can vary. Parties who dispute their own rights or the rights of others likely will be challenged to reach a mutual decision without the aid of a third party intervener. Typically parties experiencing a rights procedure issue turn to the court system and seek adjudication. Arbitrators also have authority and power to hand down a binding decision.

## Power Based

Power is narrowly defined for this context: "It is the ability to coerce someone to do something he would not otherwise do" (Ury et al., 2010, p. 4). When a person imposes authority or power over another, costing the lower power person (or threatening to cost something), it is said to be a power-based negotiation (p. 4). Power tactics of power-based negotiations are divided into two types: exchange of threats and power contests. A destructive contest determines who is the most powerful, so the challenge becomes reconciling differing points of view (p. 4).

Parties who engage in power-based negotiations use objective gauges regardless of the financial resources. People's perceptions of the incongruence of their own and the other's power leads to an incorrect conclusion (Ury et al., 2010, p. 4). Additionally, the parties are unaware of how much the other may be willing to expend or invest, and the parties may be motivated by fear because of the power imbalance which will affect the outcome of future disputes (p. 4).

### Relationship between Interests, Rights, and Power

To demonstrate the close association between interests, rights, and power, a graphic tells the story best (see Figure 9). The innermost circle is interests, the next circle is rights, and the outermost circle is power (Ury et al., 2010, p. 4). As presented, reconciliation between interests is imbedded within rights and power; likewise, rights are determined within the context of power (p. 4).

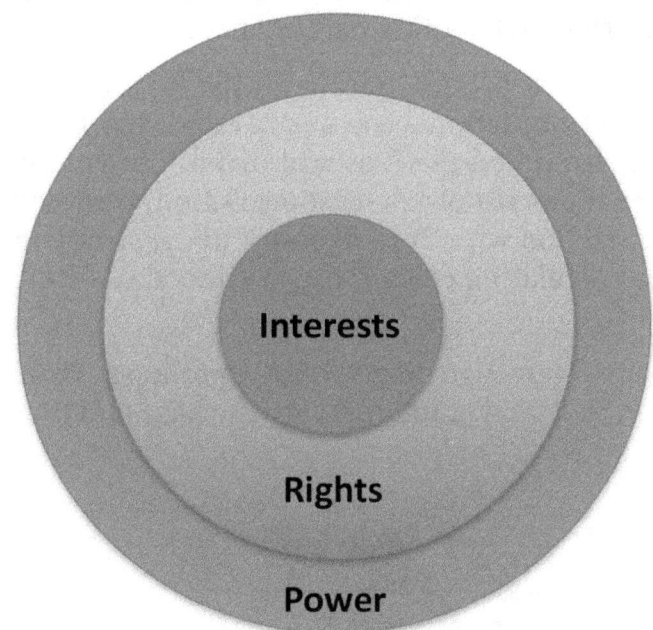

**Figure 10: Interrelationships among Interests, Rights and Power**

During the resolution process, focus may change from "interests to rights to power and back again" (Ury et al., p. 4).

### Weighing the Costs and Benefits

Each of the three types of negotiation has different costs and benefits. The four best suggested criteria to measure the costs are: "transaction costs, satisfaction with outcomes, effect on the relationship, and recurrence of disputes" (Ury et al., 2010, p. 6). It is important to realize that the four criteria are interrelated.

1. Transaction costs – costs may be of time, money, and emotional energy spent during the dispute, consumed, or destroyed; it is also important to account for opportunity costs (p. 6).

2. Satisfaction with outcomes – the parties' gratification with the results indicates satisfaction and depends on the party's perception of fairness. Even if the solution does not totally satisfy their interests, they still will be gratified by its fairness (p. 6). The fairness of the resolution process also satisfies the parties (p. 6).

3. Effect on the relationship— the long term effects on relationships is an important criterion. The solution must take into consideration its effect on the daily interaction of the parties. The solution may also vary depending on the type of relationship—interpersonal or a one-time encounter.

4. Recurrence of disputes – the proposed solution should be tested for endurance; the goal is to produce a "durable resolution" (p. 7). Sometimes resolutions do not "stick" leading to reoccurrences of disputes (p. 7). Be aware that many solutions do not prevent similar types of conflict between other parties who are independent of the original disputing parties (p. 7).

"Dissatisfaction with outcomes may produce strain on the relationship" contributing to future disputes and raising the transactional costs (Ury et al., 2010, p. 7). Typically costs rise and drop in concert and are called the "costs of disputing" (p. Therefore, when an approach is characterized as a high-cost or low-cost resolution, transaction costs are considered, as well as the dissatisfaction with the outcome and the strain on the relationship. Another consideration when calculating costs is the likelihood of future disputes and its costs (p. 7).

A graphical representation of an effective dispute system follows. Power is a small part, rights are beneath and bigger, and finally, interests are the base and the largest portion of the system.

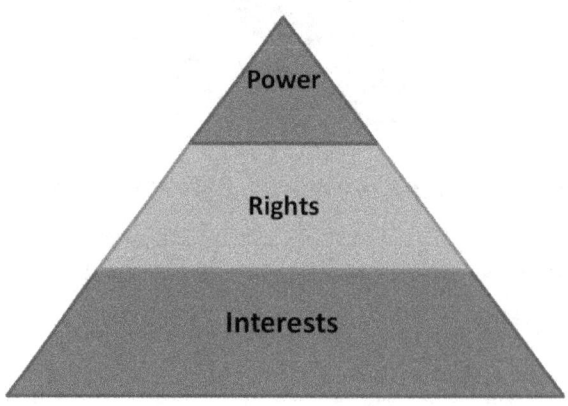

**Figure 11: Interpretation of Moving from a Distresses to an Effective Dispute Resolution System (Ury et al., 2010, p. 11).**

**Negotiation Strategies**

There are five negotiation strategies to be considered, and they are:

### 1. Accommodating

- Lose to win
- High relationship importance
- Low outcome importance

### 2. Collaborative

- Win-win
- High relationship importance
- High outcome importance

### 3. Compromise

- Split the difference
- Combination of relationship and outcome importance

### 4. Avoiding

- Lose-lose
- Low relationship importance
- Low outcome importance

### 5. Competitive

- Win at all costs, win-lose
- Low relationship importance
- High outcome importance (Lewicki, Hiam, & Olander, 2010, p. 16)

The general definitions are ideal if one issue is negotiated at a time; however, real life negotiations are usually much more complex requiring use of a mixture of the strategies (Lewicki et al., 2010, p. 17). Two fundamental concerns – "the relationship with the other negotiator and the outcome of the negotiation itself" – are dependent on personal preference (p. 14). Never forget the other party is formulating their own negotiation tactics (p. 17). Choosing which strategy to use depends on what you think the other party will use and then making adjustments accordingly (p. 17). When choosing a strategy, consider all of the following: the circumstances, preferred styles, experience, interaction of styles, and perceptions (pp. 25-28).

## Gender Differences in Negotiation Styles

Studies reveal men and women use different communication styles particularly in work settings. Deborah Tannen demonstrates these differences in her books You Just Don't Understand: Men and Women in Conversation and Talking from 9 to 5. According to Shell (2006), Tannen contends that men are more assertive, are likely to interrupt their counterpart, and focused on affirming their status; women listen more than their male counterparts, pay closer attention to emotional rapport, and will take turns talking (Shell, 2006, p. 15).

Research proves women negotiate differently than men. Typically, women choose to negotiate less often in areas of salary and promotion plus behave more cooperatively than men (Shell, 2006, p. 16). Additionally data show women react negatively when reminded of female stereotypical behavior such as being wimpy or passive; both undermine confidence and affect women's ability to use their negotiation style (p. To combat such stereotypical assertions, female negotiators can manipulate the parties' beliefs regarding women, which may give them a huge advantage when her hand is played well (p. 18).

## Cultural Differences in Negotiating Style

Culture can dictate who should be at the negotiation table. Formal cultures are sensitive to the status of the negotiators so the negotiators must be of equal status (Shell, 2006, p. 19). In contrast, less formal cultures focus on the use of functional knowledge and decision authority as criteria for selecting the negotiator. If such differences are at the same table, serious challenges can emerge leading to breakdowns in the negotiation and misunderstanding (Shell, 2006, p. 19).

"Culture issues have more to do with form than substance" (Shell, 2006, p. 20). While is does complicate the process and can cause misunderstanding and miscommunication, it is more likely that money, control, and risk are the important issues at the table regardless of where the parties are from (p. 20). The most important difference in cross-cultural negotiations (language and custom differences aside) is the party's perception of their relationship ( p. 20).

Being patient and realize the agreement is just one part of the larger picture culturally; relationships are paramount (Shell, 2006, p. 20). An effective negotiator knows his or her bargaining style, is well prepared, sets high expectations, listens patiently, and is committed to personal integrity (p. 21).

## Effective Negotiations

In the book *Getting to Yes: Negotiating Agreement Without Giving In* Roger Fisher, William Ury, and Bruce Patton suggest an effective way to negotiate. First do not haggle over positions because this is a no-win proposition (Fisher, Ury, & Patton, 1991, p. 4). The authors advocate that the best method of negotiation separates the people from the problem and focuses on the parties' interests not positions. They also suggest that brainstorming mutually beneficial options and using objective criteria are important (Fisher et al., 1991, p. 15). Remember negotiations are between emotional human beings who have values, backgrounds, and different points of view, and are unpredictable (pp. 18-19).

Human attributes can either be helpful or devastating. When relationships are built on trust, understanding, and respect, and when negotiation takes place over a period of time, it can be smoother and more effective (Fisher et al., 1991, p. 19). Conversely, people who become offended, grow angry, are depressed, feel frustrated or fearful, or are hostile, it leaves them unable to see other points of view making the negotiation process problematic (p. 19). Before, during, and after the negotiation ask "Am I paying enough attention to the people problem?" (p. 19).

### Activities

1. What negotiating style best describes you? There is no right or wrong.

2. Identify costs using the pet role-play from Appendix B7.

# Chapter 5:

# Framework of Mediation

# Framework of Mediation

**Objectives**

- Be familiar with what constitutes a successful mediation;
- Understand the mediator's and party's role;
- Know the process stages

**History of Mediation**

Mediation has a lengthy, cultural specific history. However, we will focus on its history over the last 50 years. Before 1965 mediation was primarily used in labor relations and was unheard of in other contexts (Bush & Folger, 1994, p. 1). By the late 1960s its use spread to the civic leadership and justice areas. Reformers believed it had community resource building potential in conjunction with justice. In 1970 there were a few mediation programs; however, by 1980 there were close to two hundred programs (p. 1).

Since the acceptance of mediation was growing, the number of areas in which it was used expanded to non-labor disputes such as divorce, housing, environment, organizations, institutions, small claims, personal injury, insurance, and business (Bush & Folger, 1994, p. 2). In the last 10 years attorneys and private businesses have recognized mediation's benefits and now often participate themselves. In explaining mediation, Bush and Folger note the following:

Across the mediation movement, mediation is generally understood (based on its previous use in the labor field) as an informal process in which a neutral third party with no power to impose a resolution helps the disputing parties try to reach a mutually acceptable settlement. (1994, p. 2)

**Awareness for Mediators**

Parties do not always agree to mediation, and in some circumstances it may not be appropriate, especially if there has been past physical violence. Typically such information is gained in the first contact. Mediators gain parties' consent to participate in a mediation orientation and will then ask for their commitment to participate throughout the process. A wide variety of tactics can be used to persuade the parties to try mediation such as guilt or hard sell by laying out the consequences of not participating and then selling mediation's positive advantages. However, this approach can be counterproductive. A better approach is to present the pros and cons of mediation and help the parties thoughtfully make a decision. It is the parties' sole decision to participate. The mediator's service of getting the parties to agree to participate is a first step to collaboration. It is also important to note, if parties are wavering and unsure about participating, that it may be inappropriate to move forward in the mediation process.

Mediators claim success when an agreement is made and signed. However, remember breakdowns in negotiations occurred before the mediator became involved. So even when there is no agreement, there can be positive ripple effects. Parties are looking for help and seeking a new dynamic. The parties are emotional and have ceased communicating with each other long ago. Mediators are adept at creating a safe space to resume productive communication; however, the parties may not recognize it. "What mediators offer and what disputants want are sometimes at odds and always different" (Mayer, 2012, p. 280). Parties want validation of their positions and to save face, and furthermore, want the mediator to pressure the other party into agreement (p. 280). Mediators offer attentive listening, neutrality, and resolution processes.

A mediator must remember that their third party role has limitations. Though the best solution may seem clear, mediators often do not always know the best solution to the parties' dispute. It is important to emphasize that mediators do not bring a solution. A mediator's creativity is valuable, and he or she offers thoughtful, valid suggestions. Despite the positive skills mediators possess, they do not have the power to make people reasonable (Moore, 2012, p. 275). Realize that parties may not be able to come to agreement, even when the solution seems clear.

### Finding a Mediator

How does one find a mediator? There are a number of sources to find mediators including state directories, word of mouth, the World Wide Web, and legal or social service professionals. One or both parties may find and then select a mutually acceptable mediator. The Judge may order the parties to try mediation first, thus, a mediator is assigned. In either situation, the mediator remains neutral, and does not offer legal advice or impose a solution. Additional resources applicable to the Northern Virginia area will be presented in a subsequent chapter.

### Practice of Mediation

Mediation is used in a wide variety of settings such as interpersonal, group, and government settings — all with a similar process. First, mediators analyze the dispute through gathering the facts: when, who, where, what, and how. The mediator's fact finding is neutral, and he or she refrains from passing judgment on gathered information. Second, the mediator identifies all the parties involved, even those affected indirectly. Third, the mediator assists the parties in communicating and facilitates a positive discussion.

The mediation process is explained during the orientation. First time mediation participants are apprehensive because they don't know what to expect; the orientation helps alleviate their fear. The mediator sets an agenda, formulates ground rules with party input, talks about the process, and stresses confidentiality. Examples of a few basic ground rules may include one person speaking at a time, no name calling, and refrain from inappropriate physical gestures; parties are also reminded that the mediator is neutral. An important foundation of mediation is its voluntary nature with the mediator emphasizing that the parties may opt out, halt, or complete the mediation as they wish.

Mediators need to be concerned with power imbalance. Reflect on the sources of power and how it is leveraged. It is a mediator's job to try to balance power and make sure all participate on a level playing field. All parties need to feel free to speak and participate in the mediation process. This is just a snapshot of using mediation. For the purpose of this certification course, we will concentrate on interpersonal conflict.

## Mediation Styles

Like conflict styles, mediators also have mediation styles. The recognized styles are evaluative, facilitative, narrative, and transformative.

**Evaluative**          **Facilitative**          **Narrative**          **Transformative**

**Figure 12: Spectrum of Mediation Styles**

- *Evaluative* — mediators focus on the strengths and weakness of the parties' legal cases, potential outcomes from trial, and potential settlement ranges they should consider (Mayer, 2012, p. 276).

- *Facilitative* — mediators' focus on the process with the parties at the center. Using clear communication, issues and interests are identified. Negotiation and problem solving are used to help the parties find a resolution (Mayer, 2012, p. 277).

- *Transformative* — mediators look for opportunities to empower the parties and offer them recognition (Mayer, 2012, p. 276). They do not set an agenda, reframe the issues, nor focus on the outcome.

- *Narrative* — focuses on developing a relationship between the parties making it incompatible with conflict. It is constructed on the parties' "stories of understanding, respect and collaboration" (Winslade & Monk, 2000, p. xi)". This approach strongly considers cultural narratives around ethnicity, class, gender, education, and financial resources (p. xi).

## Mediator's Role

The mediator's role is to facilitate a discussion between the parties. Through using active and reflective listening, remaining non-judgmental, and summarizing, the mediator is able to reframe the conflict story. Mediators use paraphrasing, which can bring clarity of thought. In addition, the mediator asks open-ended questions to provoke thought and highlight all relevant points.

Mediators bring the following attributes to the table:

- Change the structure of interaction
- Convey an approach to mediation
- Bring a set of skills in communication, negotiation, and problem solving
- Remain personally committed, provide vision, and humanity to the interaction
- They bring a set of values and ethics (Mayer, 2012, pp. 273-274)

Mediators do not bring the following to the table:

- The best solution
- Power to make the parties behave reasonably
- Ability to change the real circumstances the parties face
- Additional resources (Mayer, 2012, p. 275)

A couple of models help mediators understand the issues and make sure all relevant information is identified during the mediation process.

1. The Conflict Tree by Simon Fisher (Fisher, 2000)

    a.    Roots — causes

    b.    Trunk — core problems

    c.    Branches/Leaves — effects

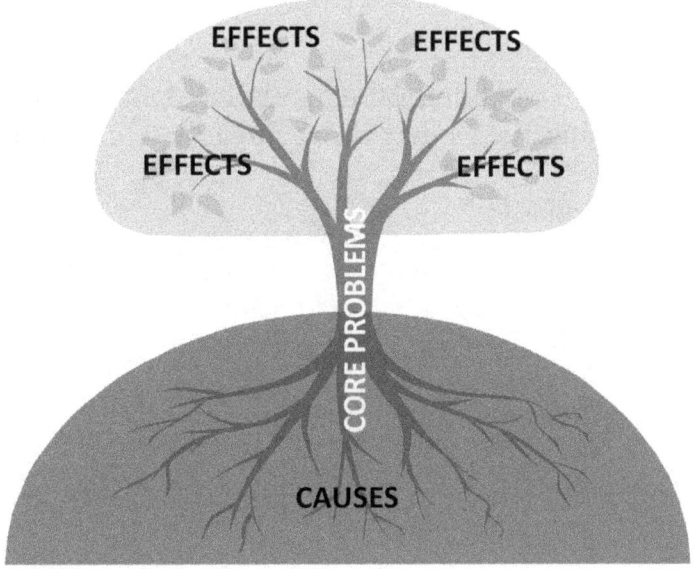

**Figure 13: Illustration of Conflict Tree by Simon Fisher**

2. Conflict Triangle by Christopher Mitchell (Walczer, Schupp, Perron, & Keathly, n.d.)

    d.     Situations

    e.     Attitudes

    f.     Behavior

**Figure 14: Interpretation of Conflict Triangle**

3. Personal Mediator Model— what helps the mediator to make sense of the dispute? The mediator is only limited by his/her imagination. The following need to be identified:

    g.     Issues/problems

    h.     Parties

    i.     Timeline

    j.     Effects of problem

    k.     What does each party hope to gain from mediation

**Party's Role**

The parties bring their story of the dispute. They also have an idea of what they want to happen in order to resolve the dispute putting them at odds with the other party. In addition to the parties' narrative, they also bring their needs, experience, knowledge, cultural norms, beliefs, and goals, which are all operating underneath the surface.

**Overview of Process Stages**

The following outline provides an overview of the mediation process stages and will be discussed in more depth in a subsequent chapter.

1. *Intake* — the mediator contacts the parties through provided information and has a brief conversation with potential parties to gather basic information and set a first appointment for orientation. It is believed that 80% of mediation work is done prior to the first meeting with the parties at the table. Unfortunately, not all mediations are set up in advance and afforded planning time. Small Claims Courts often send cases to mediation the same day they are set for trial and parties are notified 24-48 hours ahead of time. Court mediation offers parties a last opportunity to settle their dispute instead of having a solution enforced upon them and to reduce the trial docket. The Circuit, General, and Small Claims courts may refer cases to mediation. The General District Court refers cases prior to trial either before or the day of trial with the hope the parties will find a mutually acceptable solution codified in a written agreement, thus alleviating the need for a trial. Small claims cases are sent for mediation orientation and hopefully mediation the day of trial. Again, mediated cases resulting in an agreement mean one less case to be heard by the judge.

2. *Preparation* — if the mediator is assigned a case in advance then they will contact the parties ahead of the orientation to make sure there are no concerns for meeting face-to-face with the other party. The mediator will locate and secure a space for the mediation, as well as gather court paperwork and necessary forms.

3. *Gather background information* — the mediator collects court documents, giving basic information about the dispute. During the first contact the mediator will ask about resolution attempts and other helpful data.

4. *Confer with co-mediator* — some mediation services encourage co-mediation whereby two mediators share the mediation. Prior to the mediation, co-mediators decide who gives the orientation, who facilitates the discussion, who takes notes, and who drafts the agreements if one is found.

5. *Arrange the room* — the ideal room arrangement is to use a circular table so there is no perceived head. However, if that is not possible it is best to put each party beside each other facing the mediators. It prevents reaction to non-verbal communication and focuses the parties on the mediator(s).

6. *Orientation* — given at the start of the mediation session which reviews:

- Description of process
- Uninterrupted time for presenting each side
- Collaborative process
- Voluntary nature
- Option for parties to seek advice from an attorney at any time
- Reemphasis on that fact that mediators cannot offer legal advice
- Agreements reached may affect legal rights
- Confidentiality of session
- Breaks

7. Additional types of sessions
   - Caucus
   - Procedures
   - When to use
   - How long should they be
   - Separate
   - Re-establish and strengthen rapport and trust

### Will You Try Mediation?

Asking the parties to agree to give mediation a chance is critical. In order to have a successful process the parties need to "buy in." This also provides one more opportunity to remind the parties about the voluntary nature of the process. The orientation acquaints the parties with process and should put them at ease.

### Agreement to Mediate

There are several examples of "Agreement to Mediate" documents. Each covers the basic topics of the mediation process including the legal issues, confidentiality, voluntary nature, and right to have counsel review all documents. Chances are the locale where the mediator is practicing has a preferred document, so be sure to check which version of this document is required. See the example form in the appendices.

### Setting Ground Rules

Ground rules are important for the mediation operation. Rules that stifle discussion or dialogue are to be avoided; however, creating an ordered environment in which each party has the chance to address issues, needs, and goals is critical. The mediator typically has a few they prefer but will ask for suggestions of others from the parties. For instance, some basic rules may be: only one person talks at a time; no name-calling; no inappropriate gestures; and no shouting allowed. In court, the mediation process allows the plaintiff to speak first. They are allowed time to address the situation that brought them to this point, and the plaintiff is provided equal time to discuss the same. The mediator ascertains that the parties will abide by the ground rules. Remember, this is a collaborative process, so in order for it to work effectively all should agree to the adopted rules.

## Addressing the Past: Party's Narratives

People grow up listening to and telling stories. Often, the easiest way for the parties to share their version of the dispute is through story telling. Their story often follows a time-line, fills in history and context, shares their point of view of what started the dispute along with any attempts they made to resolve it, reviews why their attempts failed, and reveals any other points that are important leading to litigation.

Each party is provided the space and time to tell their specific story of the situation. However, they are asked to limit the discussion to this dispute. It is not yet the time to discuss anything further, especially settlement or agreement options. This is done for a very specific reason.

Often the mediator hears distinct and disparate stories of the same conflict. This is to be expected. People often tell their conflict story as a timeline of events, including the context of the dispute, as well as the adversary's and their placement in the dispute. Furthermore, their narrative is likely to have been rehearsed and elaborated over time (Winslade & Monk, 2000, p. 3). As each party proceeds, the mediator ensures both uninterrupted time and space to share. The mediator takes notes of the parties' specific needs, issues, goals, and emotions.

At the end of both party's respective narrative, the mediator may utilize several tools to ensure correct understanding for both him/herself and the parties. This process may include paraphrasing, summarizing, questioning, and reframing. These techniques enable the mediator to begin identifying and clarifying the needs, interests, and goals of each party. This also allows the mediation process to move forward. The chapter on mediation skill building discusses each technique in detail.

With the parties' permission, taking notes helps the mediator keep track of all major points, twists and turns of the conflict story, attempts to resolve, escalation, and path to the mediation room all of which will help clarify the dispute narrative. One of the significant tools mediators use is reflection and paraphrasing which assures understanding.

## Issue Identification and Develop Understanding

After listening to both parties' narratives the mediator identifies the issues, clarifies using open-ended questions, and uses paraphrasing to assure understanding and to reframe the main issues to be mediated. The mediator continually communicates their own understanding of the parties' agreement in order to ensure analytical accuracy and that the main issues are identified.

### Problem Solving

One of the resolution methods mediation uses is problem solving. The problem solving methodology will be discussed at length in a subsequent chapter, and it is essential you understand it by the end of this course.

### Agreement Drafting and Final Writing

The mediator's role is that of a scribe. The mediator captures both what the parties have agreed to and what they want in their mediated agreement. The mediator may suggest ways to phrase the agreement, but in the end, it needs to reflect the parties' intentions. It is helpful to write a draft first; once all changes, edits, etc., are made, and then the agreement is transcribed to the required legal form. Drafting the agreement first offers a chance to clear up misunderstandings and make changes. Moreover, writing the draft fully engages the parties, after all this is their agreement not the mediator's. The agreement should also include any verbiage required by the court.

### Other Considerations

When first contacting the parties ask how they feel about being in a room with the other party; mediators should want to make sure there is no history of abuse toward them (verbal or physical) or determine whether there is a history of violence. If there is, then using caucusing may be advisable and will be discussed later.

### Activities

1. Describe a conflict you have personally experienced or witnessed. Then identify the indicated parts using the Conflict Tree and the Conflict Triangle.

2. Draft some basic ground rules for a mediation session.

    a.

    b.

    c.

    d.


3. Write out an orientation speech covering all important elements.

# Chapter 6:

# Mediation Process and Communication

# Mediation Process and Communication

## Objectives

- Know the stages of mediation;
- Develop and improve communication skills;
- Understand neutrality

## Stages of Mediation

There are several variations of the stages of mediation. Some are succinct and straight-forward while others offer in-depth descriptions. The mediation process/stages covered in this course are Chris Moore's version known as the "Twelve Stages of Mediator Moves" (Moore, 2003, pp. 68-69). Figure 15 shows how the stages correspond to the stages Virginia advocates. The stages are as follows:

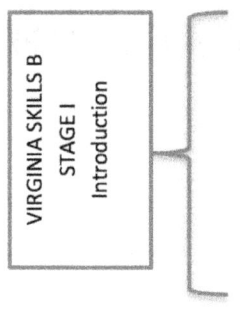

1. Establishing Relationship with the Disputing Parties
2. Selecting a Strategy to Guide Mediation
3. Collecting and Analyzing Background Information
4. Designing a Detailed Plan for Mediation
5. Building Trust and Cooperation
6. Beginning the Mediation Session

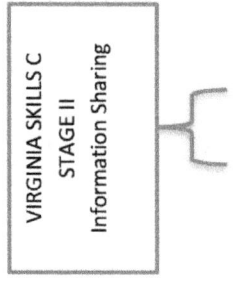

7. Defining Issues and Setting an Agenda

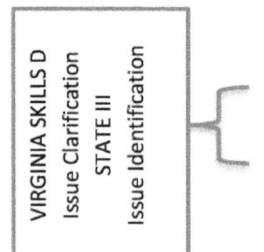

8. Uncovering Hidden Interests of the Disputing Parties

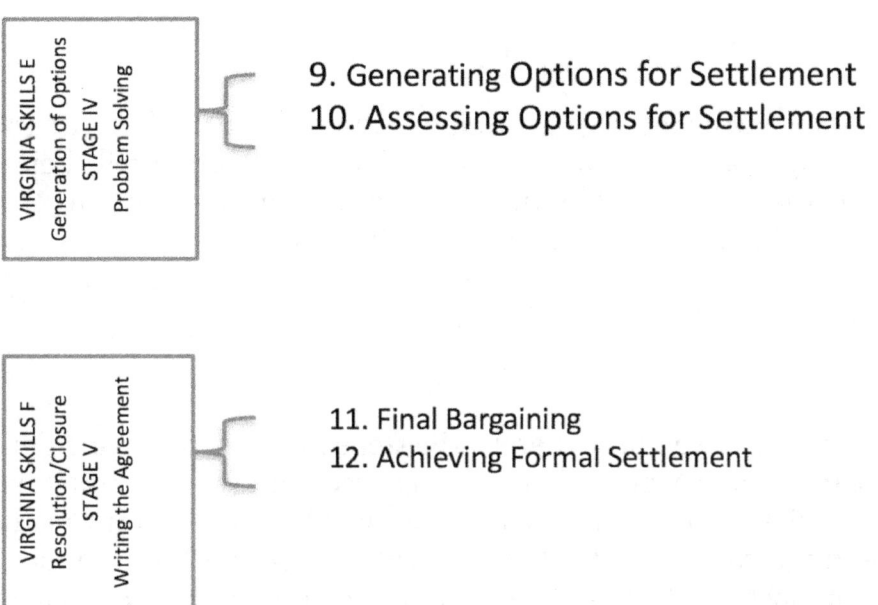

**Figure 15: Virginia's 12 Stages of Mediation**

*Note: The required skills by which a mentee is evaluated are dually labeled as Virginia Skill and Stage number. See the Mentee Evaluation Form in the Appendix F4 for an expanded explanation of each component of the skill.*

### Stage 1.

Stage 1 is the entry stage. The mediator can enter into the dispute through several ways: direct invitation from one or all the parties; referral by secondary parties; direct initiation by the mediator; or appointment by a government entity such as the court or Judge (Moore, 2003, p. 85). The tasks to be accomplished at this stage include:

- The mediator initiates contact with the parties;

- Build credibility personally, institutionally, and procedurally;

- Rapport building is critical at this stage;

- Explain the mediation process, the mediator's role, and negotiation to the parties;

- Gain the party's commitment to mediate (Moore, 2003, pp. 90-91)

### Stage 2.

Stage 2 is included in the entry stage too. Mediators are the most familiar with approaches to mediation and will educate the parties about alternatives. The most common approach we use in court mediation is the problem solving method. It will be discussed in a subsequent chapter. After the parties select the best approach and setting, the mediator will coordinate the logistics. Generally all court referred mediations take place in the court-house (Moore, 2003, pp. 102-103).

### Stage 3.

Stage 3 includes the mediator to collecting data and information from all parties (Moore, 2003, p. 118). Once they have agreed to mediate then the parties often tell their story/narrative, and it is the mediator's job to identify the issues, positions, and interests. The mediator's analysis of their stories help reframe the conflict and they begin to develop the plan or strategy leading to a resolution (p. 119). The mediator's reflective listening and questioning skills are critical at this stage is (p. 131).

### Stage 4.

In stage 4 the mediation plan is developed whereby the steps initiated by the mediator will help the parties explore options to eventually reach an agreement (Moore, 2003, p. 145). The discussion for the mediation plan is limited to what will be used in court mediation. The number of people in the room dictates the physical setting and how the mediation table will be arranged. In most court rooms the tables are rectangular, so the parties will either sit across from one another with the mediator at the head or the parties can sit side by side with the mediator sitting across from the two. Parties often choose to sit across from each other. Included and important at this stage is establishing ground rules; the mediator may offer a few and ask the parties what ground rules they would like to include.

### Stage 5.

Stage 5 may be called the conciliation stage. The mediator's facilitation of the discussion helps minimize conflict and it begins to build a psychological relationship between the parties. "Conciliation is essentially an applied psychological tactic aimed at correcting perceptions, reducing unreasonable fears, and improving communication to an extent that permits reasonable discussion to take place and in fact, makes rational bargaining possible" (Moore, 2003, p. 166). Conciliation occurs throughout the mediation and negotiation. Often strong emotions, misperceptions, negative non-verbal communication, lack of trust, and poor communication are evident by this stage (p. 166).

### Stage 6.

Stage 6 establishes a positive direction to the conflict. Common concerns have been identified and a small step towards trust begins. For court purposes, Stages 1-6 is condensed into a short period. Moore discusses the mediation orientation in this stage. Included in the orientation or opening statement are: introductions; each party's assurance they are willing to cooperate and seek a resolution; explanation of mediation and the mediator's role; statement about neutrality; description of the mediation procedure; explanation of caucus meetings; definition of confidentiality; discussion of logistics and timing; suggestions for ground rules; answers to party's questions or concerns; and secure commitment from all parties to mediate (Moore, 2003, p. 212).

### Stage 7.

Stage 7 sets the agenda and defines the issues. After listening to the parties' narratives the mediator identifies the areas of concern, seeks agreement to the issues to be addressed, and determines the order of what will be discussed first (Moore, 2003, p. 234). Framing and reframing are very important, and a skill the mediator has developed. There are three levels of reframing discussed by Moore which are: detoxification (changes verbal descriptions); definitional (changes conceptualization of dispute); and metaphorical (finds a new or altered metaphor describing the situation) (p. 238).

### Stage 8.

Stage 8 helps uncover hidden interests and the parties' agendas. Sometimes the parties are not able to identify their interests are so they need the mediator's assistance in doing so. The parties may also be reluctant to disclose their interests and goals because they believe they have more to gain by remaining quiet. Additionally, parties may be so committed to a particular outcome that it is difficult for them to separate their interests from their position.

### Stage 9.

Stage 9 is a brainstorming phase when different options for settlement may be generated. The parties' awareness that their positions are not unacceptable to the other party is a significant milestone to their willingness to find other solutions (Moore, 2003, p. 269). The mediator's job is to support the party's awareness that a variety of options should be generated and considered. Parties' leaving their unacceptable positions is critical to generating mutually acceptable options. (p. 269).

### Stage 10.

Stage 10 assists the parties with assessing their generated, acceptable resolution options. The parties work together to review their interests and how the resolution meets those interests. Reality testing using cost benefit analysis of the options is important when considering whether the selected option is their best alternative. Making modifications assure the generated options are the best resolutions.

### Stage 11.

Stage 11 is the final negotiating action; it gives the parties a last chance to express "substantive or procedural differences" between them (Moore, 2003, p. 309). Sometimes the differences are narrow so concessions gained are small. Other times the differences have been narrowed through the negotiation and details need to be worked out. Options can be unclear, vary widely, but at the same time be acceptable. The options may generate significant gain or loss of advantages in the final agreement of the selected point (pp. 309-310). Once the final agreement is reached, the details such as the deadlines need to be set; they can be fixed or flexible (p. 324). For the court's purposes, they need to be set. During closure, redefining the relationship can be helpful; it may be time for genuine and meaningful apologies or even reconciliation (pp. 341-342). Of course, the type of closure is up to the parties, and culture is an important factor (p. 346).

### Stage 12.

Stage 12 is the final activity of the mediation process; formal agreement or settlement is reached (Moore, 2003, p. 348). Moore suggests mediators consider eight important aspects for successful completion of an agreement:

1. Parties agree about the criteria to be used to measure successful compliance;

2. Parties agree to general and detailed steps required to "implement the decision";

3. The people who have the power to make the needed changes are identified;

4. The "organizational structure to implement" the settlement is identified;

5. Future changes in the parties status or agreement terms are anticipated and language is built in to accommodate such changes;

6. Language is included to manage unintended or unexpected problems that could happen after "settlement or violations of the settlement" that appear after implementation;

7. Monitoring methods are included to assure compliance and state who the monitors are;

8. The monitor's role is stated. (Moore, 2003, p. 350)

With court mediation, the Judge is the ultimate enforcer, and if the agreement is not met then the Judge will decide what the consequence will be.

Now that you understand the process, it is important to learn the skills needed to conduct an effective mediation session. These skills are learned through observation and practice. Practice, practice, practice is key to building confidence and knowledge.

### Mediation Skills

To be an effective mediator, certain skills need to be learned and perfected. This course is designed to help you master the basic skills needed to be a neutral third party. Realize that skill building is a lifelong process built on experience as well as trial and error.

The skills needed for effective mediation are communication, listening, questioning, and neutrality. Each of the skills will be explained and elaborated in the next few pages. First, the foundation of all relationships—healthy and unhealthy—is the ability or inability to communicate. Often people have poor communication skills, which lead to conflict frequently making miscommunication the source of conflict.

### Communication

The following are questions to ask while building communication skills.

- What is the basis for good communication?

- How do people connect so that each person feels genuinely heard?

- How can disputants communicate what they have to say in a conducive and effective way?

- How can a conflict resolver help turn ineffective, destructive, or nonproductive communication into more constructive exchanges? (Mayer, 2012, p. 182)

Communication aspects include:

- Verbal

- Non-verbal

- Direct

- Indirect

- Symbolic

- Concrete

- Interactive

- One-way (Mayer, 2012, pp. 182-184)

### Description of good communication

Good communication is important for good conflict management and particularly during mediation. For mediators, the art of communication is critical to know and nurture in the parties. It can be easy and simultaneously complex (Mayer, 2012, p. 182). The communication components are: speaking, listening, verbal cues, and non-verbal cues. Thankfully, communication skills can be learned, practiced, and improved (Mayer, 2012, p. 182).

The consensus among communication writers is that good communication skills are based on intention and not methods. Fortunately, it allows for mistakes despite full and focused energy to communicating effectively (Mayer, 2012, p. 183). Despite interruptions, using "I" messages, active listening, poor questioning, and boredom, as long as intention and focus are present, effective communication can be accomplished.

Bernard Mayer asserts in his book *The Dynamics of Conflict* that the following "attitudes or mind-sets" are important for effective and successful communication and in particular in conflict situations:

- Caring about what others are saying is the heart of good communication.

- There is always new information to learn from a communication.

- Good communication requires focused energy.

- Effective communication always goes two ways and requires a joint effort between speaker and listener.

- Communicating is different from persuading, evaluating, and problem solving.

- Tolerance of people's difficulty in communicating (including our own) is essential.

- The best communication occurs when we are genuine and natural. (Mayer, 2012, pp. 184-185)

Effective interpersonal communication is interactive and requires a partnership. Usually communication is neither linear nor a one-way street; it often has twists and turns. The essence of communication is teamwork; both parties working together to understand the other, not necessarily agreeing or liking each other, but connecting. However, connecting is not easy and often requires a process of listening and decoding the messages received (Mayer, 2012, p. 186). Delivering intended ideas in an understandable manner and maintaining a safe atmosphere are also part of the communication process.

Mayer describes communication as "The Communication Loop" (Mayer, 2012, p. 188). The speaker and the listener are engaged in speaking, listening, feedback, and delivery. First, the speaker needs to assist the other party in listening so they feel heard. While listening both hearing the message and offering feedback are essential to the "Communication Loop" (p. 188). Feedback is important to enhance meaning and understanding. Other parts of the communication process are: 1) delivery — refers to the pattern of speaking; 2) atmosphere — emotion or tension felt during intense exchanges; and 3) subtle non-verbal communication— body posture, gestures, etc. It is critical for the parties and the mediator to make a connection so that if there is misunderstanding, the loop offers a chance to refine meaning and understanding.

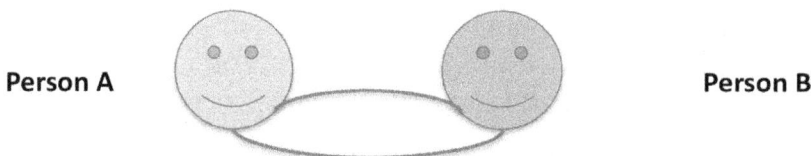

Person A          Person B

**Figure 16: Interpretation of Communication loop**

Making sure that the speaker's message is heard and understood in the manner intended, and that the listener is hearing and understanding the message as intended, is essential in mediation. One cannot assume the listener will automatically understand and decode the message as intended. People speak through their lens and listen through their lens as well. To review, the lens includes: experience, education, beliefs, values, and culture.

Blocks to communication. People often use communication barriers, which totally block their intended message. Unfortunately, the barriers tend to lower self-esteem; cause defensiveness, resistance, and resentment; and lead to defensiveness, withdrawal, or feelings of defeat and inadequacy (Bolton, 1979, p. 15).

Thomas Gordon, a communication expert, created a list of conversation spoilers — he calls the "dirty dozen"—that cause high risk of miscommunication:

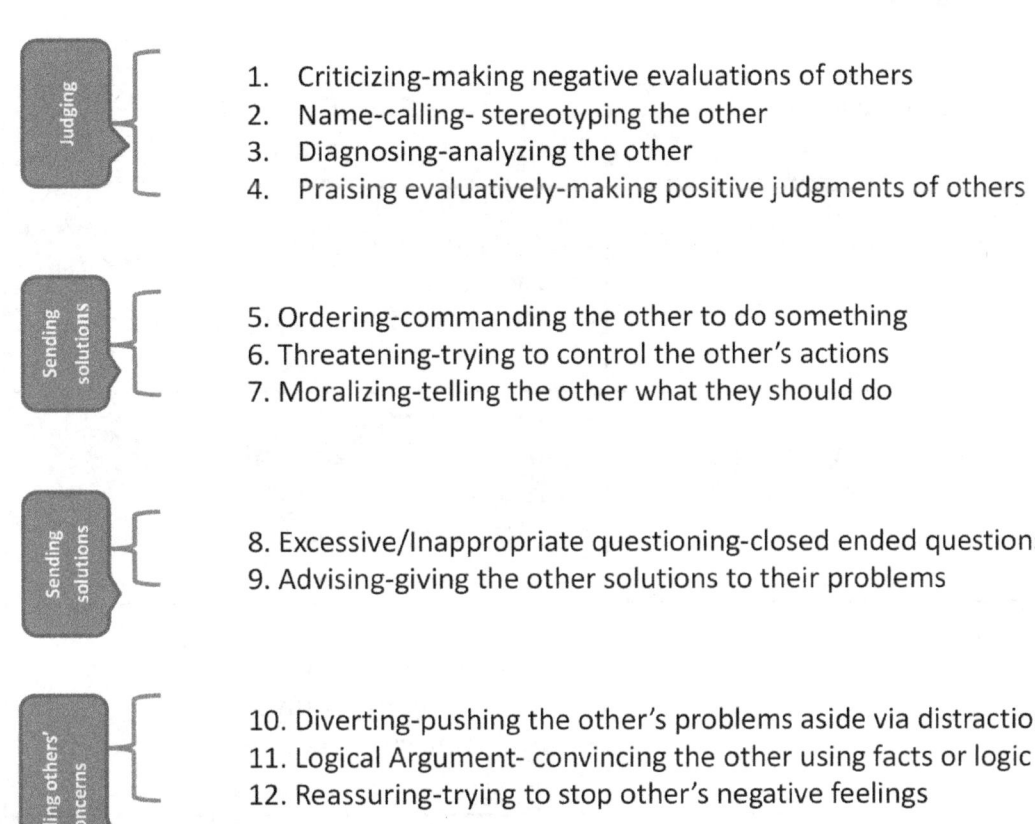

**Judging**
1. Criticizing-making negative evaluations of others
2. Name-calling- stereotyping the other
3. Diagnosing-analyzing the other
4. Praising evaluatively-making positive judgments of others

**Sending solutions**
5. Ordering-commanding the other to do something
6. Threatening-trying to control the other's actions
7. Moralizing-telling the other what they should do

**Sending solutions**
8. Excessive/Inappropriate questioning-closed ended questions
9. Advising-giving the other solutions to their problems

**Avoiding others' concerns**
10. Diverting-pushing the other's problems aside via distraction
11. Logical Argument- convincing the other using facts or logic
12. Reassuring-trying to stop other's negative feelings

**Figure 17: The "Dirty Dozen" of High Risk Communication**

## Listening

True listening is much more than merely hearing sounds which form words. Most people spend their waking hours listening but unfortunately are not good listeners. When people are not active listeners, they hear but are missing other communication components. In order to hear the entire message, the listener must pay attention to the non-verbal communication such as inflection, emotion, body language, and delivery. The ability to listen positively affects people's relationships, so it pays to perfect listening skills. According to Professor John Drakeford:

Hearing is a word used to describe the physiological sensory processes by which auditory sensations are received by the ears and transmitted to the brain. Listening, on the other hand, refers to a more complex psychological procedure involving interpreting and understanding the significance of the sensory experience. (as cited by Bolton, 1979, p. 32)

Listening and hearing are imbedded within language. The word listen is from two Anglo-Saxon words. The first is hlystan meaning "hearing" and the other is hlosnian meaning "to wait in suspense" (Bolton, 1979, p. 32). So, therefore, listening is hearing, waiting, and connecting with the speaker.

Bolton describes listening as three skill clusters presented in Table 1.

| Skill clusters | Specific Skills |
|---|---|
| <u>Attending Skills</u><br>Giving physical attention to another person | • A posture of involvement<br>• Appropriate body motion<br>• Eye contact<br>• No distracting environment |
| <u>Following Skills</u><br>Stay out of the speakers' way so as to hear the speakers point of view | • Door openers<br>• Minimal engagement<br>• Infrequent questions<br>• Attentive silence |
| <u>Reflecting skills</u> | • Paraphrasing<br>• Reflecting feelings<br>• Reflecting meanings<br>• Summative reflections |

**Table 1. Skill Clusters for Listening** (*Source: Bolton, 1979. p.33*)

## Styles of Listening

**Centered**. The Mennonites advocate a centered listening style; it helps the listener connect with the other's heart (Schrock-Shenk, 2000, p. 74). It suggests that both hearing the other's words and hearing beyond the words help the listener to understand the total meaning of the message. It asserts, "You are a person of great worth and, whether or not I agree with you, I want to hear what's in your heart" (p. 74).

**Intensive**. A distinctive listening style that advocates communication is synonymous with respect (Phillips, 2001, p. 38). Placing ourselves in another's shoes is a way to show respect plus it deepens and adds richness to the communication. Intensive listening promotes being non-critical of others who have difficulty expressing themselves perfectly. The listener is encouraged to hear beyond the spoken word and identify feelings and deeper meaning. Additionally, it restates an old adage that if one is pointing their finger at another, then there are three fingers pointing back with a twist. Northwest Indian Elder Johnny Moses says, "whatever you accuse another of is three times more true of you" (as cited in Phillips, 2001, pp. 38-39).

**Active and Reflective**. People communicate not only with words but also with facial expressions, physical gestures, and body position (Katz et al., 2011, p. 19). An attentive listener hears the words while simultaneously observing non-verbal cues, following their thoughts and feelings, and understanding the speaker's perspective. Reflective listening is more than paying attention to the message content; it also includes paying attention to feelings and then responding appropriately to what was heard (p. 19). Active listening requires demonstrated participation by giving one's full attention. The listener hears the words, observes body language, and perceives the speaker's message so it is clear they understand their point of view (p. 19).

Attending skills focus on the non-verbal message and are a component of reflective listening. When a listener uses attending skills, they give their physical and psychological attention to the speaker, which indicates that the listener is interested and is paying attention (Katz et al., 2011, p. 19). Eye contact; forward body position, absence of unnecessary movement, supportive atmosphere, and active silence all are part of attending skills (pp. 19-20).

**Paraphrasing**. The listener paraphrases the speaker's message as interpreted through the listener's lens capturing the essence of the speaker's content (Bolton, 1979, p. 61). A good paraphrase is concise. Paraphrasing only reflects the main points of the speaker's delivered message and cuts out extraneous information. Paraphrasing focuses on the content of the message and excludes any emotions. To be effective, a paraphrase should use some of the speaker's words. In order to clarify a point, the listener does not "parrot" the speaker's words exactly but summarizes the message in their own words.

**Summarization**. Summarization is a brief restatement of the speaker's message including feelings and themes of the longer conversation period rather than shorter periods (Bolton, 1979, p. 59). Typically a summary links a number of comments and feelings by condensing them into a few sentences. Summarization helps the speaker develop an integrated picture of what speakers have said (p. 59).

A good summary helps the listener convey their understanding of what the speaker said. The speaker may be better able to assimilate what they said through hearing the listener's version of what they understood the speaker to say. Effective summaries can tie loose strands of the conversation together (Bolton, 1979, p. 61).

### Questioning

The purpose of questioning is to gain additional information or to clarify points made. Depending on their focus, questions can be constructive or destructive. There are generally four types of questions:

**1. Open-ended:** Such questions invite the person to elaborate their experience, point of view, and position. A "yes" or "no" response is not appropriate, nor is a short answer (Katz et al., p. 12). It supports an answer, which has been fully explored based on their experience. Open-ended questions invite the parties to explore things about which they may be unconscious (p. 12).

*Examples:*

"Can you tell me more about......?"

"I want to understand...., can you tell me more about.....?"

"How was the.....for you?"

**2. Closed-ended**: Questions of this type elicit a short response and can change the direction of the subject or signal a different agenda. Closed-ended questions often begin with "are, do, is, where, did, was, or why" (Katz et al., 2011, p. 12). Many times, this type of question is a probe for motives or justifications and often promotes a defensive answer (p. 12).

*Examples:*

"Why did you do....?"

"Where did you get your information?"

"Are you certain the other party did....?"

**3. Challenging:** It confronts the validity or content of the message as compared to the desired outcome. It specifically relates to comments or questions that have nothing to do with the issues being discussed (Katz et al., p. 12). This type of question gets the conversation back on track and move toward a mutual goal (p. 12).

*Examples:*

"Can you help me understand....and why it is relevant to this conversation?"

"I am confused by your last statement. Can you tell me how it is relevant?"

"How is your last statement related to the outcome you desire?"

**4. Clarifying:** Such questions solicit a response that explicitly describes the person's experience accurately and with transparency (Katz et al., 2011, p. 13). It invites the person to give a full and complete account of their experience, can challenge limitations of the other, and suggests a restatement when the sentence is ill-formed for the other (p. 13). This type of question is helpful when trying to understand specifics (p. 13).

*Examples:*

"Can you help me understand what specifically is...?"

"I am curious: you think 'all', 'never', or 'always'....?"

"Would you be willing to share with me specifically...?"

**5. Impasse:** Sometimes parties become stuck and asking certain questions can help illuminate perspectives and illuminate recognized areas of common interests on which a mutual agreement can be made (Phillips, 2001, p. 127). When understanding is gained in the subtleties then the parties are freed from incorrect assumptions or judgments about the other having evil motives or just being difficult (p. 127).

*Examples:*

*They* — "How do you think the other side sees this conflict?"

*You* — "How do you see this conflict?"

*They* — "What assumptions form the bases for their view?"

*You* — "What assumptions form the basis of your view?"

*Types of appropriate questions for each step:*

- Introduction — open-ended and clarifying
- Issue Identification — open-ended, challenging, and clarifying
- Solution Development — closed-ended and clarifying
- Agreement Drafting — open-ended and clarifying
- Reflection — open-ended, challenging, and clarifying

## Neutrality

Mediators represent themselves as having no interest in the dispute they are mediating and no vested interest in the outcome (Mayer, 2012, p. 286). They have no other relationship with the parties and will not advocate for one side over the other. Mediators state that they are unbiased and impartial.

The skills needed to perform competently as a neutral mediator are:

1. Suspend judgment

2. Listen reflectively

3. Analyze problems: identify issues, separate parties from issues

4. Reframe issues in clear neutral language

5. Be sensitive to strongly felt emotions, values, culture, gender, and ethnicity

## Assertive Versus Aggressive Styles of Communicating

When a person expresses himself or herself in a self-supportive manner without hurting the rights of the other they are being assertive. Thoughts, feelings, opinions, and beliefs are expressed to the other and indicate the desired outcome without infringing on the other. Asserting ones feelings, points of view, values, and desires is an essential foundation for all interpersonal communication (Katz et al., 2011, p. 50).

A person is considered aggressive when he or she expresses himself or herself in a manner that will hurt or infringe on the other. Basically, an aggressive person invades the other's space (Katz et al., 2011, p. 50). The following table illustrates the contrast between the assertive and aggressive styles of communicating.

| Assertive | Aggressive |
|---|---|
| "State feelings, needs and wants. | "Interrupts, subordinate and stereotype. |
| Have good eye contact. | Have intense and glaring eye contact. |
| Be able to disclose information, opinions and feelings." | Conceal information, opinions and feelings." |

**Table 2. Assertive and Aggressive Styles of Communications**
(*Source: Katz et al., 2011, p. 52*)

### Framing and Reframing

Reframing is an attempt to present the conflict and issues in a manner that encourages the parties to communicate in a constructive manner (Mayer, 2012, p. 127). In short, it redefines the issues of the conflict. "Reframing is not always mutual" (Folger, Poole, & Randall, 2009, p. 88). Sometimes, there must be several iterative and interactive attempts for it to be successfully reframed (Mayer, 2012, p. 127). It can be thought of as a "dance" where one party states the issues through their lens, and in turn, the other party responds/reacts to the shared point of view; so it moves back and forth until they move forward to construct a shared frame (Folger et al., 2009, p. 89).

To further explain framing a conversation, the following components (which are part of the whole) are presented:

- *Wording* — the choice of words used to describe the issues, feelings, and goals
- Issues and ideas are further supported by their presentation
- *Constructive* — it should build a positive picture

Reframing reflects the most important needs of the parties. The levels of reframing are:

- *Detoxification* — changing the presentation of an idea, concern, proposal, or question so a party's primary interests are expressed but using non-inflammatory language, leaving out position taking or accusatory language.
- *Definitional* — focuses on redefining the issue so there is less polarization
- *Metaphoric* — using a new metaphor to describe the issues or situation, helping to alter the way it is viewed. (Mayer, 2012, pp. 201-210)

Practice of Mediation in Civil Court

## Activities

1. Write open-ended questions.

2. Write challenging questions.

3. Write clarifying questions.

4. Develop assertion messages.

5. Find a partner and practice reflective listening and paraphrasing skills using the Listening Role-Play found in Appendix B3. Reframe your partner's dispute. Reflect feelings, assertions, and values.

# Chapter 7:

# The Anatomy of Mediation

# The Anatomy of Mediation

## Objectives

- Understand the third party role;
- Understand that ethics are critical;
- Be familiar with the attorney's role

## Understanding the Role of a Third Party Intervener

Mediation is built on the premise that there will be a third party intervener. This holds true for the facilitator and arbitrator models as well. All of these methods provide essential services that help people engage in conflict resolution more effectively. While all humans experience the third party role at some point in life, the mediator role is trained and carries a tremendous amount of trust and responsibility. At various times humans are either the interveners or beneficiaries from this noble service (Mayer, 2012, p. 160).

Typically the third party considers himself or herself to be neutral, but that can change depending on the system they represent (Mayer, 2012, pp. 160-161). This course is focused on mediating for the court system, so in the court system mediators are neutral.

### Co-mediation

Often co-mediation (two mediators) is used in the court system when intervening in a conflict/dispute. There is an advantage to having two people listen; one may catch points that the other misses and vice versa. Sometimes having mediators of different genders is helpful and can help balance power. Likewise, mediators with different cultural backgrounds bring perspective to a dispute that otherwise may be missed.

Some court mediation services may use co-mediation as standard procedure while others express no preference. As stated above, there are advantages to co-mediation. However, there are some disadvantages too. For example, co-mediation can be distracting for the parties, or parties may feel ganged up on and question neutrality.

### Trust Building

Trust building demands that we be at our best. It means moving toward those whose positions differ from our own (Corcoran, 2010, p. 14). Different points of view challenge our assumptions and our worldview; we may even feel that our comfort and safety is threatened. Deciding to trust another person takes faith and belief that the person will not harm the other, and that both parties have some commonalities and shared goals.

Trust flows from openness and transparency. Conversations are comfortable when we talk with like-minded people, however, under these circumstances little changes. When there are open and inclusive conversations, trust often follows. Honest conversations invite participants to the table and promote engagement. When we engage with people who have contrary points of view, change can happen.

Trust emphasizes personal responsibility, which breaks "the cycle of denial, blame and victimhood" (Corcoran, 2010, p. 15). Leading by example and being the person we demand others to be elicits their trust. People who build trust with others often have taken a "fearless look at their own attitudes and behaviors" (p. 15). Even if trust builders do not attend or practice a particular faith, they have an inner voice that offers wise counsel and helps maintain perspective and equilibrium when life becomes difficult (p. 15).

Critical for building trust is the creation of a safe atmosphere where all feel liberty to share without judgment or shame (Corcoran, 2010, p. 15). Parties need to deeply listen to each other and ask themselves the hard questions. Parties and their relationships can be transformed in this phase.

A practical framework for building trust is a five-point frame of reference offered by Rob Corcoran.

1. "Listen to others and to the deepest thing in your heart.
2. Model the change we want to see.
3. Engage with those around us.
4. Respond to needs and challenges.
5. Risk going beyond the comfort zone." (Corcoran, 2010, pp. 202-203)

Not all people are naturally going to trust the other party they are in conflict with. Whether to trust or not depends on the willingness to let the other party control the situation. Great things can happen when parties trust each other and use empowering conflict styles like "collaboration, compromising, conceding or yielding" (Folger et al., 2009, p. 125). Conversely, when trust is low, people tend to protect themselves and use "enforcing, contending, protecting or withdrawing styles" (p. 125).

### Ethics

Mediators bring skills to the process. In addition and importantly, mediators bring their values and ethical standards (Mayer, 2012, p. 274). The ethical standards stipulate the mediator's commitment to their clients, which profoundly affects the mediation process. While the disputants may not personally adopt ethical standards, when they agree to mediate they are acknowledging the presence of standards and at some level "buy in to them" (p. 274). The ethical commitments are a foundational pillar the disputants can trust, respect, and feel comforted by. More will be discussed in a subsequent chapter.

The Society of Professionals in Dispute Resolution (SPIDR) is committed to performance principles. They are:

1. Skills necessary for competent performance as a neutral:

General

- Ability to listen actively;

- Ability to analyze problems, identify and separate the issues involved and frame these issues for resolution or decision-making;

- Ability to use clear, neutral language in speaking and (if written options are required) in writing;

- Sensitivity to strongly felt values of the disputants, including gender, ethnic, and cultural differences;

- Ability to deal with complex factual materials;

- Presence and persistence, i.e., an overt commitment to honesty, dignified behavior, respect for the parties, and an ability to create and maintain control of a diverse group of disputants;

- Ability to identify and to separate the neutral's personal values from issues under consideration;

- Ability to understand power imbalances.

For mediation

- Ability to understand the negotiating process and the role of advocacy;

- Ability to earn trust and maintain acceptability;

- Ability to convert parties' positions into needs and interests;

- Ability to screen out non-mediatable issues;

- Ability to help parties to invent creative options;

- Ability to help the parties identify principles and criteria that will guide their decision making;

- Ability to help parties assess their non-settlement alternatives;

- Ability to help the parties make their own informed choices;

- Ability to help parties assess whether their agreement can be implemented.

2. Knowledge of the particular dispute resolution process being used:

- Familiarity with existing standards of practice covering the dispute resolution process;

- Familiarity with commonly encountered ethical dilemmas.

3. Knowledge of the range of available dispute resolution processes, so that, where appropriate, cases can be referred to a more suitable process;

4. Knowledge of the institutional context in which the dispute arose and will be settled;

5. In mediation, knowledge of the process that will be used to resolve the dispute if no agreement is reached, such as judicial or administrative adjudication or arbitration;

6. Where the parties' legal rights and remedies are involved, awareness of the legal standards that would be applicable if the case were taken to a court or other legal forum;

7. Adherence to ethical standards. (*Schrock-Shenk, 2000, p. 283*)

## Understanding Some of the Deeper Aspects of the Mediation Process

**Identify positions, interests and needs.** Define what the positions, interests, and needs are; some people are unaware of their differences. Positions usually are offered in the form of statements or demands disguised as solutions. Often people think in terms of their position, which may be incomplete leaving out information, hidden agendas, and outcomes (Schrock-Shenk, 2000, p. 181). Interests are wider than positions and expressed in terms of what will satisfy their resolution (p. 181). Interests are usually underneath their positions and will include things such as needs, concerns, and hopes; helping the disputants understand their interests can lead to self-awareness and personal empowerment, unlock creativity, and recognize other's needs (p. 181). The first question to ask about an issue being raised- is it something that is negotiable? Things that can be negotiated are behaviors, things, and structures/systems (pp. 172-176). More discussion about 'interests' is found in Chapter 7.

**Reframing**. Reframing is a method of restating a disputant's stated position in a way the speaker feels validated and moves away from a particular point of view in order to respond in a more constructive way (Schrock-Shenk, 2000, p. 185). Ways to reframe include going from general to specific; identify underlying feelings; launder/neutralize attacks; identify hidden offers/points of agreement/commonalities; respond to triangulation attempts; respond to speaking for others; respond to contradictory stories; and respond to blaming statements (p. 185).

**Lead a brainstorming session to elicit creative options.** During brainstorming the mediator elicits ideas for settlement without evaluating their worth. Encouraging the disputants to be creative is helpful. The problem needs to be framed in a "how-to" plan; welcoming each idea and listing it on paper encourages disputants to build on each other's ideas (Schrock-Shenk, 2000, p. 187). Try to keep this activity short.

**Help parties identify their BATNA and items that are non-negotiable.** BATNA is an acronym for Best Alternative to a Negotiated Agreement, meaning if an agreement cannot be found then identify the next best course of action. Issues that typically cannot be negotiated are truth, fault and punishment, addiction, power differences, abusive behavior, absence of decision maker, people who will be affected by the decision, issues requiring disclosure and investigation, and lack of disputants' awareness of the complexities of the issues or legal remedies (Schrock-Shenk, 2000, p. 176). When evaluating the generated list of ideas place a plus or minus beside each idea; list the potential impact by each and list benchmarks to evaluate the idea's success (p. 187).

**Consensus building.** The mediator builds on points of agreement to find a mutually beneficial resolution.

**Separate issues extraneous to the central mediated issue.** Unimportant things must be addressed later; put them aside so the disputants do not become sidetracked.

**Help parties draft a realistic, implementable agreement.** The points of the agreement must be doable. Timelines, payment amounts, and other terms need to be executable. In the agreement stage of the mediation process it is important to be specific and clear about deadlines. In addition, the agreement should be balanced; stated positively; be realistic, simplistic, and clear; spell out "intangibles"; contemplate the future; and lastly, signed by everyone in order to be enforceable (Schrock-Shenk, 2000, p. 189).

### Attorneys and Other Professionals in Mediation

Attorneys are trained to be an advocate for their client in contrast to a mediator who is there to facilitate a process in a neutral fashion and not advocate for either party or any particular outcome. Other professionals such as counselors or therapist are also advocates for specific issues or overall well-being, and it is unnatural for them to remain impartial.

Please note: mediators are not to practice law or give legal advice even if they are an attorney. When they are in the mediator role they are not to offer legal advice. Please refer to the appendices for guidelines about the unauthorized practice of law.

### Activities

1. Set a mediation session agenda.

2. Draft an opening statement.

3. Identify the positions, interests, and needs of the disputants in the pet story found in Appendix B7.

| | Positions | Interests | Needs |
|---|---|---|---|
| **Plaintiff** | | | |
| **Defendant** | | | |

4. Still using the pet story, identify common interests.

5. Draft an agreement encompassing the common ideas, list of doables, and the specifics of the agreement to be satisfied.

# Chapter 8:

# The Mediator's Character

# The Mediator's Character

## Objectives

- Understand the personal qualities needed to be a mediator;
- Know your personal conflict management style;
- Learn how to adapt their practice to work with to other conflict management styles;

Little is written about a mediator's personality and characteristics that help bring a positive discussion and can influence the mediation session. Some of the helpful attributes cited in Bringing Peace Into The Room by Bowling and Hoffman are first be at peace with yourself and the world around you; know your experience impacts the mediation process; and remain at peace despite feelings being triggered related to your own personal conflicts during the session (Bowling and Hoffman n.d., 14). The ability to transcend your own conflicts and feelings is no small fete. No group of phrases, physical gestures or behaviors make this possible rather the ability lies within your own personal qualities that bring an air of calm to the room (n.d.14). Let's call it salve; salve soothes wounds; you are the salve to the parties.

This chapter is meant to spur self-reflection and encourage you to seek personal growth. It is not meant to be a guide how to grow but does offer a few ideas how to achieve that. Find your own path-just do it!

## Know Thyself

Numerous testing instruments exists to help a mediator identify personal traits: strong and those that need work. Some of them are the Myers-Briggs Type Indicator, the Minnesota Multiphasic Personality Inventory and the Revised NEO Personality Inventory. Taking one of these is helpful and offers one some general parameters. There are numerous testing opportunities and resources found on the World Wide Web. Less recognized but particularly applicable to mediation are conflict style, conflict management, or negotiation style testing instruments. One in particular this author found helpful is the Conflict Management Style by Katz although there are others such as Ron Kraybill and the Mennonite Conciliation Service's Personal Conflict Style Inventory (Mennonite Conciliation Service 2000, 64-66); the Thomas-Kilmann Conflict Mode Instrument; and the Gilmore-Fraleigh Style Profile (60).

What attracts people to mediation? For most mediators it's the idea of helping a fellow human being in crisis. Other things that contribute to a person's desire to mediate are-they themselves are a high conflict person and are trying to figure out how not to be; or they were raised in a high conflict family and were the peacemaker; or were introduced the wonders of mediation through their professions. This is in no way meant to be an exhaustive list of how mediators find their practice it is only meant to offer a few ideas.

According to some experience mediators there are stages which the mediator hones their skills.

Bowling and Hoffman identify "Three Stages of Development" a mediator typically follows:

- Stage 1- Skills Training  Mediators study techniques including all the skills used in a mediation session, some are active listening, framing/reframing, paraphrasing, summarizing, identifying interests and needs, setting an agenda, brainstorming and finding solutions. They read about mediation, continue taking training courses and seek out opportunities to practice.

- Stage 2- Additional Training  Some mediators seek to understand how and why mediation works. They may immerse themselves in research of applicable theories, other methods or types of mediation, connect with professional and ethical standards and generally develop a deeper understanding of mediation. Their goal is to increase their effectiveness as a mediator.

- Stage 3- Personal Development  A few mediators seek personal growth that helps them become aware of how their own personal qualities influence the mediation process and the parties. At this stage the mediator accepts responsibility for their personal development as a mediator. This is an endless process; there is always more to learn about developing a deeper understanding of oneself; and to become more authentic. *(Bowling and Hoffman n.d., 15-17)*

Having a deep understanding of yourself provides robust knowledge learned through experience of how to help others. Self-reflection is an ongoing process and not a one and done scenario. By combining self-awareness, skill training and ongoing pursuit of deeper self-evaluation, you as a mediator will bring "Peace Into The Room" (Bowling and Hoffman n.d.).

Self-awareness may also be called mindfulness. Only humans are capable of being mindful. Its characteristics are nonreactive and non judgmental. One teacher of mindfulness Jon Kabat-Zinn describes mindfulness as "paying attention in a particular way: on purpose, in the present moment, and nonjudgmentally" is distracting and can be self-defeating. It interferes with acceptance of oneself and of others. Being aware of the destructive patterns of "thought, emotional reactions and assessment" and counteracting them with mindfulness is a positive solution (62).

## Mindfulness

Buddhist scholar and monk Nyanaponikda Thera states mindfulness is the unfailing master key for knowing the mind and is thus the starting point; the perfect tool for shaping the mind, and is thus the focal point; and the lofty manifestation of the achieved freedom of the mind, and is thus the culminating point (Kabat-Zinn 2015, 1481).

Cultivating mindfulness may be intentional in the beginning. It can involve awareness and acknowledgement of inner experiences like emotions, thoughts, and behavior (HuÃàlsheger, et al. 2013, 311). Mindfulness is processing what is happening in the moment without imposing judgment, analysis, or reflection and one is present in the moment not thinking about the past or fantasizing about the future (311). After a while with practice, it can become spontaneous, seemingly happens with little effort. It may be refined through deliberate practice and can bring one into deeper wisdom and compassion helping to break one misperceptions and lack of vision.

Mindfulness brings awareness and insight. By embracing mindfulness one can examine closely what is important to their wellbeing and then how it intersects with helping others heal and transforming relationships both interpersonally and globally (1483).

Mediators engage in emotional labor. They often manage emotional labor because typically their clients are in a high state of emotion and the mediator must manage the party's emotions as well as their own. Dealing with highly emotional people can lead to emotional exhaustion for the mediator and eventually burnout (HuÃàlsheger, et al. 2013, 310). It is important for the mediator to engage in self-care. Using mindfulness can pay dividends not only in their mediation practice but also in their personal lives. Research has shown that mindfulness is powerful in promoting mental and physical health for a wide range of people in a variety of settings (321). The third stage of mediator development is differentiated by continually seeking deeper knowledge and awareness.

## Mediator's Personal Qualities

First a list of qualities immersed in a sense of humor will be helpful. Such a list was constructed by William E. Simkin and Nicholas A. Fidandis in 1986 in an effort to share the qualities an effective mediator needs. They are:

- The patience of Job
- The sincerity and bulldog characteristics of the English
- The wit of the Irish
- The physical endurance of a marathon runner
- The broken-field dodging abilities of a halfback
- The guile of Machiavelli
- The personality-probing skills of a good psychiatrist
- The hide of a rhinoceros
- The wisdom of Solomon (*Bowling and Hoffman n.d., 19*).

Two of the most significant things the mediator can bring are their physical presence and qualities/characteristics their physical presence brings (21). The mediator's personal qualities can influence the parties and in turn the parties influence the mediator. Positive characteristics the mediator can bring is: being centered, being connected to one's own values and beliefs as well as their higher purpose, making contact with other's humanity, and being consistent (27-28). "We accord our clients the respect of behaving in a manner that creates safety and inclusion for them as individuals, regardless of their background, appearance, or station in life" (28). Another worthwhile discussion relating to mindfulness is one about emotional intelligence.

## Emotional Intelligence

In 1995 Daniel Goleman wrote the bestseller *Emotional Intelligence* and aroused the collective intelligence of researchers (Bowling and Hoffman n.d., 151). Goleman defines emotional intelligence (EQ) as "the capacity for recognizing our own feelings and those of others, for motivating ourselves, and for managing emotions well in ourselves and in our relationships" (152). Goleman's book pushed the study and field of emotional intelligence into the public space.

Harvard professor Howard Gardner wrote about multiple intelligences in 1983 and spurred the concept of emotional intelligence its field. Gardner argued there are other forms of intelligence in addition to cognitive intelligence called "personal intelligences" (151). They are divided into two groups: interpersonal and intrapersonal (151). Interpersonal intelligence is explained as "the ability to understand and relate to other people" (151). Intrapersonal intelligence is defined as "the ability to understand and manage one's internal feelings" (151). Several researchers Reuven Bar-On and Peter Salovey along with Jack Mayer published studies about emotional intelligence. Bar-On developed a measurement instrument called EQ while Salovey and Mayer worked together to study how seemingly very smart people can do things that appear stupid (151).

The research shows that emotional intelligence is both teachable and learnable, anyone motivated to increase their EQ can (152). An individual can improve their EQ and enhance their performance and success in life.

Twenty competencies jointly come from Goleman and his colleagues and depend on a set of learned skills that serve holistically as building blocks for the particular competency. The success one realizes from mastering one competency is significant and if one masters a "cluster of related competencies" the secondary payoff is even larger (153). The twenty competencies Goleman and his colleagues identified are divided into four categories: self-awareness, self-management, social awareness and social skills. Each of these categories has personal attributes associated or "clustered" with them and they are:

- Emotional self-awareness
- Accurate self-awareness
- Self-confidence
- Self-Management
- Self-control
- Trustworthiness
- Conscientiousness
- Adaptability
- Achievement orientation

- Initiative
- Social Awareness
- Empathy
- Organizational awareness
- Service orientation
- Social Skills
- Developing others
- Leadership
- Influence
- Communication
- Change catalyst
- Conflict management
- Building Bonds
- Teamwork and collaboration (153-154)

## What does this have to do with the Mediator?

Mediators create a safe space for the parties to express their emotions. Because mediators are at some level in tune with emotions they are able to recognize the partys emotional blocks and help them overcome them. At the base of most conflicts is an emotional block impeding objective discussion between the parties. One of the mediators roles is to encourage the parties to explore and express their emotions; with the mediator serves as an active listener thus fulfilling the needed role of someone to listen (154). One caveat to mediating safely is there is no threat or past physical violence in the relationship of the parties.

Discussion regardless of the emotional intensity typically brings new information to light and maybe illuminate new paths to resolution. By encouraging parties to share their experience along with why they feel the way they do; what is happening in their lives as a result of the conflict and bringing clarity to their position can help remove the block (155). When the mediator is highly emotional intelligent they are typically more comfortable with the parties expressing emotion.

Some mediators feel that emotional expressions are not necessary; typically they are attorneys or are somehow attached to the legal field (not receptive to emotional discussions) (155). Of course there are other mediators who are not attached to the legal field who are also uncomfortable with emotional expression because they themselves are afraid of emotion, so fear expression of emotions in others (155). Realize, the parties are likely to be emotional, have a strong desire to share their emotions and when they are cut off or denied the opportunity to express them it can derail the mediation process.

## Preparing Mind and Body Prior to Mediation Session

Developing a routine prior to each and every mediation session is helpful. Whether it is using mediation, prayer, music or reading, engaging in something that promotes self validation, connects one to the universe, settles their thoughts and emotions, and generally promotes inner peace, it is helpful to engage in such a practice. Connecting with the universe is an individual endeavor and cannot be directed, dictated or codified in some mediation certification course, it is a personal voluntary pursuit. The important point here is to develop a routine that promotes the mediator's inner peace.

### Activities

1. What brings you inner peace?

2. If you have a centering routine, explain what it is and how you may improve it?

# Chapter 9:

# Problem Solving

# Problem Solving

## Objectives

- Be familiar with problem solving method;
- Know how to manage strong emotions;
- Be able to balance power;
- Know when to use caucusing;
- Understand the ethos of finding an agreement

Conflict is not a static phenomenon. Issues, needs, and circumstances are all subject to change throughout a dispute. Furthermore, each party possesses their own interpretation of who is right, of the wrongdoing committed, and of what would constitute resolution. As previously discussed, mediation is one of many ways to constructively engage in a resolution process. It is a method through which a third party aids disputants in a discussion about future possibilities.

As conflict is a dynamic event, mediation must be equally flexible in order to facilitate a new understanding between parties. Mediators must be able to control the process, listen, communicate effectively, and above all remain patient. This section will reflect on many topics already covered. It will address them in relation to problem solving during mediation. Please refer to prior chapters in this manual for more detailed discussion on specific concepts.

## Managing Difficult Emotions

Emotions are ever present in human affairs. They may be positive or negative. Frequently, people will keep emotions hidden and strive to be calm and rational individuals; however, conflict has a way of creating and exposing emotion. In fact, Moore (2012) states that, "Emotions are the energy that fuels conflict" (p. 13).

While emotions may flare at any point during the mediation, it is possible that they will arise while sharing stories of the conflict. In some cases, mediation is the first contact the parties have had with one another in some time. Past hurt and anger may come to the forefront during the outset of a meeting.

Mediators should remain aware of emotions present during a session, and use judgment in determining where intervention is necessary. Maintaining a productive process is essential to mediation. Picard (2002) points out that it is easier to prevent parties from "losing it" than it is to regain control over the process once it is lost (p. 134).

Managing difficult emotions will help maintain a positive environment for clear communication and joint problem solving. Moore (2003) offers several suggestions for promoting a positive emotional climate.

- Prevent interruptions or verbal attacks;

- Encourage parties to focus on the problem, not one another;

- Translate value-laden or judgmental language into less emotionally charged language [see framing and reframing];

- Affirm clear descriptions or statements, and gestures made in good faith without siding on substantive issues [see paraphrasing and summarizing];

- Remind parties of established ground rules;

- Intervene to prevent conflict escalation, abuse, or violence [see caucusing]. (p. 229)

Picard (2002) offers additional advice on managing emotions. She asserts that it is necessary to be direct and intervene in cases of accusatory, blaming, and critical statements. When doing so, it is important to be understanding and acknowledge emotions present before redirecting difficult emotions (p. 134). Piccard presents several types and levels of intervention that a mediator deems appropriate in a situation.

- *Body language*: Use body orientation or gestures to intervene.

- *Acknowledgement*: Voice recognition of present emotions, and perhaps explore roots or sources of the emotion. For example, "It is clear you are angry and that tells me how important this issue is to you. What is it that is triggering you to feel this way?"

- *Normalize*: Assure parties that emotions often arise during conflict and such emotions are to be expected. For example, "When people get angry or feel defensive, it is typical of them to interrupt especially when they do not agree. If you can hold your comments, I will make sure you have time to respond afterwards."

- *Educate*: If accusatory or offensive language is used, inform the parties how it may affect the process. Aid the party in restating or reframe when such language is used. For example, "Words like 'idiot' create defensiveness. Is there any way you can state what you are feeling more neutrally? What is it that is frustrating you?"

- *Venting*: Encourage rational versus emotional discussion. For example, "It seems what was said a few minutes ago was really triggering and upsetting you. Perhaps you can tell them what you are reacting to?"

- *Confronting discrepancy*: Assist parties in understanding how behavior and difficult emotions may be hindering the process. For example, "When you say you are upset to me [mediator], tell the other party instead" also, "When you say you are angry, you smile. Why?"

- *Offer a break*

- *Recognize difficulty and point out progress*: For example, "This hasn't been easy for either of you, and there is certainly more to discuss. However, consider the progress we have made...." (Picard, 2002, p. 134-135)

While difficult emotions will arise, keep in mind emotions may also be constructive to the process. Mayer (2012) asserts that while emotions may fuel conflict, they may also aid in de-escalating conflict (p. 14). There is always a chance that emotions may aid in reestablishing the parties relationship or may help in identifying issues, needs, and goals, which need to be discussed.

## Balancing Power in the Room

Power, like emotion, is ever present in human affairs. It is a basic function of human interaction and interpersonal relationships. Power is present during conflict. Mayer (2012) describes power as the "currency" of conflict (p. 67). In fact, parties must have at least some form of power to utilize, even if it is slight, for conflict to occur (p. 69). Fundamentally, power may be understood as the ability to influence an outcome (Moore, 2003, p. 377).

There are numerous sources of power one may draw upon. Several authors (Mayer, 2012, p. 74-77; Moore, 2003, p. 378; Picard, 2002, p. 130) combine to create a wide picture of the various sources of power in the list that follows. However, this list is not comprehensive.

- *Formal authority* — Authority granted by an institution;

- *Legal prerogative* — Customs, rules, and laws provided and outlined by legitimate institutions that provide the ability for action, decisions, and outcomes;

- *Information* — Knowledge as a source of power, especially when knowledge is hidden or unknown to the other party;

- *Associational influence* — Power derived by connections to individuals with other sources of power, generally to a greater degree, such as individuals in positions who can generate or sway decisions or outcomes.

- *Resources* — Access to money, time, labor, etc.;

- *Rewards and sanctions* — The ability to grant or withhold rewards and the ability to impose negative consequences on another;

- *Nuisance* — Ability to irritate;

- *Procedural power* — Ability to influence or control a process;

- *Habitual power* — Power derived from opposing change. It is usually easier to maintain the status quo than it is to enact meaningful change. This is often referred to as the power of inertia;

- *Moral power* — Power through appealing to beliefs or values;

- *Personal characteristics* — Power derived from an array of personal characteristics such as intelligence, stamina, communication skills, or strength;

- *Perception of power* — Belief that one possesses power, and then persuading another party that the power is legitimate or real;

- *Definitional power* — Ability to define issues, situations, the conflict itself, or outcomes in a beneficial way to a party.

Sources of power are what parties in conflict wield or draw upon to achieve desired goals and outcomes. They are not mutually exclusive or zero-sum.

It is not whether power is used in conflict, but how and to what degree (Mayer, 2012, p. 67). As such, a mediator,primary concern is not the presence of power; rather it is the distribution or the symmetry of power in the relationship amongst parties. This is, of course, among the many reasons that make conflict resolution, regardless of technique, a difficult and complex process.

Successful mediation presupposes that parties are negotiating on relatively equal terms (Picard, 2002, p. 131). It is significant to consider the power dimensions present during mediation as major imbalances in power may hinder the overall process. Furthermore, major imbalances in power will almost certainly mitigate or prevent helpful outcomes or agreements amongst parties.

Achieving a perfect balance of power during mediation is impossible. Sources of power are vast and continually shift, as it is not a fixed commodity. In a perfect scenario, a mediator would successfully shift the power dynamic between parties from "power over" into a "power with" dynamic (Picard, 2002, p. 131). This would aid parties in seeing the conflict as a mutual problem to resolve together, as opposed to a situation to be won.

However, a more practical objective is to generate a more symmetrical power relationship by lessening the impact of power imbalances. To do so, the mediator should ensure equal time for parties to tell their story and to state interests (p. 131). Another strategy is to slow the process and aid a weaker party in expressing concerns (p. 131). Sometimes simply moving closer to a party, shifting seating arrangements, changing one's tone of voice, or calling for a break may shift power imbalance within mediation (p. 131).

### Caucusing

So far we have discussed how to manage difficult emotions and power during mediation. A mediator must be creative, flexible, and firm when maintaining control of a session. However, there are situations where the emotions are too great and the power imbalances are too large for the mediator to mitigate in the room. Either will stall the mediation process. Thus, when the mediator feels either has become sufficiently hindering, it is time to separate the parties.

Often when powerful emotions are present or there is a wide power imbalance, the effect goes beyond stalling the process itself. It may not only make the mediation difficult due to interruptions or barbed comments, but may also cause interests, needs, and goals to

---

be unrealized by either party. Resolution and possible agreements are left unnoticed, as neither party is able to sufficiently focus on the future.

Caucusing is a technique that separates the parties yet allows the mediation to continue. During a caucus the mediator meets with each party separately. The overarching goal in doing so is to restore a productive process and resume facilitating constructive communication between parties.

The purpose of caucusing transcends simply separating unruly or difficult parties. Other purposes of caucusing may include:

- Check each side's perspective

- Helping each party to check the reality of their position

- Explore new possibilities of movement between parties

- Discover concerns that have yet to surface

- Clarify perceptions and uncover resistance to movement

- Identify mediator-party issues that need to be addressed

- Allow parties to discuss options without being scrutinized by the other party (Piccard, 2002, p. 126)

When conducting a caucus, there is a wide array of factors to keep in mind.

- Always meet with both sides

- Be aware of time spent with each party and try to maintain parity in time spent with each party

- Be sure to clarify and understand what information parties want shared, as well as information they wish to remain confidential

- Consider when it is appropriate to reconvene joint mediation, and how to do so smoothly (Picard, 2002, p. 127)

Simply creating space between parties and providing a forum for the mediator to have single party interaction may sufficiently shift the dynamic between parties and thereby allow the mediation process to move forward. The separation may allow interests, needs, and goals to be identified that were suppressed by the presence of the other parties. Consequently, caucusing may be a powerful tool in shifting mediation from focusing on the past towards discussing the future.

### Discussing the Future

After each party has shared their respective narratives, a mediation session can move towards discussing the future. The narratives and stories each party recited included many of the needs, issues, and goals they hope to address. Moving towards the future requires parties to identify interests in order to develop possible agreements. However, do not expect this to be an easy or linear process. Remember to be patient as parties may be stuck in the past and may need creative help in identifying sufficient terms for agreement.

At its core mediation is a problem solving process and presents opportunities for "establishing, defining, building, or terminating relationships" (Moore, 2003, p. 232). Both of these aspects occur within the discussion of the interests that parties bring to the table. For the parties involved bargaining may be a difficult process, especially if they solidified into respective positions.

## Shifting Positions to Interests

Positions are far more difficult to negotiate than interests. Piccard (2002) defines positions as "ideal outcomes from one party's point of view" (p. 123). Parties solidified into positions want results and to win. Furthermore, they find these positions to be justified due to the history of a conflict.

Hidden beneath positions are interests. For any position, there may be an array of interests that construct the position a party has taken. Furthermore, these interests may overlap with that of the other party. Piccard (2002) asserts that through examining underlying interests, there are often more commonalities than opposition (p. 123). As a problem solver, the key is to aid the parties in identifying such interests.

Moore (2003) asserts that parties rarely identify issues in a clear or direct fashion (p. 252). The lack of clarity may exist for several reasons, for example:

- Parties may be unaware of their genuine interests;

- Parties have been hiding interests under the assumption that this strategy may aid them in achieving a more unilaterally beneficial agreement;

- Parties have strongly solidified into overall positions and are unable to identify specific interests;

- Parties may be unaware of procedures for exploring interests (Moore, 2003, p. 252)

Any of these items may bring mediation to gridlock; however, there are techniques available to aid parties in moving forward. Such techniques intentionally seek to get parties to start separating positions, interests, and needs from one another. This may enable interests to be identified and help the mediation process to move towards agreement. The techniques include:

- *Interest oriented discussion* — To do this, a mediator asks disputants to refrain from discussing issues and positions and instead focus on identifying interests that would make a settlement satisfactory.

- *Testing* — A mediator listens carefully to a party's statement and then restates the interests heard to the party. Through trial and error, the mediator and party can grasp underlying needs and interests.

- *Brainstorming* — This is an excellent way to aid parties in beginning to think constructively about interests. Encourage parties to be creative and ask parties to withhold critical evaluation of options. In a short period of time, create a list of interests.

- *Caucusing* — If parties are unable or unwilling to discuss interests with another party present, then caucusing is an option. Separating parties may create a space where a party and the mediator(s) can discuss the future without the scrutiny of another party present.

- *Identifying BATNA* — The "Best Alternative to a Negotiated Agreement" of BATNA is that which the parties find to be acceptable circumstances should no agreement be found. Identifying this for each respective party may help them sift through their interests and possibly separate negotiable items from nonnegotiable items. (Moore, 2003, p. 257-259)

Included within all of these are the mediator skills such as listening, the ability to utilize open questions to stimulate conversation, paraphrasing and summarizing, and reframing. As issues are discussed remind parties that disagreement is to be expected. Help parties understand that while interests may seem opposed, there will often be mutually agreeable solutions that will address each party's needs.

## Finding Agreements

Once interests are identified, it may help to create a joint problem statement. This statement will include both individual and joint interests that parties hope to address (Moore, 2003, p. 264). Steps to create a joint problem solving statement are:

Identify and restate each party's interest, and receive confirmation from them that interests are properly identified.

Restate the interests of both parties in a joint problem statement. For example, "We are looking for an acceptable solution that does X for party A, and Y for party B."

Ask the parties if the statement of the problem and the identified interests are accurate. If they are not, ask the parties to modify the statement until it is mutually acceptable. (Moore, 2003, p. 265)

Once this statement is complete, it may be possible to begin exploring the interests in further detail. Moore suggests that mediators aid parties in "looking for objective standards, criteria, or principles that could create the framework for a solution" (p. 265)

As interests and understanding solidify, agreements may begin to surface. Again, this is not necessarily a linear process. Parties may identify interests and inch toward agreement only to regress to positions or disagree over the past. However, if interests are identified and negotiation between the parties has taken place, then it is time to begin testing and formulating agreements.

## Impasse

Even with the best intentions by all parties and the mediator, the process may reach an impasse. This occurs when parties become stuck or fixated on issues, positions, interests, or the past, or parties may simply feel unable to move forward with the process. Mayer (2012) states "impasse can be rooted in the structure of the conflict as well as in the emotions, values, communication skills, problem solving capacities, or perceptions of the disputants" (p. 249).

Fundamentally, impasse occurs because one or both parties have needs they feel will not be properly addressed by moving forward in the process (Mayer, 2012, p. 250). As a creative problem solver, do not view impasse as the end of the process. In mediation, parties possess the final word on when the process is finished; however, viewing impasse as being stuck may be an incorrect metaphor (Moore, 2012, p. 246). Rather, try to understand what the impasse is accomplishing for the parties, and work constructively towards moving forward.

When working through an impasse, it is helpful to remember the following:

- Impasse is ok.

- Parties may have good reason for being in an impasse.

- The mediator can help but is unable to solely identify the reasons or solutions to the impasse.

- Anxiety and fear are not helpful, and may be the cause of impasse.

- Impasse is a natural and frequent part of the conflict process.

- There may not be an immediate solution, but this does not prevent creative attempts to work through impasse. (Mayer, 2012, p. 255 - 257)

It is important to view impasse as an opportunity rather than a block. The hesitance to move forward in the process may signal a range of unaddressed needs for one or both parties. As such, impasse is a natural barometer for the overall process of mediation. It is an occurrence that may prevent unhelpful agreements.

## Reality Testing

At this point, the parties are happy they have reached an agreement tentatively. Unfortunately, their expectations may not be compatible with a realistic agreement. They are hopeful so they may make unreasonable demands such as time in which to pay or how payment is to be made. These unrealistic expectations can derail an agreement. It is important that the mediator be the voice of reason and emphasize that reasonableness should prevail. Mediators can ask the following questions to help the parties gauge their demands' reasonableness:

1. If you were in the other party's shoes, would you accept the proposals you are making?

2. Is the offer fair?

3. Will the people associated with the parties who could be affected by the terms of agreement support the proposal?

4. Is it legal?

5. Is the tentative agreement within norms of society for similar types of cases and agreements? (Moore, 2003, pp. 304-305)

## Reaching Agreements

As the process moves forward, agreements may emerge. By this point parties have addressed the past, discussed interests and needs, and have worked through any impasse that has occurred. With all of the information that has emerged, it is not time to begin placing it into an agreement for the future.

Any agreement should specify "WHO is agreeing to WHAT, WHERE, WHEN, and HOW" (Schrock-Shenk, 2000, p. 189). The mediator may suggest ways to state agreements; however, it must accurately reflect what the parties are comfortable agreeing to. An effective agreement will:

- Be specific and clear about deadlines

- Be balanced

- Be positive

- Be realistic

- Be clear and simple

- Name intangible items such as apologies if the parties wish

- Address the future

- Be signed by everyone present (Schrock-Shenk, 2000, p. 189)

It is not uncommon for parties to regress even after the agreement is written. There may be last minute concerns or issues that arise. Patience is the key, as mediators often need to write and rewrite agreements several times before parties agree. Above all, it is critical that parties fully understand all the terms they are agreeing to, and that the terms are realistic. In the courts, a mediated agreement may be a binding contract.

**Activities**

1. Two parties' emotions are escalating, what techniques could be used to restore calm?

2. Draft a sample agreement for the Mother-Son Role-Play found in Appendix B4.

# Chapter 10:

# Document Writing

# Document Writing

## Objectives

- Know how to fill out the required forms;

- Understand the mediator's role when writing the agreement

## Intake Form

Most mediation service agencies have a pre-printed intake form which they use. Included in the form are the intake date, case number, Judge's name, code numbers, plaintiff and defendant's names, address, and phone numbers. A brief description of the case from each point of view is also included. There will be a series of things to check off such as agreement or no agreement, additional session dates, and so forth. The mediator's name and certification number is also included. Attached is a sample used in the Alexandria Mediation Service for Alexandria City General District and Small Claims Court (see Appendix I).

## Agreement to Mediate

The mediator should begin the orientation process in which the Agreement to Mediate is an integral part. As the mediator begins the parties should also be mindful of the appropriateness of mediation.

The Agreement to Mediate in Virginia must include a number of details as spelled out by the ethical guidelines. The following details and essential information court mediation must be included:

- The mediator does not provide legal advice;

- Any mediated agreement may affect the legal rights of the parties;

- Each party may consult with an attorney at any time during the mediation process and is encouraged to do so;

- The mediation is confidential except in a few circumstances (see the Agreement to Mediate in the appendix for specifics).

All mediation services have an agreement to mediate however the structure may vary. Every agreement to mediate also includes confidentiality provisions with some exceptions; refer to statute § 8.01-576.10 in Appendix C1. There is a duty to report that mediators are bound by statute. See the Duty to Report in the Appendix C2. There is a sample of Alexandria Mediation Service's Agreement to Mediate in Appendix J, which is used by the Alexandria City General District and Small Claims Court.

## Report to the Court

This document informs the Judge whether or not mediation was tried, and if tried whether or not the result was successful; refer to statute § 8.01-576.5 in Appendix C1. If it failed, the Judge will likely move into the trial phase or, at their discretion, set another date for trial. Attached is a sample report used in the Alexandria Mediation Service for Alexandria City General District and Small Claims Court (see Appendix J).

## Mediation Agreement

Reaching an agreement means success. The state does not prescribe the Mediation Agreement document's format; however, the court may require certain language be included. The form used may include legal language given to the Mediation Provider. It typically wants a brief description of the type of case: contract, personal loan, consumer, etc. The document has space to write out the agreement in detail including who, what, when, where, and how. Attached is a sample used in the Alexandria Mediation Service for Alexandria City General District and Small Claims Court (see Appendix J).

## Reviewing Your Role as the Scribe

Remember your role is to listen and write exactly what you are told by the parties. You are reminded that you may not practice law; refer to Appendix E: Guidelines to Avoid the Unauthorized Practice of Law. You may suggest being very detailed, but the agreement is theirs not yours. Remember you also want to adhere to the Ethics; refer to Appendix D2 Standards of Ethics and Professional Responsibility For Certified Mediators. You may disagree with the terms, feel the agreement is unfair to one party, or feel that it is unenforceable; however, it is their agreement and if they are happy, then accept that this is what they want written.

Things you may do as a scribe are:

- Ask questions for clarification
- Be specific and realistic
- Strive for balance
- Help parties to deal with people who ask about the agreement
- Set date for future evaluation/return to court
- Encourage having the agreement reviewed by an attorney
- Note that agreements can be changed in the future if all agree

## Mediation Agreement Satisfaction Letter

Not all courts have such a form. However, the court in Alexandria has asked the Mediators to give this form to the party receiving compensation so the court is notified when the agreement is satisfied. It notifies the court that all terms are complete so the case may be dismissed. Refer to Appendix J; these forms are used in the Alexandria Mediation Service for Alexandria City General District and Small Claims Court.

## Evaluation Forms

Each party will receive an evaluation form to inform the state, the mediation service, and perhaps the mediator about how the parties felt about mediation. This form has two sides that need to be filled out. The state uses this form to track mediation success. Attached is a sample used in the Alexandria Mediation Service for Alexandria City General District and Small Claims Court (see Appendix J).

# Chapter 11:

# Consideration of Ethics

# Consideration of Ethics

## Objectives

- Know the Virginia Standard of Ethics and Professional Responsibility;
- Understand the different points of view with neutrality;
- Understand what confidentiality is;
- Be able to identify conflicts of interest;
- Understand culture in mediation;
- Know what the unauthorized practice of law is

One of the most important principles mediators bring to a mediation session is ethics. Ethics include values, integrity, and quality assurance. As mediators certified by a state or another organization, mediators abide by performance-based standards. Ethics from various sources that encompass the best of mediation and mediators will be discussed in this chapter.

## Common Ethics Across Mediation Theories

**Disputant autonomy.** Disputants attend mediation voluntarily, so they are self-ruling. The disputants are to be given maximum control and choices; the mediator is not in control (Waldman, 2011, p. 3). The parties are allowed to present their point of view of the conflict in their preferred manner. Fairness is emphasized; disputants are encouraged to tap into their own sense of fairness.

**Procedural fairness.** The process needs to be designed in an optimal, fair manner so an equitable result is reached. Settlements are likely to be fairer and more satisfying when the mediation procedures promote confidentiality; disputants are treated with respect; mediators maintain a professional posture; mediators shy away from personal relationships with the clients; and clients truly feel they have been listened to and understood (Waldman, 2011, p. 4).

**Substantive fairness.** A fair outcome can be achieved through the mediated agreement and result (Waldman, 2011, p. 5). There is some debate in the mediation field about fairness of the outcome. The goal is for the disputants to design a resolution that is fair; however, sometimes disputants for one reason or another will agree to terms that are not necessarily in their best interests.

Several questions mediators should ask themselves about the disputants are:

- Do the disputants have the capacity to participate in the mediation session?
- Are the disputant autonomous of anyone or anything?
- Are disputant's emotions interfering with their autonomy?

- Is there a power imbalance?
- Are there implications of criminal behavior?
- Are the disputants being truthful?

The Virginia Standards of Ethics and Professional Responsibility for Certified Mediators are the standards to which all Virginia Court Mediators are required to adhere. Please refer to Appendix D2 for the governing standards.

The values the Mennonite Conciliation Service offers are universal and applicable. They are as follows:

- "We bring the value of working with, of sharing power with others.
- We bring curiosity and a genuine interest[s] in working with a catalyst for the fulfillment of the parties' desires where those desires are legal, fundamentally fair, and not harmful to others or self.
- We bring [an] awareness that much of your work involves healing.
- We bring an attitude of inquiry, realizing that the parties are the experts on their conflict, and have given us the privilege of witnessing their attempts to find resolution.
- We bring an awareness of the importance of culture, not only culture as ethnicity, but culture as gender, class, sexual orientation, organizational affiliation, age, generation, country of origin, and many other things.
- We bring an interest in learning, as those who seek to help always do.
- We bring some skills in communication, in perceiving where communication between others is not effective, and some ways of going around the impasses.
- We bring respect for the stories of others.
- We bring an attitude of acceptance, seeking to facilitate the creation of a climate of respect among all those present.
- We bring a willingness to secure a safe environment in which to work, through agreement on ground rules and the creation of an atmosphere of shared respect for all assembled.
- We bring hope, for those in conflict who have tried and not found the way through, may have lost it, but only temporarily.
- We bring tools, an understanding of human systems of interaction, and the experiences of negotiating through other's conflicts and our own.
- We bring theoretical understandings that convert to practice and inform our interventions.
- We bring a deep faith in the resilience of the human spirit."(Schrock-Shenk, 2000, p. 279)

---

## Neutrality

The concept of being neutral is debated; some believe it is not a "constructive goal"as it seems to cause injury to peacemaking's aspirations. It seems to confuse mediators with their tasks, block sincere leaders from acting on their own beliefs of justice, and harm the creditability of the entire enterprise of peacemaking in communities (Schrock-Shenk, 2000, p. 291).

Some maintain people who are attempting to be neutral do so because there is no alternative. However the Mennonite Conciliation Service proposes such alternatives (Schrock-Shenk, 2000, p. 291). First they offer what the feel is the problem with neutrality.

Neutrality is thought to be an illusion; no human is capable of being detached or objective (Schrock-Shenk, 2000, p. 291). This is recognized by social and natural scientists in recent years; it is better to be reflective about the mediator's motivating values and share those openly than pretend to have no values or be neutral (p. 291).

Father Albert Nolan of the Institute for Contextual Theology in Johannesburg, South Africa holds another perspective stating "it [contextual theology] makes reconciliation an absolute principle that must be applied in all cases of conflict"(Schrock-Shenk, 2000, p. 291). Nolan believes conflicts are caused by misunderstandings; both sides are equally culpable, and if the two sides get together the misunderstanding will be cleared up (p. 291). He gives an example where this would be totally false, for instance "one side is right and the other wrong, one side is being unjust and oppressive and the other is suffering injustice and oppression. In such a case.. "not taking sides would be quite wrong"(p. 291).

The Mennonites suggest that mediators should not hide their values, and instead be explicit about them. Mediators need to be clear and articulate about their motives and what they want others to do if they are going to participate in the process if they want our support (Schrock-Shenk, 2000, p. 291).

James Laue and Gerald Cormick recommend intervention that is guided by values of freedom, justice, and empowerment. Justice is a primary value with freedom and empowerment helping to create justice (Schrock-Shenk, 2000, p. 291). Laue and Cormick state that: "The single ethical question that must be asked of every intervener in community disputes at every decision-making point in the intervention is: Does the intervention contribute to the ability of relatively powerless individuals and groups in the situation to determine their own destinies to the greatest extent consistent with the common good?" (as cited in Schroc-Shenk, 2000, p. 291)

Interveners should analyze the context and choose the appropriate intervention method. Laue and Cormick have identified five roles universally played by interveners:

- "The activist works closely with the powerless or non-establishment party in a conflict"(Schrock-Shenk, 2000, p. 291). The activist is typically a member of the non-establishment group or is close to them.

- An advocate plays a similar role to the activist and champions one side. However, the advocate is detached, serves more as an advisor or consultant, and does not necessarily personally identify with the group with which they are working.

- Since mediators are not involved personally with the disputants, it gives them a "more general, less party-parochial view of conflict"(Schrock-Shenk 2000, p. 292). Usually the mediator is acceptable and has the assurance of the disputants.

- A researcher may come from a variety of backgrounds such as social science, policy, media, or trained observation and provides an independent evaluation of a conflict. The researcher will analyze the conflict in broad terms and is able to empathize with all the disputants.

- An enforcer brings coercive power and can be a formal agency of social control within a larger system such as the police or courts but can also be a funding agency or arbitrator. There are aspects of this in many conflicts but usually not total (Schrock-Shenk, 2000, pp. 291-292).

Mediators need to advocate for the mediation process, which promotes fairness, freedom, justice, and empowerment. This advocacy is considered as an alternative to neutrality. It will enable the mediator to stand for a number of principles related to the process such as "conduct of participants, parties represented at the table, negotiator mandates, access of constituencies of decision-making, access of negotiators to constituencies, power, problem-solving approaches, information and accountability"(Schrock-Shenk, 2000, p. 292).

## Confidentiality

Confidentiality is a cornerstone of mediation and is so important that it is covered in the opening statement. People are often fearful to disclose private information for many reasons, for example, the information may be relevant to their case and they feel it may be used against them during a trial. The mediator assures them that within the mediation session what is said, documents shared, and findings are not to be discussed or used outside the mediation session. However, there are some exceptions to the confidentiality generally centered on criminal activity and the mediator's right to defense against complaints. Of course, all this depends on the jurisdictional laws.

The Model Standards of Conduct for Mediators, a widely recognized ethics code, state that a mediator is to "maintain the reasonable expectations of parties with regard to confidentiality"(Waldman, 2011, p. 247). Generally, the Mediation Codes of Conduct advance confidentiality by stressing the following:

Confidentiality promotes a disputant's honest and open communication in mediation and supports alternative dispute resolution (ADR) methods. Without the protection of confidentiality, it is likely the disputants would be hesitant or even unwilling to discuss their interests that could help bring resolution.

If a mediator disclosed their recollections or notes of the mediation session, it could jeopardize their stance of neutrality, be misunderstood as showing bias and prejudicial to one of the disputants.

Trust could be seriously eroded in the mediation process if confidentiality was compromised even in just one or two cases; and potentially damage ADR methods in general. (Waldman, 2011, p. 247)

It is important to remember the jurisdictional laws are to be complied with first and then let the codes of conduct guide the mediation practice.

## Conflicts of Interests

Along with neutrality and impartiality, disputants must be able to trust that their mediator does not have preconceived notions of how the settlement negotiations should proceed. They also must be confident the mediator is not supporting one side over the other. It is, therefore, imperative the mediator conduct themselves and the process in an unbiased manner so as not to appear to favor one side over the other. In short, mediators should not appear to play favorites. "Proscriptions against conflicts of interest are designed to avoid inappropriate alliances between mediator and disputant, as well as the appearance in appropriateness of alliances"(Waldman, 2011, p. 277).

So how can such alliances form? Some of the alliances may be based on "preexisting personal, professional, or financial relationships with the parties or others close to the parties"(Waldman, 2011, p. 277). Such relationships may influence the mediator's impartiality or neutrality; thus, favoritism may enter in. It causes ethical dilemmas for the mediator. In such a situation, is the mediator prohibited from taking the case? How is the perception of bias combatted if the mediator knows of or about the parties? There are guidelines provided under the Model Standards and state regulations.

Some potential alliances may be short such as a conversation in a grocery store or information volunteered at an athletic event. Surely we are not considering those as potential conflicts of interests. "A reasonable person would not think those transient and shallow connections would lead a mediator to consciously or unconsciously try to benefit such an attenuated acquaintance"(Waldman, 2011, p. 279).

Questions a mediator should ask themselves when thinking about past relationships:

- Do I know these mediation parties or their intimates, and if so, what is the nature of our relationship? It is trivial and superficial or important and profound?

- Will our past contacts and current feelings toward one another sway my behavior?

- Even if our relationship has no effect on how I actually conduct the mediation, would observers, finding out about my connections with the participants, naturally conclude that I must have preferred one side over the other? (Waldman, 2011, p. 280)

Mediators must be careful not to forge interpersonal relationships with the disputants during mediation. Interpersonal, professional, or financial relationships should be avoided during the mediation process. Accepting gifts at the end of a session should also be avoided (Waldman, 2011, p. 280).

## Multicultural Mediation

Mediating disputes when the parties are from dissimilar cultures, speak different languages, and have different behavioral norms requires additional considerations. Sometimes cultures clash causing some ethical challenges. Recall the earlier discussion about how disputants view life through their lens and part of the lens is culture. "Experts in intercultural negotiation have identified a series of cultural features that influence disputing style. These features reflect different cultural conceptualizations of identity, language, and structure"(Waldman, 2011, p. 307). Below are some features to explain where cultures tend split:

- Sense of identity: Individualistic or collectivist?

- Rules: Universalist or particularist?

- Status and power: Low power distance or high power distance?

- Use of language: Low context or high context?

- Structure and time: Monochromic or polychromic?

- Attitude toward uncertainty: Low uncertainty avoidance or high uncertainty avoidance? (Waldman, 2011, pp. 307-308)

It would be easy to reduce a culture to a few traits and features however, that is ill advised. Humans are a collection of culture influenced by family, religion, and profession, so a succinct description is shortsighted. Refrain from stereotypical or rigid thinking.

Hal Abramson who is an experienced cross-cultural mediator suggests that mediators adopt a four-step approach to cross-cultural negotiations. He advises that mediators:

- "Understand their own culture,

- Research the other culture,

- Bridge any cultural gap, and when appropriate,

- Consider withdrawal"(Waldman, 2011, p. 311).

There are a number of resources to consult to help the mediator understand an unfamiliar culture; however, there is no one definitive source.

## Unauthorized Practice of Law Issues

Mediators are not to offer any legal advice. At times it is difficult for an attorney mediator; however, the two roles must be separated in a mediation session. Mediators may refer the parties to legal aid, to their attorney, or to the local bar association. Parties are encouraged to seek legal advice, but a mediator cannot provide it. Please refer to the appendices for additional critical information on the Virginia guidelines.

## Activities

1. Name the top three values you believe you possess?

    1.

    2.

    3.

2. Are the following conflicts of interest?

    a. Your coworker's uncle is the plaintiff in a small claims case that you have been assigned to. The uncle mentions he has heard about your mediation skills and hopes you will mediate his case when he checks in.

    b. Parents of a classmate of your child come to you for custody mediation. You have seen the parents at PTA meetings, but there is no other contact. Your children are not playmates.

    c. In addition to mediation, you are a realtor who regularly refers clients to allied housing services. One of the service providers you personally have used and to which you have referred clients is the defendant in a case that has been assigned to you.

    d. A woman gets into a friendly chat with a young girl sitting next to her on the plane. They are travelling to an international destination, which is the child's home country. They talk about school and favorite toys. The young girl shares that she raises guinea pigs and is quite proud. The woman asks what her favorite guinea pig's name is, and the little girl looks horrified and says they don't have names. The woman retorts, "You don't name your guinea pigs?" The young girl begins to cry. Someone leans over and whispers in the woman's ear "they raise guinea pigs to eat and sell for food." Whoops! What can be said to calm the young girl and restore a smile?

3. Write a personal statement reflecting your ethics.

# Chapter 12:

# Benefits of Role-Playing in Mediation Training

# Benefits of Role-Playing in Mediation Training

## Objectives

- Be familiar with the importance of role-play;
- Be able to debrief a role-play

Role-plays are designed to simulate realistic cases a mediator is likely to encounter. The intention is to help the participants practice essential skills of reflective listening; paraphrasing; framing/reframing; questioning; position, needs and interests identification; and eliciting commonalities upon which a mutually beneficial resolution can be built.

Initially, participants may feel awkward when playing a role. They must ignore their own instincts and values to adopt their characters persona. The participants will think about how their character will act and think; creativity is beneficial. The role may feel "fake"or compelled. The role may even touch a personal experience causing a flood of thoughts and feelings, but remember, this is like drama—it is not real.

## Disputant Suggestions

Read through your character's description. Do your best to adopt the character's persona—thinking, feeling, and acting as the character likely would. Be creative; add any details that will help convey your character's position. Try to be realistic and believable. Balance between being passive, unreasonable, congenial, and aggressive. The goal is to make this a learning experience, not to give the mediator a really difficult time.

## Mediator Tips

If you are co-mediating, decide who is going to conduct the opening, questioning, paraphrasing, brainstorming, etc. Share with each other your mediation styles and decide how to balance if the styles are different. Set up the room and create a safe space. Decide how the process will unfold, set the agenda, and make sure all supplies are available.

Chances are during the role-play there may be some confusion and frustration. There may also be some laughter as everyone is becoming comfortable with his or her roles. Remember this is all part of the learning process.

This is a collaborative effort between the disputants and mediators. Co-mediating can add additional frustration but is critical to learning. Better to practice it here than to get in the middle of a real mediation and encounter issues never experienced or thought through.

## Tips for All

Center yourself before starting and to offer time to transition into the roles. This is a learning process so it may take time and several role-plays to become comfortable with the training tool. It can be transformative, thought provoking, and emotional. Refer to the role-play analysis questions in Appendix A1.

Stay in the role and try not to break character. Confusion and frustration are natural but will pass. If someone does leave his or her role, attempt to get back into character as soon as possible.

Your trainers will be observing and are there to help. They will offer constructive feedback. During the role-play tune them out. They should not intervene except in rare circumstances, i.e. impasse. They may offer suggestions that will return you to the role-play.

## Debriefing the Role-Play

When the role-play time ends, take a few moments to relax by taking deep cleansing breaths, stretch, walk around, or do whatever will help. The other participants are doing the same thing so no need to feel that the process is being halted.

In the role-play debrief, the discussion reviews what worked, what didn't work, what feelings and emotions were present, and how the process was experienced. Refer to Appendix A2 for a summary of debriefing questions. Try not to revisit the problem presented in the scenario and continue with resolution; this is not the purpose. Feedback is important and may be offered by any and all present.

The three main focus areas for questions asked:

1. How did the disputants feel? Did the feelings change during the role-play? How and why?

2. What went well? For disputants? For mediators? Did everyone feel safe? What helped move the process forward? How did the natural strengths of each participant help or hinder?

3. What could be changed in the future? What could the mediators have done differently that would have helped? How could trust and safety be increased? What did not go well? What could have been tried and possibly helped? What was difficult about co-mediating?

Role-plays are essential for learning. It helps to learn both skills and the process. Participants may discover some things about themselves that they were previously unaware of. Journaling right after a role-play can also be helpful to the participants. Consider questions such as: "What needs to be improved or things to be learned?"and "What touched the participants at their core?"(Schrock-Shenk, 2000, pp. 314-316).

# Chapter 13:

# Professional Association and Resources for Mediators

# Professional Association and Resources for Mediators

### Objectives

- Be familiar with the professional associations and resources for mediators;
- Review the states who offer reciprocity;
- Know where to find blog sites for mediators

Listed below are a few of the numerous professional associations for mediators. Each may require membership fees or some other form of monetary compensation; however, they each offer training and networking opportunities. This is not to be considered a comprehensive list, nor is it an endorsement of any organization listed below. Research any organization thoroughly to ensure it will fulfill your individual needs or desires.

### Virginia Mediation Network (VMN)
### www.vamediation.org

The Virginia Mediation Network is an association of professional mediators in Virginia with the expressed purpose to "exchange ideas, enhance skills, increase public understanding and acceptance of mediation, act as a resource about mediation, and promote professional interests and skills of mediators"(VMN, n.d.). In order to proactively advance the organizations goals, the VMN organizes bi-annual professional conferences, promotes mediation through the work of its committees, and offers a searchable database of mediators.

A list and description of the various VMN committees can be found on the website under the VMN Board and Committees link. There is also a searchable database of mediators under the "Find a Mediator"link. Both LJ Pendlebury and Dr. Pamela Struss are listed there. Most of the literature and resources provided seem to give the organization a heavy emphasis on family law mediation.

There are three membership categories with assorted benefits. The first is the basic membership ($125 per year), which provides reduced rates for conferences, tele-seminars, and a basic listing in the "find a mediator"search database. The second is the enhanced membership ($175 per year), which provides all benefits of the basic package, as well as a more robust listing in the "find a mediator"search database. The final membership is for students ($50 per year) and provides the benefits of the basic membership without a listing in the "find a mediator database."This membership level is available to full-time students and new mediators within three months of completing the 20-hour training regimen.

### Association for Conflict Resolution
### www.acrnet.org

The Association for Conflict Resolution is a professional organization enhancing the practice and public understanding of conflict resolution. It is the largest professional organization of mediators, arbitrators, educators, and other conflict resolution practitioners. It was formed in 2001 through the merger of the Academy of Family Mediators (AFM), the Conflict Resolution Network (CREnet), the National Institute for Dispute Resolution (NIDR), and the Society of Professionals in Dispute Resolution (SPIDR).

The primary activities of the association include conferences, professional interest sections, regional chapters, committees, and initiatives. It provides a lengthy and robust discussion of ethical practice during dispute resolution (http://www.acrnet.org/Page.aspx?id=1960). It also offers a wide variety of membership types, as well as access to meaningful resources for practitioners. Overall, it is an excellent and well-integrated resource for all conflict practitioners. The link for the Washington, DC chapter is found at http://www.mediate.com/dcacr/)

### Mediators Beyond Borders International
### www.mediatorsbeyondborders.org

The vision of Mediators Beyond borders International is to build a more peace "able"world. Its mission is to build local skills for peace and promote mediation worldwide. In order to do so the organization focuses on two strategies. The first is strategy building, which includes projects to improve local mediation and organizational skills. The second is advocacy projects, which seek to promote mediation worldwide.

The MBB also offers "direct services, training and coaching in third party facilitated conflict resolution processes designed to reach agreement, resolve conflicts, solve problems, build trust and heal relationships"(MBB, 2014, para. 3). MBB is a tax exempt, not-for-profit NGO with a wide array of membership opportunities.

### Mediators Without Borders
### www.mediatorswithoutborders.com

Mediators Without Border is similar in name to the previous organization, but is an entirely separate organization. It should not be confused with MBB. This organization is primarily geared towards training for various dispute resolution practices.

**(A complete list of classes and training can be found at http://mediatorswithoutborders.com/course-offerings).**

### Cutting Edge Law
### www.cuttingedgelaw.com

This organization is designed specifically for lawyers; however, its purpose is to forge an understanding of lawyers as problems solvers. Rather than the adversarial approach, the practice of law can become one that is both "cutting edge"and forward thinking.

---

While not specifically a mediation resource, it does offer a wide array of information on alternate dispute resolution. In addition, it serves as a great resource for individuals considering law school who have an interest in alternate dispute resolution.

### Reciprocity Between States

### Virginia
### (See: http://www.courts.state.va.us/courtadmin/aoc/djs/programs/drs/ mediation/ certification_process/certification_requirements.html)

Section 4 (p. 9) outlines Virginia's reciprocity rules. The Dispute Resolution Services of the Office of the Executive Secretary (DRS) may "waive or partially waive training and mentorship requirements based on an applicant's background and experience, and may require additional or advanced training, observations and/or co-mediations as a condition of any waiver."

Essentially the DRS, and only the DRS, have the authority to grant reciprocity to mediators trained outside the Virginia requirements. They will account for experience, but there is no guarantee as it is considered on a case-to-case basis. See:

http://www.courts.state.va.us/courtadmin/aoc/djs/programs/drs/mediation/training/ tom.pdf

### North Carolina
### (See: http://www.nccourts.org/Courts/CRS/Councils/DRC/MediatorCert/ Default.asp)

This state does not seem to have reciprocity. However, there are some loopholes worth mentioning. Of the four types of mediation recognized by North Carolina, the "family financial mediator"does not need to be state certified so long as the mediator is chosen by the parties involved (refer to: http://www.nccourts.org/Courts/CRS/Councils/DRC/ FFS/Certification/Apply/Default.asp). However, the website does recommend that all mediators be certified, and highly recommends that parties consider state certified mediators.

The remaining three areas of mediation recognized in North Carolina have specific training requirements. The prerequisite threshold for mediators is similar to that of Virginia. Mediators must possess a bachelor's degree, or prove competence in written and oral skills if the individual does not possess a bachelor's. Furthermore, there are specific training requirements for certification.

Here, the mediator trainees are required to list training programs and training experience to be considered for certification. While reciprocity is not specifically mentioned, perhaps Virginia certified mediators can list experience and training completed to be considered by North Carolina as having satisfied the training and experience prerequisites. Please refer to http://www.nccourts.org/Courts/CRS/ Councils/DRC/Documents/ msc_rule8B2c.pdf.

## Maryland
(See: http://www.courts.state.md.us/macro/becomingmediator.html)

There are currently no certification requirements to act or work as a private mediator in Maryland. However, to mediate cases from the Circuit Court there is both training and education al requirements.

Like the other states, there is no direct route to reciprocity. However, according to section 17-104 (p. 652) the basic mediation program requirements listed is highly similar to that of Virginia's current mediation training handbook.

Furthermore, the requirements listed in rule 17-205 (p. 659) seem highly similar to those of Virginia. Other than familiarization with Maryland court procedures, it is possible that qualified Virginia mediators meet all prerequisites for training and certification. Please refer to http://www.courts.state.md.us/macro/ pdfs/201301title17scanned.pdf.

## Mediation Training Institute
(See: http://www.mediationworks.com/medcert3/staterequirements.htm)

According to my research it seems that the only state that even mentions reciprocity is Virginia. However, after several hours of reviewing state certification requirements, and trying to find overlap in certification requirements, the aforementioned website was found.

It compiles the requirements per state to receive mediation cases from each respective state. The website claims that the report was completed by the University of Arkansas' Institute of Government. In referencing the states already presented here, I found that the information matches up. Unfortunately, there is still no mention of reciprocity between states in certifications.

## Online Guide to Mediation
(http://mediationblog.blogspot.com/2007/01/mediator-certification-getting-accurate.html)

While I am not familiar with the author, this blog article summarizes the issues surrounding mediator certification and practice. Based on my research, it seems credible.

It seems that there is no shortage of organizations offering training in mediation. While I am sure many of these organizations do offer relevant training, it is up to the trainee to determine the validity of each claim. Each state requires training for court appointed mediators among other requirements respectively. As such, the mediator must be careful of the training programs selected. I would recommend that each person contact the court, or use a list of relevant training resources provided by the state to select training resources. If mediation is to become a robust system of formal dispute resolution, there must be a formal system of reciprocity. Unfortunately, at the moment this does not exist.

# Chapter 14:

# Summary

# Summary

## Objectives

- Give yourself applause — you have finished the basic education!

- Congratulations, now get the observations and co-mediations done;

- Join a wonderful group of people

Conflict is part of the human experience. People often view conflict/disputes negatively as a failure to manage themselves and their relationships effectively. However, conflict can be positive and bring about change.

People often use a particular method or style when engaging in conflict. The conflict styles are accommodating, avoiding, compromising, collaborating, and competition. A person's chosen conflict style depends on their level of concern for others versus themselves.

Most interpersonal conflicts are a result of unmet human needs including physiological, safety and security, love and affection/belongingness, esteem, and self-actualization. Other causes can result from differences in values, goals, data, and interests. Often the conflict is expressed in terms of a position, and upon closer analysis, interests and needs are found at the root. Interests are driven by needs and the position is the visible expression of needs and interests.

Culture can also contribute to conflict. There can be misunderstanding and miscommunication based on whether people are oriented toward a collectivist/high context culture or toward an individualist/low context culture. It is helpful to understand basics about cultural norms. Such knowledge and understanding are particularly helpful in Northern Virginia because it is so multicultural.

There are numerous tools available to the conflict resolver; however, in this course we focused on mediation and to a lesser degree negotiation. Mediation is typically voluntary and is a confidential process. The mediator is a third party neutral with no interest in the outcome and is there to assist the parties with a discussion to focus on finding a solution that will meet all parties' needs and interests.

In the role of a mediator, one can use a variety of styles of mediation selecting from evaluative, facilitative, transformative, and narrative. For court purposes, the mediators use a combination of facilitative and narrative. The mediator's role is to bring an approach through process; reframing of the issues to lessen the we/they stance; a skill set of communication, negotiation, and problem solving; personal commitment to help and do no harm; ethics and guidelines as set by the state; and best acceptable practices.

Conversely, it is important to remember that a mediator is neither judgmental nor do they bring a ready-made solution. They also do not have the power to make the involved parties reasonable or change the circumstances of what happened. In addition, the mediator does not bring additional resources.

The party's role is to be willing to discuss what happened from their perspective. They also need to have an idea of what they wish to happen in order to resolve their dispute. Generally, it helps if the parties have an idea of what their needs and interests are; however, the mediator may have to assist them in such identification. Remember the parties will bring their culture, that is, their values and traditions, experience, and expectations with them as well which will influence the mediation process.

Mediation follows a process which involves intake, preparation, information gathering, conferring with a co-mediator, setting arrangement, orientation, and the session(s). After the orientation, the mediator will invite the parties to mediate. Once they have agreed, the parties will set ground rules with a few suggestions from the mediator. The parties will each share their points of view, issues will be identified, and understanding gained. Using problem solving, options for solutions will be generated and then the best solutions that are mutually beneficial and agreed to will be drafted in the mediation agreement. Such agreements may be reached in one session, or it may take multiple sessions. Remember to make sure all parties feel secure with the others in the room.

Being a mediator is both rewarding and frustrating. However, at the end of the day helping the parties learn to communicate, recognize conflict behavior, and resolve their disputes is worthwhile and is only measured in heart language. Empowering people is an awesome feeling.

# References

American Arbitration Association, American Bar Association, & Association for Conflict Resolution. (2005). *Model standards of conduct for mediators.* Retrieved from http://www.americanbar.org/content/dam/aba/migrated/dispute/documents/model_standards_conduct_april2007.authcheckdam.pdf

Augsburger, D. W. (1992). *Conflict Mediation Across Cultures: Pathways and Patterns.* Louisville, KY: Westminster/John Knox Press.

Bolton, R. F. (1979). *People Skills: How to Assert Yourself, Listen to Others and Resolve Conflicts.* New York: Simon & Schuster.

Burton, J. (1990). *Conflict: Resolution and Prevention.* London: MacMillan Press LTD.

Bush, R. A. B., & Folger, J. P. (1994). *The Promise of Mediation: Responding to Conflict Through Empowerment and Recognition* (1st ed.). San Francisco, CA: Jossey-Bass.

Commonwealth of Virginia. (2009). *Forms and applications to be used for mediation.* Retrieved http://www.courts.state.va.us/courtadmin/aoc/djs/programs/drs/mediation/forms/adr1004proc.pdf (accessed November 23, 2013).

Commonwealth of Virginia. (2011a). *Forms and applications to be used for mediation.* Retrieved http://www.courts.state.va.us/courtadmin/aoc/djs/programs/drs/mediation/forms/home.html

Commonwealth of Virginia. (2011b). *Standards of ethics and professional responsibility for certified mediators.* Retrieved http://www.courts.state.va.us/courtadmin/aoc/djs/programs/drs/mediation/soe.pdf

Commonwealth of Virginia. (2011c). *Guidelines for the Certification of Mediation Training Programs.* Retrieved http://www.courts/state.va.us/courtadmin/aoc/djs/programs/drs/mediation/training/guidelines_for_cert.pdf (accessed January 17, 2014).

Commonwealth of Virginia. (2013). *Child abuse and neglect hotline.* Virginia Department of Social Services, Child Protective Services. Retrieved from http://www.dss.virginia.gov/family/cps/index2.cgi

Corcoran, R. (2010). *Trustbuilding: An honest conversation on race, reconciliation, and responsibility.* Charlottesville, VA: University of Virginia Press.

Fink, L. D. (2003). *Creating significant learning experiences: An integrated approach to designing college courses* (1st ed.). San Francisco, CA: Jossey-Bass.

Fisher, R., Ury, W., & Patton, B. (1991). *Getting to yes: Negotiating Agreement Without Giving In* (2nd ed.). New York: Penguin Books.

Fisher, S., Abdi, D. I., Ludin, J., Smith, R., Williams, S., & Williams, S. (2000). *Work with conflict: Skills and strategies for action.* London: Zed Books.

Folger, J. P., Poole, M. S., & Stutman, R. K. (2009). *Working through conflict: Strategies for relationships, groups, and organizations* (6th ed.). Boston, MA: Pearson.

Hocker, J. L., & Wilmot, W. W. (2014). *Interpersonal conflict* (9th ed.). New York: McGraw Hill.

Katz, N. H., Lawyer, J. W., & Sweedler, M. K. (2011). *Communication and conflict resolution* (2nd ed.). Dubuque, IA: Kendall Hunt Publishing Company.

Kettner, P. M., Moroney, R. M., & Matin, L. L. (2013). *Designing and managing programs.* Los Angeler: SAGE Publications.

LeBaron, M. (1994). *Conflict resolution and analysis as education: Culturally sensitive processes for conflict resolution.* Victoria, British Columbia: Institute for Dispute Resolution, University of Victoria.

Lewicki, R. J., Hiam, A., & Olander, K. W. (2010). *Selecting a strategy*. In R. J. Lewicki, D. M. Saunders, & B. Barry (Eds.), Negotiation: Readings, exercises and cases (6th ed., pp. 14-29). New York: McGraw-Hill.

Mayer, B. (2012). *The Dynamics of conflict resolution: A guide to engagement and intervention* (2nd ed.). San Francisco, CA: Jossey-Bass.

Mediators Beyond Borders International [MBB]. (2014). *MBB services*. Retrieved from http:// mediatorsbeyondborders.org/home/services/

Mennonite Conciliation Service. (2000). *Mediation and Facilitation Training Manual* (4th ed.). Akron, PA: Mennonite Conciliation Service.

Moore, C. W. (2003). *The mediation process: Practical strategies for resolving conflict* (3rd ed.). San Franscisco, CA: Jossey-Bass.

Office of the Executive Secretary, Supreme Court of Virginia. (2009a). *Forms and applications used for mediation*. Retrieved from http://www.courts.state.va.us/courtadmin/aoc/djs/ programs/drs/mediation/forms/home.html

Office of the Executive Secretary, Supreme Court of Virginia. (2009ba). *Virginia's judicial system*. Retrieved from http://www.courts.state.va.us/main.htm

Phillips, B. A. (2001). The mediation field guide: Transcending litigation and resolving conflicts in your business or organization. San Francisco, CA: Jossey-Bass.

Picard, C. A. (2002). *Mediating Interpersonal and Small Group Conflict* (Rev. & updated ed.). Ottawa, Canada: Golden Dog Press.

Schrock-Shenk, C. (Ed.). (2000). *Mediation and facilitation training manual: Foundations and skills for constructive conflict transformation* (4th ed.). Akron, PA: Mennonite Conciliation Service.

Shell, G. R. (2006). *Bargaining for advantage: Negotiation strategies for reasonable people* (2nd ed.). New York: Penguin Books.

Smith, A. L., & Smock, D. R. (2008). *Managing a mediation process*. Washington, DC: United States Institute of Peace.

Ury, W. L., Brett, J. M., & Goldberg, S. B. (2010). *Three Approaches to Resolving Disputes: Interests, Rights and Power*. In R. J. Lewicki, D. M. Saunders, & B. Barry (Eds.), Negotiation: Readings, exercises and cases (6th ed., pp. 1-13). New York: McGraw-Hill.

Virginia Mediation Network [VMN]. (n.d.). *Welcome to the Virginia Mediation Network*. Retrieved from www.vamediation.org

Walczer, H., Schupp, C., Perron, C., & Keathley, P. (n.d.). *The Structure of International Conflict* by C. R. Mitchell. George Mason University, School of Conflict Resolution-CONF 210. Fairfax, VA: George Mason University.

Waldman, E. (2011). *Mediation ethics: Cases and commentaries* (1st ed.). San Francisco, CA: Jossey-Bass.

Winslade, J., & Monk, G. (2000). *Narrative mediation: A new approach to conflict resolution* (1st ed.). San Francisco, CA: Jossey-Bass.

# Appendices

# Appendix A: Questions to Analyze Parties and Role-Plays

## A1. Role-Play Analysis Questions

As you are participating in role-plays, ask yourself the following questions or think about the following subjects with regard to each party:

| | PARTY 1 | PARTY 2 |
|---|---|---|
| What is each party's position? | | |
| What interests are being affected? | | |
| Analyze which needs are being affected (based on Hierarchy of Needs): <br><br> • Physiological <br> • Safety/ Security <br> • Love/ Affection/ Belongingness <br> • Esteem <br> • Self-Actualization | | |
| What is each party's culture? <br><br> • Direct <br> • Indirect <br> • Low/ Individualist <br> • High/ Collectivist | | |
| What is the relationship of the parties? | | |
| What are the issues? | | |
| Can intervention help? | | |

## A2. Role-Play Debriefing Questions

The questions to ask are:

1. How did the disputants feel? Did the feelings change during the role-play? How and why?

2. What went well? For disputants? For mediators? Did everyone feel safe? What helped move the process forward? How did each participant's natural strengths help or hinder?

3. What could be changed in the future?

4. What could the mediators have done differently that would have helped?

5. How could trust and safety be increased?

6. What did not go well?

7. What could have been tried and possibly helped?

8. What was difficult about co-mediation?

# Appendix B: Role-Plays

## B1. Car Repair Role-Play

This role-play is designed to identify costs, positions, interests, and a mutually beneficial solution for both parties. The mediator will be challenged by the unreasonableness of one of the parties and their unrealistic expectations.

Participants: Elizabeth Smith-Consumer and Chris Kindly-Car Repair Shop Owner

Amount of Case: $1400

Issue: Faulty car repair

### Plaintiff

Elizabeth Smith owned a 1996 Dodge with in excess of 260,000 miles. It was her sole means of transportation to get to work 15 miles from where she lived. She lived between two metro lines both over five miles away; there is bus service, however, her hours make the public transportation commute difficult. She is very dependent on her car. She is not highly compensated so purchasing a newer car is not possible at the current time.

Recently the alternator stopped working. She walked to a gas station close to her home to ask for help. She explained to the owner, Chris Kindly, that she didn't have a great deal of money and really was dependent on her car, so therefore, she needed it fixed. The car was fixed; however, she demanded the old alternator back. The repair bill was $275 plus the core charge of $55 that would be refunded to the gas station when the old alternator was returned. She was not asked to pay the $55.

About four months after the alternator was repaired the car broke again. The battery was discharging which the replaced alternator caused so the car broke again. She was convinced that the car repair shop was trying to rip her off. Instead she went to another shop, and they charged her $650 to replace the alternator and battery. She was without her car for a week and had to use a taxi to get to work. She is suing Chris Kindly for $1400 to reimburse the new repair bill (the repair Chris had performed) and taxicab fare.

### Defendant

Chris Kindly owned a gas station and a tow truck and employed several mechanics. His station is in a prime location, and he has been in business for 29 years. He sells lots of gasoline monthly and had a loyal customer base.

Elizabeth Smith came to his station about five months ago for the first time. She is an older woman and, judging from the condition of her car, was financially challenged. He noticed she was not wearing a wedding ring so he assumed she was single. She seemed like a nice lady, and he took pity on her. He agreed to send a tow truck to pick up her car and offered her a ride back home.

The car was in sad shape, and he fixed her car as inexpensively as possible. He passed on his discount to her, did not charge for the tow truck, and discounted the labor. The bill should have been $490, but he only charged her $275. When she demanded the old alternator, he was shocked but returned it and said he needed to charge her the $55 core charge; she refused to pay it. He installed a rebuilt alternator to save her money; typically, they last the same amount of time as a new one. But occasionally one goes bad quickly. Mr. Kindly offers a 12K and 12 month warranty on his work and offered to replace the bad alternator at no charge.

# B2. Landlord-Tenant Role-Play

This role-play is designed to be similar to cases filed and assigned in General District Court. It offers a chance for a mediator to practice reflective listening, paraphrasing, questioning, and helping the parties to resolve their dispute.

<u>Participants</u>: Bertie Crook-Landlord and Sally Brown-Tenant

<u>Amount of Case</u>: $8000

<u>Issue</u>: Broken lease, & remaining rent

## Plaintiff

Sally Brown moved to Arlington, VA from Chicago, IL for a new position working for the school system. She was a new graduate and was excited about her first job after college. Human Resources gave her a list of apartments and real estate professionals who could help her locate housing. Being adept at using the internet to find out about the area she stumbled across a website featuring an apartment complex with full color pictures and tons of information. She decided it would be the perfect place so she rented a one-bedroom one-bath apartment sight unseen and had no information about the neighborhood. A corporation with a challenging reputation managed the complex. They did a credit check on Sally, and all seemed perfect.

In August, Sally moved in and found the complex to be different than the website representation. The pictures were older and were taken after a renovation 10 years ago. The grass was gone, what shrubs were left were sickly, and the paint on the building was chipping and missing. Unfortunately, she had signed a year lease and was stuck. She noticed a group of young men hanging out, and it looked like they were sharing a funny cigarette. Sometimes they would cat-call to her; she would step up her pace to get inside.

In September, she got up as usual, got ready for work, and walked to her car. When she got close to the car she noticed a window busted out. Sally was alarmed and visibly shaken when she got to work. The principal of the school stopped her as she walked in and inquired about why she was so upset. She explained, and he suggested that she call the apartment manager and report what happened. He also called the police, and they took a report.

In October, the young men's taunting escalated. They were more aggressive verbally and began following her to her apartment. Then one day it turned violent. One young man followed her. She ran and got to her apartment and tried to close the door, but he busted it open. He assaulted her, beat, and punched her. He told her it was payback for reporting the broken window, and he blamed her for a drug bust the previous week. He did not sexually assault her this time but said he would the next time. She was so scared; she did not call anyone.

The next morning she reported for work, and the principal was horrified to see her. Her eyes were swollen, and her face was bruised. She was walking with a limp and generally was in bad shape. He called the police, and they called an ambulance who took her to the hospital. She had bruised ribs, her cheek was cracked, and one leg was strained. The principal was furious. He called the apartment manager who offered sympathy but refused to let her out of the lease. Another older teacher took the young teacher in while she healed. The principal called a realtor and asked for guidance. The realtor suggested that there are a couple of clauses the apartment is in violation of and they could try to break the lease that way.

Sally Brown filed a suit to terminate her lease and the judge sent the case to mediation.

## Landlord

Sonaste Apartment Manager, Bertie Crook, rented a newly painted unit to Sally Brown. Sally asked if the web pictures were an accurate representation and Bertie said "Of course!" The apartment complex was offering a special rate of $50 security deposit, no pet deposit, and a discounted rent of $75 off a month. Sally did not have a great deal of money so the rent and deposits sounded perfect. Mrs. Crook said the deal was only good for the next 3 days, so Sally felt pressured. Ther e was an online application and a way to pay the deposit and rent via credit card through the web. Sally jumped right on the deal and was proud for finding a great deal, after all it was about $250 cheaper than any other apartment. The rent was $1000 a month. Having saved so much money, she was excited about buying a new car after she worked for about four months.

Bertie Crook was understanding about the car window and said she would have a talk with the boys. When she was told about the taunting again, she said she would talk to the boys again. When the beating was reported she was sympathetic but said there was no way she would let Sally out of the lease. She had nine months left on the lease and was obligated to pay it regardless. She said she could move out but still would be responsible for the remaining rent. Sonaste Apartments would not budge from their position.

## B3. Listening Role-Play

This is a narrative to train mediators to listen reflectively, as well as practice paraphrasing and clarifying positions. Listen for positions, interests, and needs.

<u>Participants:</u> Captain Tim Valiant-Husband & Mrs. Valiant-Wife

<u>Issue</u>: Fidelity and separation

### Captain Tim Valiant

Tim Valiant, an Army Captain, returned home from a nine-month deployment. He was excited to see his wife as they had gotten married a year before he was deployed. They had dated during college, and their families had developed a friendship. He anticipated and fantasized about how he would hold her in his arms as soon as they were dismissed and allowed to reunite with their loved ones. He also had decided they should work on expanding their family; it was time for a child. The deployment had been stressful. They had through live combat; several members of his platoon had been seriously hurt by an IED but were recovering. During the long days, he and his buddies discussed many things, but the "dads" always talked about their children. Captain Valiant wanted to be a dad; he wanted pictures in his wallet, homemade cards, and videos on his phone.

Captain Valiant came from a military family. His dad was a General, and his mom had been the loyal, supportive wife. He wanted to recreate the wonderful loving atmosphere he grew up in. His mom was active with the other wives, worked part-time, and volunteered with the family support unit on base.

The day came to see his wife and what a great day it would be. Once they were dismissed he took his wife and kissed, hugged, and held her. He noticed she looked a bit heavier but just thought it was the chunky sweater she was wearing. When they got home the intimacy continued. She definitely had gained weight.

### Wife

Mrs. Valiant missed her husband terribly. She did not grow in a military family. Tim's deployment was tough on her. She received a phone call from her old high school flame who was passing through town. They had dinner and the old flame was rekindled. She was so lonely. The old flame was in town for 2 weeks for business.

She had a lapse of judgment and after a passionate night she was left with a memorial. Her hips had spread and her chest was noticeably larger, but he would not complain. After all she had been stressed and worried with him gone. After a few days he noticed her tummy seemed to be growing quickly, and she kept putting her hand on her stomach.

He finally asked if her stomach was hurting. She retorted "no" and smiled worriedly. He asked what was wrong; she stated she was pregnant. He was elated and said "I am going to be a daddy!" Reality quickly set in, and he asked when she was due; she said in four months. The wheels began to spin—due in four months. He had been gone nine months and so she was already five months along. His happiness soon turned to horror, anger, and sadness — the baby was not his. He stated what he suspected — the baby is not mine? She said "no" and that it belonged to a high school boyfriend who had passed through town. She said she was lonely, and before she knew it they were intimate and she must have gotten pregnant. She had stopped taking her birth control since Tim was gone.

# B4. Mother-Son Role-Play

This role-play simulates a highly emotionally charged interpersonal dispute. Often when cases involve family members they can be extremely emotional. Caucusing could be used here.

Participants: Barbara Winter- Mother and Brian Winter- Son

Issue: Son's employment & contributions to house

## Mother

Barbara Winters was a hard-working mom with one son, Brian. Her ex-husband, the son's dad, had abandoned her and the boy when the boy was 14 years old. He met a younger woman on a business trip. He was quite successful so he paid for a townhome for Barbara and the son to live in. He paid child support diligently, spent very little time with the son, and when the son turned 18 years old, he stopped any contact.

The son was a bright student but got bored easily. He started community college and had excellent grades. He worked part-time to pay for gas, insurance, and social outings. Barbara was happy to pay for the utilities, taxes, and property insurance while her son was in school. The son took a computer gaming class and became hooked on gaming. He designed and played games morning, noon, and night. He quit his job as it interfered with this gaming design. He explained that he was designing new games and was confident a company would soon hire him for his design abilities. After 18 months he still had not been hired and was bringing in no income. Brian just turned 23 years old. Mom was concerned about his unemployment and suggested he find some type of job. He stayed up late and slept until noon daily. He stopped helping around the house and was not paying for his personal expenses. She was fed up and decided to throw him out of the house. She filed an eviction proceeding with the court.

## Son

Brian Winters was an above average student with a high IQ. He was excellent at math and science. His teachers recognized him for his academic prowess, and they thought he was bound for great achievements. Brian and his dad had been very close when Brian was young. However, that changed when his dad met the new girlfriend and no longer had time for Brian. Brian really missed his dad and believed he must have done something wrong.

Going away to college was out of the question because his dad's financial support stopped and his mom could afford community college if he lived at home. He started community college and did well. He worked part-time at a media store to earn some money to pay for

136

necessities and his social life. He completed junior college and moved on to a local university. He took a gaming class his second semester and found his passion. He loved gaming and was adept at design and writing code. He breathed gaming. He was convinced he could make a living at designing games and began sending out resumes for jobs. He quit his part-time job to pursue gaming; he continued school but did not take a full load every semester. He was comfortable; mom kept a roof over his head and cooked wonderful meals—life was great. Despite his best efforts, he still had not gotten the job of his dreams. He was frustrated with his mom and just felt like getting a meaningless job was pointless. He was sick of her nagging.

# B5. Needs, Interest, and Positions Role-Play

This role-play is designed to increase the participants' ability to identify and distinguish needs, interests and positions.

<u>Participants</u>: John-Husband and Susan-Wife

<u>Issue</u>: HVAC's use

### John

John is happily married to his princess Susan in February. Shortly after the wedding they purchased a home during late winter and moved in. By the end of March the weather had turned pleasant, and as usual Susan opens all the windows to let fresh air in after turning the HVAC system off.

John has serious allergies and uses a number of drugs to help him control the symptoms. In fact, John had insisted that an electronic filter be installed on the HVAC system to filter out allergens. When John returns home after a long day of working and commuting, he begins shutting all the windows and turns on the HVAC system. John's suffering includes watering swelling eyes, runny nose, and excessive sneezing. One day John became so frustrated he slammed the windows and grumbled under his breath, "I should move!" John was frustrated and felt physically awful.

### Susan

Susan was a happily married newlywed and looking forward to making their house a home. Susan grew up in the country where windows were left open, clothes hung out after washing and food came from the garden.

Susan was walking in as John was grumbling. She returned home from running errands to find the house closed up and was perplexed as to why. When she overheard John's remark, she began to cry. Susan was confused and hurt.

# B6. Personal Loan Role-Play

This role-play involves co-workers who must continue to work together after the case is heard. Emotions can be high but the parties may be guarded. Questioning is important as well as helping parties to remember when they had a good friendship.

<u>Participants</u>: Nina Fink-Plaintiff and Mary Crockett-Defendant, Co-Workers

<u>Amount of Case</u>: $750

<u>Issue</u>: Personal loan

## Plaintiff

Nora Fink works at Big Money Real Estate Development Corporation. She is an administrative assistant to the CFO and has been with the company for 18 years. Her kids are grown, and she is expecting her first grandchild. Nora was married, but her husband passed away after a long fight with cancer. She is comfortable financially but by no means wealthy. Nora noticed that Mary was very upset one morning a while after she began working there. Nora was concerned and tried to console Mary. She let Mary volunteer what was wrong. When Mary explained that her landlord was being difficult and was refusing to continue working with her because of habitually late rent. Nora felt badly for Mary and offered to lend her the $750 as long as it was paid back within 15 days. Nora gave Mary a check on the second of the month, and the rent was paid to the landlord.

Nora became concerned by the 20th of the month when Mary had not paid her back. Mary was avoiding Nora. Nora had left a couple of notes on Mary's desk to please come talk to her. Finally five days later, Mary talked to Nora and explained she didn't have all the money to pay her back. It was one of her children's birthdays, and she had a party for the child which took most of the child support. Nora was perturbed but agreed to let her pay the money back over time. Mary gave Nora $150 and promised to pay $150 a month until paid in full. After the initial payment Nora did not receive any additional payments. After numerous attempts to work with Mary, Nora filed a suit to be repaid the balance of $600.

## Defendant

Mary Crockett was recently hired by the Big Money Real Estate Development Corporation to be an accounts payable clerk. She was young and single with three children. She had been awarded child support and typically received the money monthly but always late. She paid her rent with the child support money, so frequently the rent was 10 days late, and she incurred late charges as result. One morning about five months after she began her job, she arrived in tears. She was a mess, makeup running down her face, eyes swollen, and depressed.

Mary's landlord had threatened that if she was late one more time, he was going to start eviction proceedings. It was the second of the month and still no child support. She needed a temporary loan to pay the rent and then would immediately pay it back soon as the child support came. Mary needed $750. Mary was thrilled when Nora offered to lend her the money and had full intention of repaying the money as soon as she received the child support. In the meantime her oldest child turned seven and wanted to have a party at the Mousey Cheese Restaurant like all of his friends. Mary wanted to give her child his dream, so she took the child support money received on the eighth of the month and paid upfront for the party to be held on the 15th. Mary thought surely since Nora was a mother and soon-to-be grandmother, she would be willing to wait for her money. She had $150 left so she would give that to Nora and work out a payment plan. In the meantime, Mary moved to a larger more expensive apartment which left no extra money to pay Nora back. She did not know what to do, so she avoided Nora.

# B7. Personal Property Pet Role-Play

This role-play is extremely emotional and involves animals. The mediator will be challenged by the highly volatile nature of the parties.

<u>Participants</u>: Tim Hill-Plaintiff and Colin Neal-Defendant, ex-significant others

<u>Amount of Case</u>: $1250

<u>Issue</u>: Custody of dog and repayment of expenses

### Plaintiff

Tim Hill met Colin Neal at a festival and after one year decided to move in together. They were very close intimate friends for 10 years. Seven years ago they purchased a townhouse together. Several months before Tim and Colin bought their home, Colin bought a Bichon Frieze puppy named Duke; he was a lively and loving puppy. Tim quickly became attached to Duke also. Tim worked out of their home part-time, so Duke was his co-worker. They spent loads of time together. In fact, Duke turned to Tim before pestering Colin to go outside or for food.

Tim and Colin begin to have relationship issues. Tim agreed to keep Duke. Tim fed him, and took him to the veterinarian and the groomers. Tim offered numerous times to have Colin visit Duke, but he always had some excuse. Months went by and still no visits. In the meantime, Duke and Tim were very attached to each other.

Colin called and demanded Duke back. Tim was upset about relinquishing Duke and asked to be reimbursed for all his care. Tim was stunned and retorted, "Where have you been? And you have never shown interest. I have fed Duke, have paid for all his medical care, and had him groomed regularly." Tim called several times to recover his money and also ask for a visit with Duke. All attempts were ignored. As a result, Tim grew angry and decided to file a small claims suit to either ask for the dog to be returned or to recover the money.

### Defendant:

Colin was having problems at work and was just generally in a bad mood. Colin eventually decided Tim was the problem and decided to move out into his own place. His new place would not accept pets.

Colin's life improved, work was better and the depression lifted. He had moved on with life. In a chance meeting, he met Beverly. They began seeing each other on a regular basis and decided to be exclusive. After a quick worldwind dating period they living together.

Colin told Beverly about Duke and they decided they wanted his dog back. Two and a half years later, Colin called out of the blue demanding Duke. After a heated phone call, Tim said the only way Colin would get Duke back was to agree to pay him back for all of Duke's expenses.

Colin decided he would pay Tim for all the expenses to meet Tim's demand. Colin got Duke back and intended to repay Tim. However, Colin never had the money to repay Tim. Colin and Beverly love to have fun, took quick weekend trips and they loved to shop.

# B8. Questioning Role-Play

This role-play is designed to practice questioning to clarify positions and interests. Mediators should practice open-ended questions.

Participants: Priscilla Kennedy and Cindy Rockefeller, Roommates

Issue: Home cleaning

### Priscilla

Priscilla Kennedy moved here recently to start a graduate degree. Through the universities website, she found a gal who was also starting her graduate degree, and they decided to share an apartment. She was moving to the area from New York, just outside of Manhattan. Priscilla is organized and goal oriented, and enjoys Friday night television to unwind from the week. Priscilla is frustrated with her new roommate, Cindy Rockefeller.

### Cindy

Cindy Rockefeller moved to the area from Massachusetts. Cindy is a free spirit and spontaneous, and loves to have fun. By Friday night she is ready to party. Cindy is not a neat freak and clutter is acceptable. Its not big deal if there are dishes in the sink, clothes hung over chairs and shoes by the door.

# B9. Consumer Rug Role-Play

Mediators often have other professions and occasionally may encounter people from their ,"other lives." There is a dilemma about impartiality if they are asked to mediate a case when they have a relationship with one of the parties. This role play examines this dilemma.

Participants: Brett & Sally Moore, couple and Salam, the owner of a rug company

Mediators: mediator (realtor), and co-mediator

Amount of Case: $2500

Issue: Rug cleaning and its destruction

### Plaintiff

Brett and Sally Moore purchased an antique rug at an estate sale. It was room size and in its earlier days was vibrant and beautiful. The rug was approximately 100 years old and now a bit frayed and very dirty. They were not worried about the condition as they were going to take it to a Persian rug cleaner who was touted to be the expert in repairs and cleaning.

Brett and Sally were very unhappy with the condition of the rug after cleaning. The couple filed a small claims suit alleging lack of care and ruining their rug. They sued for the cost of the rug, the cost of cleaning, and their time off work for their court appearance.

### Defendant

Salam Rugs and Custom Cleaning was a family business started by the grandfather and handed down to the son and then to the grandson. They were well known and respected. Realtors, insurance companies, and interior designers often recommend them.

The Moore's took their antique rug to Salam Rugs to have it cleaned and repaired. Salam cleaned it, however, after cleaning one portion of the rug was basically thread bare. There was no pile left, and so the only things showing were the warps and wefts (off white thick thread). Salam attempted to appease them to no avail.

### Other Information

The Vernon County Mediation Service serves the Small Claims-General District Court of Vernon County. They have a number of mediators who volunteer to mediate cases assigned by the Judge to the mediation service. On this day four mediators showed up to help the disputants find a solution to their cases.

One of the mediators is also a realtor in her "other life." She was assigned the case with the Moores and the Salam Rugs. She was very familiar with Salam Rugs and regularly refers her clients to them. Often a co-mediator is also assigned, and so it is with this case. This posed a dilemma for the realtor mediator in deciding how to handle this mediation.

# B10. Contracts Downsizing while Grieving Role-Play

This role-play will help participants understand that it is not the role of the mediator to offer advice, coerce, or push a client into a settlement.

Participants: Lou Gambrell- father & Mr. Gambrell, his son and Sally Smith apartment manager

Amount of Case:

Issue: Termination of contract- lease

## Plaintiff

Sally, the apartment manager showed Mr. Gambrell several apartments in July. She found Mr. Gambrell to be a sweet elderly gentleman but seemed bewildered after losing his wife. He explained he wanted to sale his home and leave the memories behind. He also talked about making his life less complicated and wanted a smaller space.

After several separate conversations, Mr. Gambrell selected an apartment and agreed to pay $1100 a month and sign a year's lease. Unfortunately Mr. Gambrell became ill, had to live in a rehab center for a short period of time. Mr. Gambrell's son advised us what happened but looked forward to his dad being able to stay at the apartment after a recuperation period.

Unfortunately, Mr. Gambrell never returned, his son moved him out of the apartment. He was in charge of his dad's financial affairs and stopped paying the rent. The apartment owners took Mr. Gambrell to court and sued for the balance of the rent owed.

## Defendant

Louis Gambrell recently lost his wife of 52 years. His home held lots of memories, and it became too painful to stay there. Without talking to his children, he decided to put his house on the market and move into an apartment. The apartment complex had been beautiful in its early years but was aging much like him. It was a short walk to the Potomac River, and in fact, there was a park along the river. He imagined himself going to the park and walking his four-legged companion.

He told his children about his plans and shortly afterwards he received a respectable offer on his home. He moved out right before the closing. When he arrived with all his possessions in a rental truck, the apartment complex did not resemble the picture he had remembered. The building was in disrepair, groups of late-teen/twenty-year-old males were hanging out and were very adept at wolf whistles. He went to the office to pick up his key and inquired about the difference from what he remembered. The manager said a remodel project was scheduled in the next few weeks.

Several weeks later he got ready for his walk to the park and went downstairs to find that a tire was flat and a side window shattered. He called a car emergency service to change the tire and put plastic over the window. He notified the apartment manager about the incident.

A month later, on a sunny autumn Sunday he was returning to his apartment after taking a walk. He began to feel dizzy and sat down on the porch. A young man approached him and asked if he was okay. He explained he wasn't feeling well and asked if the young man could help him get upstairs. As they were climbing the stairs Mr. Gambrell passed out. An ambulance was called, and he was taken to the hospital. At this point in time he still had six months on the lease.

Mr. Gambrell's son notified the apartment complex about what happened, and explained to them that they were going to move Mr. Gambrell to assisted living. He had a stroke, would not be able to climb stairs, and now needed help with daily living chores. The apartment manager replied that he still had to fulfill his lease, and they would hold him responsible for the balance of the rent owed. His well-being was at stake so they moved him anyway.

### Other Information

The case was assigned to mediation. The mediators decided to use caucusing because Mr. Gambrell was physically and emotionally fragile. He tried to explain what happened, however, his speech was greatly affected. His son had given 30-day notice as required by the lease; however, it was five months before the lease was to expire.

In a separate caucus the mediators met with the apartment complex owners. The owners wanted their money plus court costs and interest. They refused to budge off the amount they wanted.

The mediators met again with Mr. Gambrell and advised that the apartment complex owners wanted all their money. They asked him if there was some amount of money he was willing to counter offer. One of the mediators talked about what a trial would be like, and Mr. Gambrell worried about the toll a trial would take on his health and well-being. The mediator mentioned he did sign a lease which was a contract. He asked how much he wanted to counter with. The elderly man began to cry and shake. His son waited outside for his dad because the mediator said the son was not a party to the suit.

# B11. Employer/Employee Wage Role-Play

This role-play will address past due wages, mistreatment of employees and immigration status.

Participants: Jose Pena, employee-Plaintiff and Joe Schmoe, Cheaper 4 U Construction Company-Defendant

Amount of Case: $4000

Issue: Failure to pay for hours worked

### Jose

Jose moved to Virginia from El Salvador. He initially was given a visitor's visa. He overstayed his visa but was making excellent money all cash. Most of the money he made he sent back to his family. He rented a house along with 6 other countrymen. Jose was a talented carpenter and made beautiful cabinets. Recently at another carpenter's referral he went to work for Joe. He worked for Joe and the agreement was he would be paid every 2 weeks in cash. After a month Jose still had not been paid. He was getting desperate for the money and after Joe once again did not pay him as promised, he quit and went to work for another construction company. Jose found out he could file a case in court and no questions would be asked about his immigration status.

### Joe

Joe saw Jose's work on a job he had done the framing for. He was impressed with his work. Joe asked Jose if he would work for him on an upcoming job. Joe promised a $200 a week raise and that he would pay in cash every two weeks.

Joe found out that Jose had overstayed the visa and thought Jose would not have any recourse to collect the wages owed him. So he decided to not pay at least not now. He believe with his immigration status he did think he would file a suit and risk being deported.

# B12. Home Repair Role-Play

This role-play will address incomplete home repair, deposits collected and homeowner frustration with work not being complete.

<u>Participants</u>: Mark and Ann Lowe, homeowner-Plaintiff and Jack Sprat, owner-Expert Bathrooms Inc.

<u>Amount of Case</u>: $5000

<u>Issue</u>: Bathroom remodel not complete

## Mark and Ann

Mark had heard from a coworker about Jack's company and his exceptional work. They were excited about the bathroom remodel and it would be done in time for their family and company to arrive for Thanksgiving. They explained their time frame and Jack believed it would be no problem to meet their requirements.

The remodeling job was going very well. By mid October it looked like the job would finish ahead of time. The only things left were the bathroom cabinet, hardware and molding. Jack called and apologized for not mentioning he would be away for 5 days but believe all was under control. Ann was a weary but felt assured because the job had gone well. The molding was to be installed during the time Jack was gone and the cabinet was to be installed during the time as well.

Ann had gotten the carpenter's phone number so they could coordinate the installation. Ann left numerous messages for the carpenter and he never called her back. She was angry but there was no way to contact Jack. When Jack checked his messages when he returned he got an ear full of hostility.

He called the carpenter and asked why he had not responded to the Lowes and offered not reasonable excuse. By November 10th, the cabinet, molding and hardware were still not installed. Ann was furious and had threatened to post bad reviews on line, not pay the balance due and was abusive.

## Jack

Jack has been remodeling bathrooms for many years with a list of happy customers. He has reliable sub contractors and generally there are no issues. Recently is carpenter has a serious medical issue and is not able to work for a while. He had gotten the lead on a carpenter and decided to try him out on this job. All his other subs were the ones he had used for years.

The Lowes had been referred to Jack by a co-worker and prior customer. They met and talked about what the Lowes wanted, decided on the design and materials plus time frame.

It was August and the Lowes needed it to be finished by the second week of November. It all seemed reasonable and the Lowes signed the contract.

Jack had given his wife a special birthday present in May, it was a 5 day cruise in the Caribbean and the reservations were for the last of October. Jack had forgotten to mention it to the Lowes but felt it would be no problem.

The job started in September and the work was being complete according to schedule. By mid October, all the major tasks of the job were finished. The remaining tasks were the crown molding, the cabinet and the hardware for the door. Jack contacted the carpenter who assured him it would be finished while he was away.

Jack had received the scheduled payments as per the contract. However when he returned from the cruise, the job was not complete and the Lowes were angry.

## More Information

The cabinet, molding and hardware were installed, and the job was complete the weekend before Thanksgiving. Ann and Mark withheld the final payment, equal to 1/3 of the job because the agreed completion date was missed. The bathroom looked great.

# B13. Personal Property Role-Play

This role-play will demonstrate the return of personal property and a counter suit.

Participants: Becky Plummer-plaintiff and Sharon Wolfe-defendant

Amount of Case: $700

Amount of Countersuit: $900

Issue: Collector Barbies & unpaid share of utilities

## Becky

Becky loved Barbies and had an extensive collection of Christmas Barbies. Recently Becky moved out of Sharon's apartment after a dispute over utility bills. Becky moved all of her belongings out but discovered she had left one box behind of 6 Barbies, years 2005-2011. When Becky discovered the missing box she called Sharon to ask if she had seen it. Indeed Sharon had discovered it and was waiting for Becky to call.

Becky asked if she could come get them the next weekend and Sharon said yes! Sharon did remind Becky about her unpaid share of the utilities. Becky had planned to pay Sharon back but after going to a collector Barbie show, she found several Barbies she was missing so bought them, they cost her $900. She knew Sharon would understand and they could work out a payment plan.

## Sharon

Sharon was happy to find a roommate, her last one moved overseas. She met Becky through some friends. Becky had relocated to the area and needed to share housing costs. Sharon was under lease and could not move for another 9 months. Becky moved in and was an ideal roommate, she paid her share of the bills and kept her room tidy. Becky had a good job, ideal to support her Barbie collecting. Sharon and Becky lived together for 26 months and Becky overspent at a Barbie Festival. She did not have the money to pay her full rent and utiliites $900. She promised to pay Sharon when her tax refund was received. Instead of paying Sharon she spent the money again on Barbies. Sharon was so angry. They had an argument and Becky moved out.

Finding the box of Barbies, Sharon decided to hold them hostage until she got her money. Sharon filed a counter suit seeking recovery of the money and would return the dolls when she gets her money.

The mediator was assigned both cases and will work with the ladies to have the Barbies returned to Becky and Sharon to be paid back for the utilites.

# B14. What is Difficult about Co-Mediation

This role-play will help mediators establish their plans when co-mediating.

<u>Participants</u>: Frank Ross and Alicia Borden, co-mediators

<u>Issue</u>: Clashing styles

## Frank

Frank is an attorney and mediator. He has been practicing law for 20+ years. He liked helping parties resolve their disputes without going thru a trial. He was fairly new to mediation but was excited engaging in this form of dispute resolution.

## Alicia

Alicia has a background in human resources and had been mediating for 18 years. She has been a court certified mediator for 16 years. Alicia was also certified as a mentor and conducted continuing education programs. She was very knowledgeable about the mediation process.

## More Information

Frank and Alicia were assigned to co-mediate a case together. They agreed who would conduct the opening and how the process would progress. All was going well when inadvertently Frank gave the plaintiff legal advice. Alicia gently reminded the parties they could provide legal information but not advice. Frank asserted I know what I am saying and the plaintiff doesn't have a case.

The mediation process had progressed well and the parties had reached a tentative agreement when the plaintiff decided to try and nibble for a little more money. Frank was frustrated and loudly protested saying "you don't have a case, you will lose in court, stick with the agreement".

The defendant decided to not be agreeable after all he now believed he would prevail in a trial.

# Appendix C: Commonwealth of Virginia Laws

## C1. Mediation

### About

Mediation is an alternative dispute resolution (ADR) process in which a trained neutral mediator facilitates communication between the parties and, without deciding the issues or imposing a solution on the parties, enables them to understand and to reach a mutually agreeable resolution to their dispute. It helps the parties understand and recognize their underlying needs, overlapping interests and areas of agreement. In Virginia the mediation process is voluntary and confidential.

Contact Information

    A. Director - Paul F. DeLosh, (804) 786-6455

    B. Dispute Resolution Services Manager - Sally P. Campbell, (804) 786-6455

### Referrals

Form DC-400, "Order of Referral," is used in any contested civil matter or for selected issues in a civil matter, when the court on its own motion or the motion of the parties refers the matter to an orientation session pursuant to Section 8.01-576.5 of the Code of Virginia.¬†The orientation session is conducted by a neutral or intake specialist at no expense to the parties to assist them in determining whether their case is suitable for a dispute resolution process such as mediation. The cost of any subsequent dispute resolution proceeding is as agreed between the neutral and the parties. Procedures for the referral are printed on the reverse side of the form.

8.01-576.4. Scope and definitions. The provisions of this chapter apply only to court-referred dispute resolution services. As used in this chapter:

"Conciliation" means a process in which a neutral facilitates settlement by clarifying issues and serving as an intermediary for negotiations in a manner which is generally more informal and less structured than mediation.

"Court" means any juvenile and domestic relations district court, general district court, circuit court, or appellate court, and includes the judges and any intake specialist to whom the judge has delegated specific authority under this chapter.

"Dispute resolution proceeding" means any structured process in which a neutral assists disputants in reaching a voluntary settlement by means of dispute resolution techniques such as mediation, conciliation, early neutral evaluation, nonjudicial settlement conferences or any other proceeding leading to a voluntary settlement conducted consistent with the requirements of this chapter. The term includes the orientation session.

"Dispute resolution program" means a program that offers dispute resolution services to the public, which is run by the Commonwealth or any private for-profit or not-for-profit organization, political subdivision, or public corporation, or a combination of these.

"Dispute resolution services" includes screening and intake of disputants, conducting dispute resolution proceedings, drafting agreements and providing information or referral services.

"Intake specialist" means an individual who is trained in analyzing and screening cases to assist in determining whether a case is appropriate for referral to a dispute resolution proceeding.

"Mediation" means a process in which a neutral facilitates communication between the parties and, without deciding the issues or imposing a solution on the parties, enables them to understand and to reach a mutually agreeable resolution to their dispute.

"Neutral" means an individual who is trained or experienced in conducting dispute resolution proceedings and in providing dispute resolution services.

"Orientation session" means a preliminary meeting during which the dispute resolution proceeding is explained to the parties and the parties and the neutral assess the case and decide whether to continue with a dispute resolution proceeding or adjudication. (1993, c. 905; 2002, c. 718.)

§ 8.01-576.5. Referral of disputes to dispute resolution proceedings.

While protecting the right to trial by jury, a court, on its own motion or on motion of one of the parties, may refer any contested civil matter, or selected issues in a civil matter, to an orientation session in order to encourage the early resolution of disputes through the use of procedures that facilitate (i) open communication between the parties about the issues in the dispute, (ii) full exploration of the range of options to resolve the dispute, (iii) improvement in the relationship between the parties, and (iv) control by the parties over the outcome of the dispute. The neutral or intake specialist conducting the orientation session shall provide information regarding dispute resolution options available to the parties, screen for factors that would make the case inappropriate for a dispute resolution proceeding, and assist the parties in determining whether their case is suitable for a dispute resolution process such as mediation. The court shall set a date for the parties to return to court in accordance with its regular docket and procedure, irrespective of the referral to an orientation session. The parties shall notify the court, in writing, if the dispute is resolved prior to the return date.

Upon such referral, the parties shall attend one orientation session unless excused pursuant to § 8.01-576.6. Further participation in a dispute resolution proceeding shall be by consent of all parties. Attorneys for any party may participate in a dispute resolution proceeding.

(1993, c. 905; 2002, c. 718.)

§ 8.01-576.6. Notice and opportunity to object.

When a court has determined that referral to an orientation session is appropriate, an order of referral to a neutral or to a dispute resolution program shall be entered and the parties shall be so notified as expeditiously as possible. The court shall excuse the parties from participation in an orientation session if, within fourteen days after entry of the order, a written statement signed by any party is filed with the court, stating that the dispute resolution process has been explained to the party and he objects to the referral.

(1993, c. 905; 2002, c. 718.)

§ 8.01-576.7. Costs.

The orientation session shall be conducted at no cost to the parties. Unless otherwise provided by law, the cost of any subsequent dispute resolution proceeding shall be as agreed to by the parties and the neutral.

(1993, c. 905; 2002, c. 718.)

§ 8.01-576.8. Qualifications of neutrals; referral.

A neutral who provides dispute resolution services other than mediation pursuant to this chapter shall provide the court with a written statement of qualifications, describing the neutral's background and relevant training and experience in the field. A dispute resolution program may satisfy the requirements of this section on behalf of its neutrals by providing the court with a written statement of the background, training, experience, and certification, as appropriate, of any neutral who participates in its program. A neutral who desires to provide mediation and receive referrals from the court shall be certified pursuant to guidelines promulgated by the Judicial Council of Virginia. The court shall maintain a list of mediators certified pursuant to guidelines promulgated by the Judicial Council and may maintain a list of neutrals and dispute resolution programs which have met the requirements of this section. The list may be divided among the areas of specialization or expertise of the neutrals.

At the conclusion of the orientation session, or no later than ten days thereafter, parties electing to continue with the dispute resolution proceeding may: (i) continue with the neutral who conducted the orientation session, (ii) select any neutral or dispute resolution program from the list maintained by the court to conduct such proceedings, or (iii) pursue any other alternative for voluntarily resolving the dispute to which the parties agree. If the parties choose to proceed with the dispute resolution proceeding but are unable to agree on a neutral or dispute resolution program during that period, the court shall refer the case to a neutral or dispute resolution program who accepts such referrals, on the list maintained by the court on the basis of a fair and equitable rotation, taking into account the subject matter of the dispute and the expertise of the neutral, as appropriate. If one or more of the parties is indigent or no agreement as to payment is reached between the parties and a neutral, the court shall set a reasonable fee for the service of any neutral who accepts such referral pursuant to this paragraph.

(1993, c. 905; 2002, c. 718.)

§ 8.01-576.9. Standards and duties of neutrals; confidentiality; liability.

A neutral selected to conduct a dispute resolution proceeding under this chapter may encourage and assist the parties in reaching a resolution of their dispute, but may not compel or coerce the parties into entering into a settlement agreement. A neutral has an obligation to remain impartial and free from conflict of interests in each case, and to decline to participate further in a case should such partiality or conflict arise. Unless expressly authorized by the disclosing party, the neutral may not disclose to either party information relating to the subject matter of the dispute resolution proceeding provided to him in confidence by the other. In reporting on the outcome of the dispute resolution proceeding to the referring court, the neutral shall indicate whether an agreement was reached, the terms of the agreement if authorized by the parties, the fact that no agreement was reached, or the fact that the orientation session or mediation did not occur. The neutral shall not disclose information exchanged or observations regarding the conduct and demeanor of the parties and their counsel during the dispute resolution proceeding, unless the parties otherwise agree.

However, where the dispute involves the support of minor children of the parties, the parties shall disclose to each other and to the neutral the information to be used in completing the child support guidelines worksheet required by § 20-108.2. The guidelines computations and any reasons for deviation shall be incorporated in any written agreement between the parties.

With respect to liability, when mediation is provided by a mediator who is certified pursuant to guidelines promulgated by the Judicial Council of Virginia, then the mediator, mediation program for which the certified mediator is providing services, and a mediator co-mediating with a certified mediator shall be immune from civil liability for, or resulting from, any act or omission done or made while engaged in efforts to assist or conduct a mediation, unless the act or omission was made or done in bad faith, with malicious intent or in a manner exhibiting a willful, wanton disregard of the rights, safety or property of another. This language is not intended to abrogate any other immunity that may be applicable to a mediator.

(1993, c. 905; 1994, c. 687; 2002, c. 718.)

§ 8.01-576.10. Confidentiality of dispute resolution proceeding.

All memoranda, work products and other materials contained in the case files of a neutral or dispute resolution program are confidential. Any communication made in or in connection with the dispute resolution proceeding that relates to the controversy, including screening, intake and scheduling a dispute resolution proceeding, whether made to the neutral or dispute resolution program staff or to a party, or to any other person, is confidential. However, a written settlement agreement signed by the parties shall not be confidential, unless the parties otherwise agree in writing.

Confidential materials and communications are not subject to disclosure in discovery or in any judicial or administrative proceeding except (i) where all parties to the dispute resolution proceeding agree, in writing, to waive the confidentiality, (ii) in a subsequent action between the neutral or dispute resolution program and a party to the dispute resolution proceeding for damages arising out of the dispute resolution proceeding, (iii) statements, memoranda, materials and other tangible evidence, otherwise subject to discovery, that were not prepared specifically for use in and actually used in the dispute resolution proceeding, (iv) where a threat to inflict bodily injury is made, (v) where communications are intentionally used to plan, attempt to commit, or commit a crime or conceal an ongoing crime, (vi) where an ethics complaint is made against the neutral by a party to the dispute resolution proceeding to the extent necessary for the complainant to prove misconduct and the neutral to defend against such complaint, (vii) where communications are sought or offered to prove or disprove a claim or complaint of misconduct or malpractice filed against a party's legal representative based on conduct occurring during a mediation, (viii) where communications are sought or offered to prove or disprove any of the grounds listed in § 8.01-576.12 in a proceeding to vacate a mediated agreement, or (ix) as provided by law or rule. The use of attorney work product in a dispute resolution proceeding shall not result in a waiver of the attorney work product privilege.

(1993, c. 905; 1994, c. 687; 2002, c. 718; 2013, cc. 283, 383.)

§ 8.01-576.11. Effect of written settlement agreement.

If the parties reach a settlement and execute a written agreement disposing of the dispute, the agreement is enforceable in the same manner as any other written contract. Upon request of all parties and consistent with law and public policy, the court shall incorporate the written agreement into the terms of its final decree disposing of a case. In cases in which the dispute involves support for the minor children of the parties, an order incorporating a written agreement shall also include the child support guidelines worksheet and, if applicable, the written reasons for any deviation from the guidelines. The child support guidelines worksheet shall be attached to the order.

(1993, c. 905; 1994, c. 687.)

§ 8.01-576.12. Vacating orders and agreements.

Upon the filing of an independent action by a party, the court shall vacate a mediated agreement reached in a dispute resolution proceeding pursuant to this chapter, or vacate an order incorporating or resulting from such agreement, where:

1. The agreement was procured by fraud or duress, or is unconscionable;

2. If property or financial matters in domestic relations cases involving divorce, property, support or the welfare of a child are in dispute, the parties failed to provide substantial full disclosure of all relevant property and financial information; or

3. There was evident partiality or misconduct by the neutral, prejudicing the rights of any party.

For purposes of this section, "misconduct" includes failure of the neutral to inform the parties in writing at the commencement of the mediation process that: (i) the neutral does not provide legal advice, (ii) any mediated agreement may affect the legal rights of the parties, (iii) each party to the mediation has the opportunity to consult with independent legal counsel at any time and is encouraged to do so, and (iv) each party to the mediation should have any draft agreement reviewed by independent counsel prior to signing the agreement.

The fact that any provisions of a mediated agreement were such that they could not or would not be granted by a court of law or equity is not, in and of itself, grounds for vacating an agreement.

A motion to vacate under this section shall be made within two years after the mediated agreement is entered into, except that, if predicated upon fraud, it shall be made within two years after these grounds are discovered or reasonably should have been discovered.

(1993, c. 905; 2002, c. 718.)

8.01-581.21. Definitions. As used in this chapter:

"Mediation" means a process in which a mediator facilitates communication between the parties and, without deciding the issues or imposing a solution on the parties, enables them to understand and to reach a mutually agreeable resolution to their dispute.

"Mediation program" means a program through which mediators or mediation is made available and includes the director, agents and employees of the program.

"Mediator" means an impartial third party selected by agreement of the parties to a controversy to assist them in mediation. (1988, cc. 623, 857; 2002, c. 718.)

§ 8.01-581.22. Confidentiality; exceptions.

All memoranda, work products and other materials contained in the case files of a mediator or mediation program are confidential. Any communication made in or in connection with the mediation, which relates to the controversy being mediated, including screening, intake, and scheduling a mediation, whether made to the mediator, mediation program staff, to a party, or to any other person, is confidential. However, a written mediated agreement signed by the parties shall not be confidential, unless the parties otherwise agree in writing.

Confidential materials and communications are not subject to disclosure in discovery or in any judicial or administrative proceeding except (i) where all parties to the mediation agree, in writing, to waive the confidentiality, (ii) in a subsequent action between the mediator or mediation program and a party to the mediation for damages arising out of the mediation, (iii) statements, memoranda, materials and other tangible evidence, otherwise subject to discovery, which were not prepared specifically for use in and actually used in the mediation, (iv) where a threat to inflict bodily injury is made, (v) where communications are intentionally used to plan, attempt to commit, or commit a crime or conceal an ongoing crime, (vi) where an ethics complaint is made against the mediator by a party to the mediation to the extent necessary for the complainant to prove misconduct and the mediator to defend against such complaint, (vii) where communications are sought or offered to prove or disprove a claim or complaint of misconduct or malpractice filed against a party's legal representative based on conduct occurring during a mediation, (viii) where communications are sought or offered to prove or disprove any of the grounds listed in § 8.01-581.26 in a proceeding to vacate a mediated agreement, or (ix) as provided by law or rule. The use of attorney work product in a mediation shall not result in a waiver of the attorney work product privilege.

(1988, cc. 623, 857; 2002, c. 718; 2013, cc. 283, 383.)

§ 8.01-581.23. Civil immunity.

When a mediation is provided by a mediator who is certified pursuant to guidelines promulgated by the Judicial Council of Virginia, or who is trained and serves as a mediator through the statewide mediation program established pursuant to § 2.2-1202.1, then that mediator, mediation programs for which that mediator is providing services, and a mediator co-mediating with that mediator shall be immune from civil liability for, or resulting from, any act or omission done or made while engaged in efforts to assist or conduct a mediation, unless the act or omission was made or done in bad faith, with malicious intent or in a manner exhibiting a willful, wanton disregard of the rights, safety or property of another. This language is not intended to abrogate any other immunity that may be applicable to a mediator.

(1988, cc. 623, 857; 2002, c. 718; 2012, cc. 803, 835.)

§ 8.01-581.24. Standards and duties of mediators; confidentiality; liability.

A mediator selected to conduct a mediation under this chapter may encourage and assist the parties in reaching a resolution of their dispute, but may not compel or coerce the parties into entering into a settlement agreement. A mediator has an obligation to remain impartial and free from conflicts of interest in each case, and to decline to participate further in a case should such partiality or conflict arise. Unless expressly authorized by the disclosing party, the mediator may not disclose to either party information relating to the subject matter of the mediation provided to him in confidence by the other. A mediator shall not disclose information exchanged or observations regarding the conduct and demeanor of the parties and their counsel during the mediation, unless the parties otherwise agree.

However, where the dispute involves the support of minor children of the parties, the parties shall disclose to each other and to the mediator the information to be used in completing the child support guidelines worksheet required by § 20-108.2. The guidelines computations and any reasons for deviation shall be incorporated in any written agreement by the parties.

(2002, c. 718.)

§ 8.01-581.25. Effect of written settlement agreement.

If the parties reach a settlement and execute a written agreement disposing of the dispute, the agreement is enforceable in the same manner as any other written contract. If the mediation involves a case that is filed in court, upon request of all parties and consistent with law and public policy, the court shall incorporate the written agreement into the terms of its final decree disposing of a case. In cases in which the dispute involves support for the minor children of the parties, an order incorporating a written agreement shall also include the child support guidelines worksheet and, if applicable, the written reasons for any deviation from the guidelines. The child support guidelines worksheet shall be attached to the order.

(2002, c. 718.)

§ 8.01-581.26. Vacating orders and agreements.

Upon the filing of an independent action by a party, the court shall vacate a mediated agreement reached in a mediation pursuant to this chapter, or vacate an order incorporating or resulting from such agreement, where:

1. The agreement was procured by fraud or duress, or is unconscionable;

2. If property or financial matters in domestic relations cases involving divorce, property, support or the welfare of a child are in dispute, the parties failed to provide substantial full disclosure of all relevant property and financial information; or

3. There was evident partiality or misconduct by the mediator, prejudicing the rights of any party.

For purposes of this section, "misconduct" includes failure of the mediator to inform the parties at the commencement of the mediation process that: (i) the mediator does not provide legal advice, (ii) any mediated agreement may affect the legal rights of the parties, (iii) each party to the mediation has the opportunity to consult with independent legal counsel at any time and is encouraged to do so, and (iv) each party to the mediation should have any draft agreement reviewed by independent counsel prior to signing the agreement.

(2002, c. 718.)

# C2. Mediators' Duty to Report

Certified mediators have a duty to report similar to teachers, physicians, etc. The statute § 63.2-1509 spells out our obligation as mediators.

§ 63.2-1509. Requirement that certain injuries to children be reported by physicians, nurses, teachers, etc.; penalty for failure to report.

A. The following persons who, in their professional or official capacity, have reason to suspect that a child is an abused or neglected child, shall report the matter immediately to the local department of the county or city wherein the child resides or wherein the abuse or neglect is believed to have occurred or to the Department's toll-free child abuse and neglect hotline:

1. Any person licensed to practice medicine or any of the healing arts;

2. Any hospital resident or intern, and any person employed in the nursing profession;

3. Any person employed as a social worker;

4. Any probation officer;

5. Any teacher or other person employed in a public or private school, kindergarten or nursery school;

6. Any person providing full-time or part-time child care for pay on a regularly planned basis;

7. Any mental health professional;

8. Any law-enforcement officer or animal control officer;

9. Any mediator eligible to receive court referrals pursuant to § 8.01-576.8;

10. Any professional staff person, not previously enumerated, employed by a private or state-operated hospital, institution or facility to which children have been committed or where children have been placed for care and treatment;

11. Any person 18 years of age or older associated with or employed by any public or private organization responsible for the care, custody or control of children;

12. Any person who is designated a court-appointed special advocate pursuant to Article 5 (§ 9.1-151 et seq.) of Chapter 1 of Title 9.1;

13. Any person 18 years of age or older who has received training approved by the Department of Social Services for the purposes of recognizing and reporting child abuse and neglect;

14. Any person employed by a local department as defined in § 63.2-100 who determines eligibility for public assistance;

15. Any emergency medical services provider certified by the Board of Health pursuant to § 32.1-111.5, unless such provider immediately reports the matter

directly to the attending physician at the hospital to which the child is transported, who shall make such report forthwith;

16. Any athletic coach, director or other person 18 years of age or older employed by or volunteering with a private sports organization or team;

17. Administrators or employees 18 years of age or older of public or private day camps, youth centers and youth recreation programs; and

18. Any person employed by a public or private institution of higher education other than an attorney who is employed by a public or private institution of higher education as it relates to information gained in the course of providing legal representation to a client.

This subsection shall not apply to any regular minister, priest, rabbi, imam, or duly accredited practitioner of any religious organization or denomination usually referred to as a church as it relates to (i) information required by the doctrine of the religious organization or denomination to be kept in a confidential manner or (ii) information that would be subject to § 8.01-400 or 19.2-271.3 if offered as evidence in court.

If neither the locality in which the child resides nor where the abuse or neglect is believed to have occurred is known, then such report shall be made to the local department of the county or city where the abuse or neglect was discovered or to the Department's toll-free child abuse and neglect hotline.

If an employee of the local department is suspected of abusing or neglecting a child, the report shall be made to the court of the county or city where the abuse or neglect was discovered. Upon receipt of such a report by the court, the judge shall assign the report to a local department that is not the employer of the suspected employee for investigation or family assessment. The judge may consult with the Department in selecting a local department to respond to the report or the complaint.

If the information is received by a teacher, staff member, resident, intern or nurse in the course of professional services in a hospital, school or similar institution, such person may, in place of said report, immediately notify the person in charge of the institution or department, or his designee, who shall make such report forthwith. If the initial report of suspected abuse or neglect is made to the person in charge of the institution or department, or his designee, pursuant to this subsection, such person shall notify the teacher, staff member, resident, intern or nurse who made the initial report when the report of suspected child abuse or neglect is made to the local department or to the Department's toll-free child abuse and neglect hotline, and of the name of the individual receiving the report, and shall forward any communication resulting from the report, including any information about any actions taken regarding the report, to the person who made the initial report.

The initial report may be an oral report but such report shall be reduced to writing by the child abuse coordinator of the local department on a form prescribed by the Board. Any person required to make the report pursuant to this subsection shall disclose all information that is the basis for his suspicion of abuse or neglect of the child and, upon request, shall make available to the child-protective services coordinator and the local department, which is the agency of jurisdiction, any information, records, or reports that document the basis for the report. All persons required by this subsection to report suspected abuse or neglect who maintain a record of a child who is the subject of such a report shall cooperate with the investigating agency and shall make related information, records and reports available to the investigating agency unless such disclosure violates the federal Family Educational Rights and Privacy Act (20 U.S.C. § 1232g). Provision of such information, records, and reports by a health care provider shall not be prohibited by § 8.01-399. Criminal investigative reports received from law-enforcement agencies shall not be further disseminated by the investigating agency nor shall they be subject to public disclosure.

B. For purposes of subsection A, "reason to suspect that a child is abused or neglected" shall include (i) a finding made by a health care provider within six weeks of the birth of a child that the results of toxicology studies of the child indicate the presence of a controlled substance not prescribed for the mother by a physician; (ii) a finding made by a health care provider within six weeks of the birth of a child that the child was born dependent on a controlled substance which was not prescribed by a physician for the mother and has demonstrated withdrawal symptoms; (iii) a diagnosis made by a health care provider at any time following a child's birth that the child has an illness, disease or condition which, to a reasonable degree of medical certainty, is attributable to in utero exposure to a controlled substance which was not prescribed by a physician for the mother or the child; or (iv) a diagnosis made by a health care provider at any time following a child's birth that the child has a fetal alcohol spectrum disorder attributable to in utero exposure to alcohol. When "reason to suspect" is based upon this subsection, such fact shall be included in the report along with the facts relied upon by the person making the report.

C. Any person who makes a report or provides records or information pursuant to subsection A or who testifies in any judicial proceeding arising from such report, records, or information shall be immune from any civil or criminal liability or administrative penalty or sanction on account of such report, records, information, or testimony, unless such person acted in bad faith or with malicious purpose.

D. Any person required to file a report pursuant to this section who fails to do so as soon as possible, but not longer than 24 hours after having reason to suspect a reportable offense of child abuse or neglect, shall be fined not more than $500 for the first failure and for any subsequent failures not less than $1,000. In cases evidencing acts of rape, sodomy, or object sexual penetration as defined in Article 7 ( § 18.2-61 et seq.) of Chapter 4 of Title 18.2, a person who knowingly and intentionally fails to make the report required pursuant to this section shall be guilty of a Class 1 misdemeanor.

E. No person shall be required to make a report pursuant to this section if the person has actual knowledge that the same matter has already been reported to the local department or the Department's toll-free child abuse and neglect hotline.

(1975, c. 341, § 63.1-248.3; 1976, c. 348; 1978, c. 747; 1993, c. 443; 1994, c. 840; 1995, c. 810; 1998, cc. 704, 716; 1999, c. 606; 2000, c. 500; 2001, c. 853; 2002, cc. 747, 860;

2006, cc. 530, 801; 2008, cc. 43, 268; 2012, cc. 391, 504, 640, 698, 728, 740, 815; 2013, cc. 72, 331.)

### Child Abuse & Neglect Hotline

### About the Hotline

The Virginia Department of Social Services operates a statewide Child Protective Services (CPS) Hotline 24/7 to support local departments of social services by receiving reports of child abuse and neglect and referring them to the appropriate local department of social services. The CPS Hotline is staffed by trained Protective Service Hotline Specialists.

Anyone can report suspected child abuse or neglect to a local department of social services or to the CPS Hotline. Callers will be asked to provide as much information as possible about the child, the alleged abuser and the incident. You are not required to give your name when you make the report, but if you do identify yourself, the local department of social services will be able to contact you for further information if needed and will be able to inform you of actions that were taken.

Each report is sent to the proper local social service agency to be evaluated to determine whether the report information meets the legal definition of child abuse or neglect and whether CPS has the authority and responsibility to conduct a family assessment or an investigation to determine the child's immediate safety needs and to determine if the family needs services.

### Criteria for Child Abuse

- Alleged victim is under the age of 18 at the time of the report

- Alleged abuser is in a caretaking role

- Alleged abuse or neglect meets the definition of abuse or neglect as defined by the CPS laws, regulations and policy

- The Virginia Department of Social Services local agency has jurisdiction to respond to the report

### Hotline Numbers

| CHILD PROTECTIVE SERVICES HOTLINES |
| --- |
| G. In Virginia: (800) 552-7096 |
| H. Out-of-state: (804) 786-8536 |
| I.  Hearing-impaired: (800)828-1120 |

CPS Hotline staff may provide general information and educational materials about child abuse or neglect to callers from the general public, child care providers, school educators and medical professionals on recognizing and reporting suspected child abuse or neglect.

CPS Hotline staff is also trained to provide crisis counseling and intervention if needed, and can provide information and referral assistance to callers to locate prevention and/or treatment programs in their area.

### Report Child Abuse/Neglect to Child Protective Services (CPS)

The Virginia Department of Social Services operates a CPS Hotline 24/7 to support local departments of social services by receiving reports of child abuse and neglect and referring them to the appropriate local department of social services. The CPS Hotline is staffed by trained Protective Services Hotline Specialists.

CPS Hotline staff may provide general information and educational materials about child abuse or neglect to callers from the general public, child care providers, school educators and medical professionals on recognizing and reporting suspected child abuse or neglect.

CPS Hotline staff is also trained to provide crisis counseling and intervention if needed, and can provide information and referral assistance to callers to locate prevention and/or treatment programs in their area.

(Commonwealth of Virginia, 2013)

# Appendix D: Standards of Conduct

## D1. Model Standards of Conduct

The following standards are from the American Arbitration Association, the American Bar Association, and the Association for Conflict Resolution as noted.

### MODEL STANDARDS OF CONDUCT FOR MEDIATORS

### AMERICAN ARBITRATION ASSOCIATION (ADOPTED SEPTEMBER 8, 2005)

### AMERICAN BAR ASSOCIATION (APPROVED BY THE ABA HOUSE OF DELEGATES AUGUST 9, 2005)

### ASSOCIATION FOR CONFLICT RESOLUTION (ADOPTED AUGUST 22, 2005)

### SEPTEMBER 2005

# The Model Standards of Conduct for Mediators 2005

The Model Standards of Conduct for Mediators was prepared in 1994 by the American Arbitration Association, the American Bar Association's Section of Dispute Resolution, and the Association for Conflict Resolution. A joint committee consisting of representatives from the same successor organizations revised the Model Standards in 2005. Both the original 1994 version and the 2005 revision have been approved by each participating organization.

## Preamble

Mediation is used to resolve a broad range of conflicts within a variety of settings. These Standards are designed to serve as fundamental ethical guidelines for persons mediating in all practice contexts. They serve three primary goals: to guide the conduct of mediators; to inform the mediating parties; and to promote public confidence in mediation as a process for resolving disputes.

Mediation is a process in which an impartial third party facilitates communication and negotiation and promotes voluntary decision making by the parties to the dispute.

Mediation serves various purposes, including providing the opportunity for parties to define and clarify issues, understand different perspectives, identify interests, explore and assess possible solutions, and reach mutually satisfactory agreements, when desired.

## Note on Construction

These Standards are to be read and construed in their entirety. There is no priority significance attached to the sequence in which the Standards appear.

The use of the term ,"shall" in a Standard indicates that the mediator must follow the practice described. The use of the term ,"should" indicates that the practice described in the standard is highly desirable, but not required, and is to be departed from only for very strong reasons and requires careful use of judgment and discretion.

The use of the term ,"mediator" is understood to be inclusive so that it applies to co-mediator models.

These Standards do not include specific temporal parameters when referencing a mediation, and therefore, do not define the exact beginning or ending of a mediation.

Various aspects of a mediation, including some matters covered by these Standards, may also be affected by applicable law, court rules, regulations, other applicable professional rules, mediation rules to which the parties have agreed and other agreements of the parties. These sources may create conflicts with, and may take precedence over, these Standards. However, a mediator should make every effort to comply with the spirit and intent of these Standards in resolving such conflicts. This effort should include honoring all remaining Standards not in conflict with these other sources.

These Standards, unless and until adopted by a court or other regulatory authority do not have the force of law. Nonetheless, the fact that these Standards have been adopted by the respective sponsoring entities, should alert mediators to the fact that the Standards might be viewed as establishing a standard of care for mediators.

## STANDARD I. SELF-DETERMINATION

A mediator shall conduct a mediation based on the principle of party self-determination. Self-determination is the act of coming to a voluntary, uncoerced decision in which each party makes free and informed choices as to process and outcome. Parties may exercise self-determination at any stage of a mediation, including mediator selection, process design, participation in or withdrawal from the process, and outcomes.

1. Although party self-determination for process design is a fundamental principle of mediation practice, a mediator may need to balance such party self-determination with a mediator's duty to conduct a quality process in accordance with these Standards.

2. A mediator cannot personally ensure that each party has made free and informed choices to reach particular decisions, but, where appropriate, a mediator should make the parties aware of the importance of consulting other professionals to help them make informed choices.

A mediator shall not undermine party self-determination by any party for reasons such as higher settlement rates, egos, increased fees, or outside pressures from court personnel, program administrators, provider organizations, the media or others.

## STANDARD II. IMPARTIALITY

A mediator shall decline a mediation if the mediator cannot conduct it in an impartial manner. Impartiality means freedom from favoritism, bias or prejudice.

A mediator shall conduct a mediation in an impartial manner and avoid conduct that gives the appearance of partiality.

1. A mediator should not act with partiality or prejudice based on any participant's personal characteristics, background, values and beliefs, or performance at a mediation, or any other reason.

2. A mediator should neither give nor accept a gift, favor, loan or other item of value that raises a question as to the mediator's actual or perceived impartiality.

3. A mediator may accept or give de minimis gifts or incidental items or services that are provided to facilitate a mediation or respect cultural norms so long as such practices do not raise questions as to a mediator's actual or perceived impartiality.

If at any time a mediator is unable to conduct a mediation in an impartial manner, the mediator shall withdraw.

## STANDARD III. CONFLICTS OF INTEREST

A mediator shall avoid a conflict of interest or the appearance of a conflict of interest during and after a mediation. A conflict of interest can arise from involvement by a mediator with the subject matter of the dispute or from any relationship between a mediator and any mediation participant, whether past or present, personal or professional, that reasonably raises a question of a mediator's impartiality.

A mediator shall make a reasonable inquiry to determine whether there are any facts that a reasonable individual would consider likely to create a potential or actual conflict of interest for a mediator. A mediator's actions necessary to accomplish a reasonable inquiry into potential conflicts of interest may vary based on practice context.

A mediator shall disclose, as soon as practicable, all actual and potential conflicts of interest that are reasonably known to the mediator and could reasonably be seen as raising a question about the mediator's impartiality. After disclosure, if all parties agree, the mediator may proceed with the mediation.

If a mediator learns any fact after accepting a mediation that raises a question with respect to that mediator's service creating a potential or actual conflict of interest, the mediator shall disclose it as quickly as practicable. After disclosure, if all parties agree, the mediator may proceed with the mediation.

If a mediator's conflict of interest might reasonably be viewed as undermining the integrity of the mediation, a mediator shall withdraw from or decline to proceed with the mediation regardless of the expressed desire or agreement of the parties to the contrary.

Subsequent to a mediation, a mediator shall not establish another relationship with any of the participants in any matter that would raise questions about the integrity of the mediation. When a mediator develops personal or professional relationships with parties, other individuals or organizations following a mediation in which they were involved, the mediator should consider factors such as time elapsed following the mediation, the nature of the relationships established, and services offered when determining whether the relationships might create a perceived or actual conflict of interest.

## STANDARD IV. COMPETENCE

A mediator shall mediate only when the mediator has the necessary competence to satisfy the reasonable expectations of the parties.

Any person may be selected as a mediator, provided that the parties are satisfied with the mediator's competence and qualifications. Training, experience in mediation, skills, cultural understandings and other qualities are often necessary for mediator competence. A person who offers to serve as a mediator creates the expectation that the person is competent to mediate effectively.

A mediator should attend educational programs and related activities to maintain and enhance the mediator's knowledge and skills related to mediation.

A mediator should have available for the parties' information relevant to the mediator's training, education, experience and approach to conducting a mediation.

If a mediator, during the course of a mediation determines that the mediator cannot conduct the mediation competently, the mediator shall discuss that determination with the parties as soon as is practicable and take appropriate steps to address the situation, including, but not limited to, withdrawing or requesting appropriate assistance.

If a mediator's ability to conduct a mediation is impaired by drugs, alcohol, medication or otherwise, the mediator shall not conduct the mediation.

## STANDARD V. CONFIDENTIALITY

A mediator shall maintain the confidentiality of all information obtained by the mediator in mediation, unless otherwise agreed to by the parties or required by applicable law.

If the parties to a mediation agree that the mediator may disclose information obtained during the mediation, the mediator may do so.

A mediator should not communicate to any non-participant information about how the parties acted in the mediation. A mediator may report, if required, whether parties appeared at a scheduled mediation and whether or not the parties reached a resolution.

If a mediator participates in teaching, research or evaluation of mediation, the mediator should protect the anonymity of the parties and abide by their reasonable expectations regarding confidentiality.

A mediator who meets with any persons in private session during a mediation shall not convey directly or indirectly to any other person, any information that was obtained during that private session without the consent of the disclosing person.

A mediator shall promote understanding among the parties of the extent to which the parties will maintain confidentiality of information they obtain in a mediation.

Depending on the circumstance of a mediation, the parties may have varying expectations regarding confidentiality that a mediator should address. The parties may make their own rules with respect to confidentiality, or the accepted practice of an individual mediator or institution may dictate a particular set of expectations.

## STANDARD VI. QUALITY OF THE PROCESS

A mediator shall conduct a mediation in accordance with these Standards and in a manner that promotes diligence, timeliness, safety, presence of the appropriate participants, party participation, procedural fairness, party competency and mutual respect among all participants.

A mediator should agree to mediate only when the mediator is prepared to commit the attention essential to an effective mediation.

A mediator should only accept cases when the mediator can satisfy the reasonable expectation of the parties concerning the timing of a mediation.

The presence or absence of persons at a mediation depends on the agreement of the parties and the mediator. The parties and mediator may agree that others may be excluded from particular sessions or from all sessions.

A mediator should promote honesty and candor between and among all participants, and a mediator shall not knowingly misrepresent any material fact or circumstance in the course of a mediation.

The role of a mediator differs substantially from other professional roles. Mixing the role of a mediator and the role of another profession is problematic and thus, a mediator should distinguish between the roles. A mediator may provide information that the mediator is qualified by training or experience to provide, only if the mediator can do so consistent with these Standards.

A mediator shall not conduct a dispute resolution procedure other than mediation but label it mediation in an effort to gain the protection of rules, statutes, or other governing authorities pertaining to mediation.

A mediator may recommend, when appropriate, that parties consider resolving their dispute through arbitration, counseling, neutral evaluation or other processes.

A mediator shall not undertake an additional dispute resolution role in the same matter without the consent of the parties. Before providing such service, a mediator shall inform the parties of the implications of the change in process and obtain their consent to the change. A mediator who undertakes such role assumes different duties and responsibilities that may be governed by other standards.

If a mediation is being used to further criminal conduct, a mediator should take appropriate steps including, if necessary, postponing, withdrawing from or terminating the mediation.

If a party appears to have difficulty comprehending the process, issues, or settlement options, or difficulty participating in a mediation, the mediator should explore the circumstances and potential accommodations, modifications or adjustments that would make possible the party's capacity to comprehend, participate and exercise self-determination.

If a mediator is made aware of domestic abuse or violence among the parties, the mediator shall take appropriate steps including, if necessary, postponing, withdrawing from or terminating the mediation.

If a mediator believes that participant conduct, including that of the mediator, jeopardizes conducting a mediation consistent with these Standards, a mediator shall take appropriate steps including, if necessary, postponing, withdrawing from or terminating the mediation.

## STANDARD VII. ADVERTISING AND SOLICITATION

A mediator shall be truthful and not misleading when advertising, soliciting or otherwise communicating the mediator's qualifications, experience, services and fees.

A mediator should not include any promises as to outcome in communications, including business cards, stationery, or computer- based communications.

A mediator should only claim to meet the mediator qualifications of a governmental entity or private organization if that entity or organization has a recognized procedure for qualifying mediators and it grants such status to the mediator.

A mediator shall not solicit in a manner that gives an appearance of partiality for or against a party or otherwise undermines the integrity of the process.

A mediator shall not communicate to others, in promotional materials or through other forms of communication, the names of persons served without their permission.

## STANDARD VIII. FEES AND OTHER CHARGES

A mediator shall provide each party or each party's representative true and complete information about mediation fees, expenses and any other actual or potential charges that may be incurred in connection with a mediation.

If a mediator charges fees, the mediator should develop them in light of all relevant factors, including the type and complexity of the matter, the qualifications of the mediator, the time required and the rates customary for such mediation services.

A mediator's fee arrangement should be in writing unless the parties request otherwise.

A mediator shall not charge fees in a manner that impairs a mediator's impartiality.

A mediator should not enter into a fee agreement which is contingent upon the result of the mediation or amount of the settlement.

While a mediator may accept unequal fee payments from the parties, a mediator should not allow such a fee arrangement to adversely impact the mediator's ability to conduct a mediation in an impartial manner.

## STANDARD IX. ADVANCEMENT OF MEDIATION PRACTICE

A mediator should act in a manner that advances the practice of mediation. A mediator promotes this Standard by engaging in some or all of the following:

Fostering diversity within the field of mediation.

Striving to make mediation accessible to those who elect to use it, including providing services at a reduced rate or on a pro bono basis as appropriate.

Participating in research when given the opportunity, including obtaining participant feedback when appropriate.

Participating in outreach and education efforts to assist the public in developing an improved understanding of, and appreciation for, mediation.

Assisting newer mediators through training, mentoring and networking.

A mediator should demonstrate respect for differing points of view within the field, seek to learn from other mediators and work together with other mediators to improve the profession and better serve people in conflict.

(American Arbitration Association, American Bar Association, & Association for Conflict Resolution, 2005)

# D2. Standards of Ethics and Professional Responsibility for Certified Mediators

## OFFICE OF THE EXECUTIVE SECRETARY OF THE SUPREME COURT OF VIRGINIA

## STANDARDS OF ETHICS AND PROFESSIONAL RESPONSIBILITY FOR CERTIFIED MEDIATORS

**Adopted by the Judicial Council of Virginia April 5, 2011**

**Effective Date: July 1, 2011**

### GENERAL

The Commonwealth of Virginia permits the referral of civil disputes pending in court to mediators certified pursuant to Guidelines adopted by the Judicial Council of Virginia. The referral of cases from the court system to mediation places an important responsibility upon persons who serve as mediators. Confidence in the mediation process and in the integrity and competence of mediators depends upon mediators conducting themselves in accordance with the highest ethical standards. These Standards are intended to guide the conduct of mediators certified pursuant to Guidelines adopted by the Judicial Council of Virginia and to promote public and judicial confidence in the mediation process.

This section and the Scope and Definitions provide general orientation. The text of the body of these Standards is authoritative and the Comments accompanying each section are interpretive.

### SCOPE AND DEFINITIONS

These Standards of Ethics and Professional Responsibility apply to all certified mediators in their capacity 1) as mediators in court-referred and all other mediations in the Commonwealth of Virginia; 2) as trainers of certified mediation courses; and 3) as mediation mentors.

Mediation, as defined in Virginia Code § 8.01-581.21, is ,"a process in which a mediator facilitates communication between the parties and, without deciding the issues or imposing a solution on the parties, enables them to understand and to reach a mutually agreeable resolution to their dispute." See also Virginia Code § 8.01-576.4.

Mediator, as defined in Virginia Code § 8.01-581.21, ,"means an impartial third party selected by agreement of the parties to a controversy to assist them in mediation." See also Virginia Code § 8.01-576.4.

These Standards recognize the need for flexibility in style and process and are not intended to unduly restrict the practice of mediation.

*Comment: It is the intent of the drafters of the Standards that the term "party" means an individual who has an issue to be resolved, and the term "participant" means everyone, other than the mediator, who participates in the process, including the parties.*

## ASSESSING THE APPROPRIATENESS OF THE MEDIATION

Prior to and throughout the mediation, the mediator should assess whether:

mediation is an appropriate process for the parties;

each party is able to participate effectively in the mediation; and

each party is willing to enter and participate in the mediation in good faith.

If in the judgment of the mediator the conditions specified in C.1. through C.3. are not met, the mediator shall not commence or continue the mediation.

*Comment: Section 8.01-576.5 of the Code of Virginia allows a court to refer any contested civil matter to a dispute resolution orientation session. "Orientation session" is defined in Section 8.01-576.4 as a preliminary meeting during which the parties and the neutral assess the case and decide whether to continue with a dispute resolution proceeding or adjudication. A major goal of the orientation session is to educate the parties about dispute resolution processes available to them, such as mediation.*

The orientation session can also play an important role as an assessment tool. Assessment as to whether a case is appropriate for a dispute resolution process, like mediation, may involve, particularly in family cases, separate screening interviews with the parties. Where appropriate, these interviews should include specific questions regarding violence and abuse (physical, emotional, and verbal abuse and/or threats), child abuse/neglect, drug and/or alcohol use, and balance of power. In cases where separate screening interviews have been conducted by an intake specialist or organization, such as a court program or community mediation center, such screening must meet the requirements of this Section. This in no way relieves the mediator from continual assessment of appropriateness throughout the mediation process. See Section K.4.

### INITIATING THE PROCESS

1. Description of Mediation Process. The mediator shall define mediation (as defined in Scope and Definitions) and describe the mediation process to the participants.

- The description of the process shall include an explanation of the role of the mediator.

- The mediator shall also generally describe his or her style and approach to mediation. The parties must be given an opportunity to express their expectations regarding the conduct of the mediation process. The parties and mediator must include in the Agreement to Mediate a general statement regarding the mediator's style and approach to mediation to which the parties have agreed.

- The mediator shall describe the stages of the mediation process.

2. Procedures

- Prior to commencement of a court-referred mediation, the mediator shall inform the parties in writing of the following:

- The mediator does not provide legal advice.

- Any mediated agreement may affect the legal rights of the parties.

- Each party to the mediation has the opportunity to consult with independent legal counsel at any time and is encouraged to do so.

- Each party to the mediation should have any draft agreement reviewed by independent legal counsel prior to signing the agreement.

In all other cases, the mediator shall inform the parties, orally or in writing, of the substance of the following:

- The mediator does not provide legal advice.

- Any mediated agreement may affect the legal rights of the parties.

- Each party to the mediation has the opportunity to consult with independent legal counsel at any time and is encouraged to do so.

- Each party to the mediation should have any draft agreement reviewed by independent legal counsel prior to signing the agreement.

The mediator should reach an understanding with the parties regarding the procedures which may be used in mediation. This includes, but is not limited to, the practice of separate meetings (caucus) between the mediator and participants, the involvement of additional interested persons, the procedural effect on any pending court case of participating in the mediation process, and the ability of any party or the mediator to terminate the mediation.

*Comment: In section D.1.a., the description of the mediation process may include an explanation of the role of the mediator as that of a facilitator, not advocate, judge, jury, counselor or therapist. The role of the mediator also includes, but is not limited to, assisting the parties in identifying issues, reducing obstacles to communication, maximizing the exploration of alternatives, and helping the parties reach voluntary agreements.*

In Section D.1.c., the stages of mediation should include at a minimum, an opportunity for all the parties to be heard, the identification of issues to be resolved in mediation, the generation of alternatives for resolution, and, if the parties so desire, the development of a Memorandum of Understanding or Agreement.

In Section D.2.b., the primary role of the mediator is to facilitate the voluntary resolution of a dispute. In order to ensure that parties make informed decisions, mediators should make the parties aware of the importance of consulting other professionals. Particularly where legal rights are involved or the parties' expectation is to enter into a binding and enforceable agreement, clear notification of the information in (b) 1-4 is essential. A mediator can most effectively verify that he or she has informed the parties of the items listed in (b) 1-4 if these items are put in writing.

## SELF DETERMINATION

Mediation is based on the principle of self-determination by the parties. Self- determination is the act of coming to a voluntary, uncoerced decision.

The mediator may provide information and raise issues. The mediator has no vested interest in the outcome of the mediation. Therefore, the mediator must encourage the parties to develop their own solution to the conflict. The mediator may suggest and explore options for the parties to consider, only if the suggestions do not interfere with the mediator's impartiality or the self-determination of the parties. The mediator may not recommend a particular solution to any of the issues in dispute between the parties or coerce the parties to reach an agreement on any or all of the issues being mediated.

The primary role of the mediator is to facilitate a voluntary resolution of a dispute. The mediator may not coerce a party into an agreement, and shall not make decisions for any party to the mediation process.

The mediator shall promote a balanced process and shall encourage the participants to participate in the mediation in a collaborative, non-adversarial manner.

A mediator must obtain consent from the parties before conducting another dispute resolution process, such as arbitration, in the same matter as the one being mediated. Prior to requesting the parties' consent, the mediator shall inform the parties of the following:

the procedures that will be used in the additional dispute resolution process, and

the implications of having the same neutral conduct both processes.

A mediator who conducts an additional dispute resolution process, in the same matter as the one being mediated, assumes different duties and responsibilities that may be governed by other professional standards.

## PROFESSIONAL INFORMATION

The mediator shall encourage the parties to obtain independent expert information and/ or advice when such information and/or advice is needed to reach an informed agreement or to protect the rights of a party.

A mediator may give information only in those areas where qualified by training or experience and only if the mediator can do so consistent with these Standards.

When providing information, the mediator shall do so in a manner that does not interfere with the mediator's impartiality or the self-determination of the parties.

*Comment: The role of the mediator differs substantially from other professional roles. Mixing the role of a mediator and the role of another professional is problematic and thus, a mediator should distinguish between the roles. For additional information, see Virginia's Guidelines on Mediation and the Unauthorized Practice of Law.*

## IMPARTIALITY

A mediator shall conduct a mediation in an impartial manner. Impartiality means freedom from favoritism or bias in word, action, or appearance. If the mediator cannot conduct the mediation in an impartial manner, the mediator shall not serve.

A mediator should avoid the appearance of partiality, as viewed by the parties, at all times in providing mediation services. A mediator shall promptly disclose any facts, including any actual or potential conflicts of interest, that are known to the mediator and could reasonably be seen by the parties as creating an appearance of partiality. This is an ongoing duty.

The parties may also raise, at any time, any concerns they may have regarding the appearance of partiality by the mediator.

After appropriate disclosure and discussion of any matters regarding the appearance of partiality on the part of the mediator, the mediator may proceed with the mediation, if the mediator and all parties agree. Otherwise, the mediator shall not serve.

Comments: A mediator should not act from favoritism or bias based on any participant's personal characteristics, background, values, beliefs, or performance at a mediation, or any other reason.

Matters that may create an appearance of partiality include, but are not limited to, (a) a mediator's involvement in, or opinions and beliefs about, the subject matter of the dispute and (b) a mediator's known current, known past, or reasonably anticipated future relationship or affiliation, whether personal or professional, with any participant in the mediation process.

A mediator should neither give nor accept a gift, favor, loan or other item of value that raises a question as to the mediator's actual impartiality or raises an appearance of partiality as viewed by the parties. However, a mediator may accept or give de minimis gifts or incidental items or services that are provided to facilitate a mediation or respect cultural norms so long as such practices do not raise questions as to a mediator's actual impartiality or raise an appearance of partiality as viewed by the parties.

In making any disclosures under this Standard, the neutral should not reveal any confidential information. Mediators should consider whether written or verbal disclosure is more appropriate, considering the situation requiring disclosure.

## CONFIDENTIALITY

In order to inform the participants about confidentiality in mediation, the mediator shall use an Agreement to Mediate that contains the statutory language relating to confidentiality and any requirements for mandatory reporting that are applicable to the mediation. In such Agreement, the mediator and parties may also agree in writing to create (a) any additional confidentiality provisions that are not inconsistent with law and (b) any additional exceptions to confidentiality. Any such additional exceptions or confidentiality provisions must be in writing and signed by the participants. The statutory language to be included from Virginia Code § 8.01-581.22 is as follows:

All memoranda, work products and other materials contained in the case files of a mediator or mediation program are confidential. Any communication made in or in connection with the mediation, which relates to the controversy being mediated, including screening, intake, and scheduling a mediation, whether made to the mediator, mediation program staff, to a party, or to any other person, is confidential. However, a written mediated agreement signed by the parties shall not be confidential, unless the parties otherwise agree in writing.

Confidential materials and communications are not subject to disclosure in discovery or in any judicial or administrative proceeding except:

- where all parties to the mediation agree, in writing, to waive the confidentiality,

- in a subsequent action between the mediator or mediation program and a party to the mediation for damages arising out of the mediation,

- statements, memoranda, materials and other tangible evidence, otherwise subject to discovery, which were not prepared specifically for use in and actually used in the mediation,

- where a threat to inflict bodily injury is made,

- where communications are intentionally used to plan, attempt to commit, or commit a crime or conceal an ongoing crime,

- where an ethics complaint is made against the mediator by a party to the mediation to the extent necessary for the complainant to prove misconduct and the mediator to defend against such complaint,

- where communications are sought or offered to prove or disprove a claim or complaint of misconduct or malpractice filed against a party's legal representative based on conduct occurring during a mediation,

- where communications are sought or offered to prove or disprove any of the grounds listed in § 8.01-581.26 in a proceeding to vacate a mediated agreement, or

- as provided by law or rule.

At the commencement of the orientation session and of any mediation, the mediator shall inform the participants of any mandatory reporting obligations of the mediator, such as the reporting of allegations of child abuse (Virginia Code § 63.2-1509).

At the commencement of the orientation session and of any mediation, the mediator shall inform the participants of any required reporting to the court in court-referred cases. For example, in reporting on the outcome of the dispute resolution proceeding to the referring court, the mediator shall indicate whether an agreement was reached, the terms of the agreement if authorized by the parties, the fact that no agreement was reached, or the fact that the orientation session or mediation did not occur (Virginia Code § 8.01- 576.9.).

The mediator shall not disclose information exchanged or observations regarding the conduct and demeanor of the parties and their counsel during the dispute resolution proceeding, unless the parties otherwise agree (Virginia Code § 8.01-576.9. See also Virginia Code § 8.01-581.24.).

The mediator should have a reasonable understanding of confidentiality in mediation.

The mediator shall promote understanding among the participants of the extent to which the mediator and the participants will maintain confidentiality.

If a mediator participates in teaching, research or evaluation of mediation, the mediator shall protect the anonymity of the participants and abide by their reasonable expectations regarding confidentiality.

Unless expressly authorized by the disclosing party, the mediator may not disclose to either party information relating to the subject matter of the mediation provided to him in confidence by the other (Virginia Code § 8.01-581.24.).

## AGREEMENT

Prior to the parties entering into a mediated agreement, the mediator shall encourage the parties to consider the meaning and ramifications of the agreement and the interests of any third parties.

The mediator shall encourage review of any agreement by independent legal counsel for each of the parties prior to the mediated agreement being signed by the parties.

If the mediator has concerns about the possible consequences of a proposed agreement or that any party does not fully understand the terms of the agreement or its consequences, the mediator may raise these concerns with the parties and may withdraw from the mediation.

## COMPETENCE

- If at the time of the referral, a mediator determines that he or she lacks sufficient med iator skill or subject-matter knowledge to effectively mediate the dispute, the mediator shall notify the parties and shall decline to mediate the dispute, unless the parties agree otherwise.

- If a mediator determines during the course of a mediation that he or she lacks sufficient mediator skill or subject-matter knowledge to effectively mediate the dispute, the mediator shall notify the parties and shall withdraw, unless the parties agree otherwise.

## QUALITY OF THE PROCESS

- A mediator shall conduct a mediation in a manner that promotes diligence, timeliness, safety, procedural fairness, and mutual respect among all the participants. A mediator should agree to mediate only when the mediator is prepared to commit the time and attention essential to an effective mediation.

- A mediator shall act consistently with all Virginia statutes governing mediation, mediators, and dispute resolution proceedings.

- A mediator should promote honesty and candor between and among all participants.

- The mediator shall terminate the mediation when, in the mediator's judgment, the integrity of the process has been compromised. (For example, by inability or unwillingness of a party to participate effectively; gross inequality of bargaining power or ability; and unfairness resulting from nondisclosure, where there is a legal duty to disclose, or fraud, by a participant.) The mediator may explain the reason for the mediator's termination, so long as the explanation is consistent with the obligations arising under these Standards, including but not limited to the obligation of confidentiality.

- Mediators shall conduct themselves in a manner that will instill confidence in the mediation process and in the integrity and competence of mediators. Mediators shall conduct mediations consistent with the proper administration of justice. For example, a mediator shall not:

a. commit a criminal or deliberately wrongful act that reflects adversely on the mediator's honesty, trustworthiness or fitness to provide mediation services, conduct mediation training programs, and/or mentor; or

b. engage in conduct involving dishonesty, fraud, deceit or misrepresentation which reflects adversely on the mediator's fitness to provide mediation services, to conduct mediation training programs, and/or to mentor; or

c. knowingly assist or induce another person to violate or attempt to violate the Standards of Ethics and Professional Responsibility for Certified Mediators.

## FEES

- A mediator shall fully disclose compensation, fees, and, charges to the parties.

- A mediator shall not enter into a fee agreement contingent on the result of the mediation or the amount of settlement because such a practice creates an appearance of partiality.

- A mediator shall not give or receive any commission or other monetary or non-monetary form of consideration in return for referral of parties for mediation services.

- Comment: Section L.3. is not intended to preclude a dispute resolution organization or program from receiving a commission or consideration for acceptance of a case which it then refers to a member of the organization's panel of neutrals.

### Advertising

A mediator shall be truthful in advertising, solicitation, information distributed electronically through a website, or other communication about the mediator's qualifications, experience, services and fees.

## COMMUNITY SERVICE

A mediator is encouraged to provide pro bono or reduced fee services to the community, where appropriate.

## ADDITIONAL RESPONSIBILITIES

These Standards are not intended to be exclusive and do not in any way limit the responsibilities the mediator may have under codes of ethics or professional responsibility promulgated by any other profession to which the mediator belongs or any other code of ethics or professional responsibility to which the mediator subscribes, such as those promulgated by the American Bar Association, the Association for Conflict Resolution or the American Arbitration Association. However, where these Standards and another code of ethics or professional responsibility conflict, these Standards take precedence.

## ENFORCEMENT OF THE STANDARDS OF ETHICS AND PROFESSIONAL RESPONSIBILITY

The Standards of Ethics and Professional Responsibility for Certified Mediators shall be enforced through the processes set out in the Procedures for Complaints Against Certified Mediators, Mediation Trainers, and Mediator Mentors available on the Supreme Court of Virginia web site (www.courts.state.va.us).

(Commonwealth of Virginia, 2011b)

# Appendix E: Guidelines to Avoid the Unauthorized Practice of Law

## PREFACE

In the Fall of 1998, the Department of Dispute Resolution Services of the Supreme Court of Virginia received a grant from the State Justice Institute to develop a set of guidelines to assist Virginia mediators in avoiding the unauthorized practice of law (UPL) when providing mediation services. The effort to secure this grant was in part a response to a 1996 Henrico County, Virginia Circuit Court case which found that a non-attorney mediator had engaged in the unauthorized practice of law by drafting legal documents and by giving legal advice to his mediation clients. This case engendered a great deal of concern within Virginia's non-attorney mediator community and led to a training conference sponsored by the Department of Dispute Resolution Services in March of 1997. This conference was designed to provide mediators with information on the UPL rules in Virginia, attorney ethics, and mediator ethics and to help them avoid illegally practicing law or violating ethical standards when conducting mediations.

It became apparent at the conclusion of the conference that a comprehensive set of guidelines that more clearly defined when mediation activities crossed the line and constituted the practice of law was needed. Thus, the purpose of the State Justice Institute project was to conduct a national research study on UPL as it relates to mediation and to develop instructive guidelines that would help mediators in Virginia understand the contours of legal practice and thus avoid practicing law when mediating disputes.

The Guidelines on Mediation and UPL project officially got underway in August of 1998. Shortly thereafter a survey (Appendix A) was sent to approximately 180 bar associations and alternative dispute resolution offices in all 50 states. The purposes in conducting this survey were to explore how the various states have addressed the potential problems of UPL and mediation and to use the information generated by the survey in the creation of UPL Guidelines for Virginia mediators. The results of this survey are reported in Appendix B to this report.

While the UPL/ mediation survey was being formulated and mailed, an advisory committee was formed to provide direction to the Department of Dispute Resolution Services in creation of the Guidelines. The committee was comprised of the members of the Virginia state Bar, judges, lawyers and mediators from throughout the Commonwealth of Virginia. This committee met monthly throughout the fall of 1998 and Spring of 1999. The members of the committee are listed below.

•Karen Asaro, Family Mediation Program Virginia Beach, Virginia

•Dotty Larson, Director Prince William county Office of Dispute Resolution, Manassas, Virginia

•Prof. Michael R. Smith, Virginia Commonwealth University, Richmond, Virginia Lead Researcher and Reporter

•Lawrie Parker, Director Piedmont Dispute, Resolution Center Warrenton, Virginia

•Yvonne DeBruyn Weight, Chair, Unauthorized Practice of Law Committee, Virginia State Bar, Alexandria Virginia

•Hon. Margaret Spencer, Richmond Circuit Court, Richmond, Virginia

•Torrence Harman, Esq., Board of Governors, Family Law Section of the Virginia State Bar, Richmond, Virginia

•Robert N. Baldwin, Executive Secretary, Supreme Court of Virginia, Richmond, Virginia

•Lawrence H. Hoover, Jr., Esq., Co-Chair Ethics Sub-Committee of Virginia State Bar-Virginia Bar Association Joint ADR Committee, Harrisonburg, Virginia

•Samuel Jackson, Esq., Chair, Standards of Practice Committee, Virginia Mediation Network, McLean, Virginia

•John McCammon, Esq., McCammon Mediation Group, Richmond, Virginia

•James McCauley, Esq., Ethics Counsel, Virginia State Bar, Richmond, Virginia

•Merry L. Hanson, Peninsula Mediation Center, Hampton, Virginia

•Hon. Ann Simpson, Fredericksburg Circuit Court, Fredericksburg, Virginia

•Geetha Ravindra, Director Department of Dispute Resolution Services, Supreme Court of Virginia, Richmond, Virginia

The Report that follows is organized into three chapters. Chapter 1 is an introduction that traces the historical development of UPL rules and helps define the specific UPL issues that are relevant to mediation. Chapters 2 and 3 comprise the Guidelines themselves. Chapter 2 discusses the difference between legal information and legal advice and gives specific examples of which mediator activities are permissible and which may constitute the practice of law. Chapter 3 discusses the issue of mediators drafting agreements for disputants without contravening the various statutes, UPL rules, and ethical standards that govern mediators in Virginia. The Standards of Ethics for Court-Certified Mediators, the Dispute Resolution Proceedings statute in the Code of Virginia and the Virginia Rules of Professional Conduct for attorneys (See Chapter I) prohibit mediators from giving legal advice or otherwise practicing law during mediation. As a result, the Guidelines make no distinction between the activities of attorney and non-attorney mediators. Conduct by non-attorney mediators that would constitute the unauthorized practice of law would constitute unethical mediation practice or professional misconduct if engaged in by attorney-mediators. Thus, the Guidelines set forth a single standard applicable to both attorney and non-attorney mediators.

Hopefully, this Report and the accompanying Guidelines will provide some insight with respect to the ongoing debate over what activities constitute the practice of law in the mediation context. Where applicable, specific examples are given and suggestions are offered to assist mediators in avoiding UPL or unethical practice. The Guidelines were prepared according to the UPL and ethical rules currently existing in Virginia and should not be read to apply outside of this context.

# Overview Of UPL And Mediation

## SECTION 1. INTRODUCTION

The American Bar Association,[1] as well as some state bar associations throughout the country,[2] have recognized that mediation is a law-related activity. Lawyers who practice mediation may be subject to the rules of professional responsibility that govern attorney conduct in their respective states. Because disputing parties typically bring legal disputes into mediation, mediators may be called upon to provide law-related information to the parties or to provide legal evaluations of the parties' positions. When these law-related activities occur during mediation, they may raise for all mediators issues of unethical mediation practice, conflicts of interest for attorney-mediators, and issues of the unauthorized practice of law (UPL) for non-attorney mediators. This chapter discusses the historical development of UPL enforcement, the approaches used by the various states in defining the practice of law, and how UPL and mediation are regulated in Virginia.

## SECTION 2. THE LEGAL AND HISTORICAL CONTEXT OF UPL ENFORCEMENT

During the United States' first 100 years of existence as an independent nation, the legal profession was largely unregulated. Colonial era restrictions on admissions to the bar and on those who could appear before tribunals were lifted by most of the newly formed states. Coinciding with the organization of professional bar associations at the state and local levels following the Civil War, states began to pass UPL legislation restricting the law-related activities of non-lawyers. Most of these early statutes were limited in scope and merely prohibited court appearances by persons who had not been admitted to the bar.[3]

The Depression era of the 1930s saw a significant increase in the enforcement of UPL statutes and in the passage of new, more expansive prohibitions against UPL. The new laws in many jurisdictions were, by today's standards, broadly worded and prohibited the unauthorized practice of law without defining precisely what was meant by that phrase. The public policy rationale for more expansive UPL enforcement was the protection of the public and the preservation of the lawyers' professional independence, which was also thought to benefit clients.[4] More recently, the American Bar Association Commission on Nonlawyer Practice has recommended a somewhat narrower approach to protecting the public from nonlawyers engaged in law-related activities. This ABA commission recommends that states consider regulating UPL when a nonlawyer activity poses a serious risk to a consumer's life, health, safety, or economic well-being.[5]

Since the passage of more expansive and non-specific UPL statutes following the Depression, courts have struggled to define the unauthorized practice of law on a case by case basis. In attempting to reach a workable definition of UPL, courts and bar associations in the various states have usually adopted one of five different "tests."[6]

### The "Commonly Understood" Test

The "commonly understood" test[7] defines the practice of law as being comprised of activities that lawyers have traditionally performed. The leading case that adopts this approach is State Bar v. Arizona Land Title & Trust Co.[8] In that case, the Arizona Supreme Court held that the practice of law consists of those activities, "whether performed in court or in a law office, which lawyers customarily have carried on from day to day through the centuries."[9] Under this test, no distinction is drawn between litigation and court-related activities and activities that involve giving legal advice and drafting legal instruments.[10]

The "commonly understood" test is subject to a number of exceptions recognized by courts. For example, some courts permit non-lawyers to perform activities usually performed by lawyers if those activities are incidental to the non-lawyers' professions.[11] The justification for this exception is that too broad a definition of the practice of law would severely limit the common business practices of other professionals, including real estate agents, accountants, and investment counselors, and therefore would not serve the public interest.[12]

In Commonwealth v. Jones & Robins, Inc.[13], the Supreme Court of Virginia placed its imprimatur on this line of reasoning by holding that real estate agents can prepare contracts for the sale of real property. The court reasoned that to deny real estate agents this ability would severely impact their business and would run counter to the long-standing practice among real estate agents of preparing sales contracts.[14]

Another exception to the "commonly understood test" allows non-lawyers to provide services that are commonly understood as the practice of law so long as those services do not involve difficult or complex questions of law.[15] For example, in Agran v. Shapiro,[16] a California appellate court ruled that the preparation of simple income tax forms was not the practice of law. Similarly, the Minnesota Supreme Court has held that only the resolution of complex tax questions constitutes the practice of law.[17]

### The "Client Reliance" Test

A second test used in defining the practice of law asks whether a client believes that he or she is receiving legal services. Under this approach, a person is practicing law if others believe that the person is engaged in the traditional role of giving legal advice.[18] The focus of this test is on whether the client relied on the services rendered and thus requires an inquiry into the client's state of mind.

In State Bar v. Arizona Land Title & Trust Co[19] the Supreme Court of Arizona noted that "reliance by the client on advice or services rendered . . . [is pertinent] in determining whether certain conduct is the purported or actual practice of law."[20] In that case, the court held that certain activities of real estate title companies constituted the practice of law both because they were activities that lawyers have traditionally performed and because customers of title companies rely on those activities as legal services.

In his Williamette Law Review article on party empowerment and mediation,[21] Donald Weckstein defines legal advice "as the application of general principles or statements of law to a particular person's transactions or activities, with the mutual expectation of influencing that person's legal behavior."[22] Thus, under this definition, both client reliance and the intent of the purported attorney are relevant in determining whether a person has engaged in the practice (or unauthorized practice) of law.

### The "Application of Law to the Facts" Test

Another test used by courts to define UPL identifies the practice of law as relating the general body of legal knowledge to the facts of a particular case or to the specific legal problems of a client.[23] Some courts, for example, have approved of the sale of "divorce kits" on the ground that they merely provide legal information to purchasers.[24] Other courts have concluded that the selection of

certain forms to include in divorce kits necessarily involves the giving of legal advice because it involves the application of law to a particular problem (divorce).[25]

Presumably under this test, merely stating what the law is on a general legal topic would not constitute UPL. A person engages in the practice of law only when he or she takes a generally applicable legal principle, applies it to the facts of a specific case, and thereby reaches a legal conclusion. However, as the cases mentioned above illustrate, stating a general legal principle in the context of a dispute involving that same principle may be viewed by a court as applying law to fact.

### The "Affecting Legal Rights" Test

A fourth test used by courts to define the practice of law is the "affecting legal rights" test. [26] Under this test, a person engages in the practice of law if he or she provides services that affect another's legal rights.[27] Thus, the drafting of contracts - or settlement agreements - clearly affects the legal rights of those bound by the contracts. Likewise, providing legal information or advice, to the extent that someone acts upon the information or advice, also affects legal rights. Because almost any activity from investment advice to counseling forgiveness and reconciliation can potentially affect someone's legal rights, this test is among the broadest of the approaches used by courts to define UPL.[28]

### The "Attorney-Client Relationship" Test

The fifth test used by courts to determine what constitutes the practice of law focuses on the existence of an attorney-client relationship.[29] According to this test, there must be a personal relationship tantamount to that of attorney and client before the practice of law is implicated.[30] An example of such a test can be found in the Unauthorized Practice Rules of the Supreme Court of Virginia.[31] Subsection B of Part Six provides that "it is from the relation of attorney and client that any practice of law must be derived."

### SECTION 3. UPL IN THE CONTEXT OF MEDIATION

Mediation is a process for resolving disputes. Some of those disputes have already ripened into lawsuits by the time they reach mediation; others have not yet resulted in a lawsuit but may end up in litigation if not successfully mediated. In either case, legal norms are likely to play an important role in the dispute. If one of the parties has already filed suit, then that party, and probably the other as well, has already defined the dispute in legal terms, thus calling for the resolution of legal issues. Even if a lawsuit has not yet been filed, one or both of the disputants are likely to have preconceived ideas about the proper legal resolution of the issues involved.

As parties enter into the mediation process, they often ask questions or raise issues about their legal rights and responsibilities. They may ask their mediator to assist them in evaluating or clarifying their legal positions. Similarly, mediators may find it useful to ask reality-testing questions of the parties that implicate legal issues. The providing of legal information and the asking of reality-testing questions are valuable to the mediation process in that these activities promote informed and considered decision-making by the parties. If a settlement is reached, the mediator may be asked or may take it upon herself to assist the parties in committing the agreement to writing, which is useful in helping the parties clearly articulate, remember and remain committed to the settlement reached during the mediation. The effectiveness of the mediation process is thus served when the mediator is permitted to provide appropriate legal information and to memorialize the parties' settlement.

Depending upon how the practice of law is defined in a given jurisdiction, a typical mediation session may involve a range of activities by the mediator that approaches the practice of law. The following are the two most common categories of mediator activities that may potentially involve the practice of law:

- Applying law to facts
- Drafting settlement agreements that may be viewed as legal instruments

Mediation practitioners, state bar ethics committees, and academic commentators are currently engaged in a heated debate over the question of whether any or all of the activities listed above constitute the practice of law. Representative of one side of this debate is Professor Carrie Menkel-Meadow.[32] Professor Menkel-Meadow argues that when a mediator evaluates the strengths and weakness of a client's case by applying legal principles to specific facts he or she is engaged in the practice of law.[33] She is concerned that mediation clients may be injured by reliance on erroneous information given to them by non-lawyer mediators,[34] and she believes that current ADR guidelines and rules of ethics do not adequately address the practice of law issues inherent in mediation.[35]

On the opposite side of the spectrum, Donald Weckstein[36] encourages mediators - both lawyers and non-lawyers alike - to actively evaluate the strengths and weaknesses of the disputing parties' cases by applying legal principles to the facts in the mediation.[37] He argues that "legal advice" should be construed narrowly for UPL purposes and that it requires both the mediator and the person receiving the advice to have a mutual expectation that the advice given will influence the recipient's behavior.[38]

Under his approach, a non-lawyer mediator would be free to employ a wide range of evaluative techniques during mediation without engaging in the practice of law.

## SECTION 4. THE VIRGINIA RULES ON MEDIATION AND THE PRACTICE OF LAW

The Virginia appellate courts have not yet weighed in on the question of what mediator activities constitute the practice of law. The issue of the unauthorized practice of law was also not considered by the Joint Virginia State Bar - Virginia Bar Association Joint Committee on ADR during the development of the dispute resolution proceedings statutes (Section 8.01-576.4 et seq. of the Code of Virginia). However, a variety of court rules, state statutes, standards of ethics, and Virginia State Bar legal ethics opinions have addressed the unauthorized practice of law generally, and some of these rules deal directly with issue of mediation and the practice of law.

### Court Rules and Their Interpretation

Supreme Court of Virginia Rule Part 6, § I serves as the primary source for regulating the unauthorized practice of law in the Commonwealth. In addition, § 54.1-3904 of the Code of Virginia makes it a misdemeanor to practice law without being authorized or licensed to do so. Finally, the Supreme Court of Virginia has made clear that courts of the Commonwealth have the inherent power to enjoin the unauthorized practice of law when it occurs.[39]

Part 6, § I (B) states that "the relation of attorney and client exists, and one is deemed to be practicing law, whenever he furnishes to another advice or service under circumstances which imply his possession and use of legal knowledge." (See Appendix B for the full text of the Rule). In addition, this Rule provides that a person is practicing law whenever

1. One undertakes for compensation, direct or indirect, to advise another, not his regular employer, in any matter involving the application of legal principles to facts or purposes or desires [or]

2. One, other than a regular employee acting for his employer, undertakes, with or without compensation, to prepare for another legal instruments of any character, other than notices or contracts incident to the regular course of conducting a licensed business.

The case law on UPL in Virginia is largely undeveloped. In only two cases has the Supreme Court of Virginia addressed the unauthorized practice of law. In one case, the court approved of real estate agents preparing simple contracts of sale, options, and leases.[40] In the second case, the court held that an association of credit providers could not act as an intermediary in employing lawyers on behalf of creditors whom it was representing in the collection of debts.[41] Thus, Virginia appellate courts have been largely silent on UPL issues and have never specifically addressed UPL as it relates to mediation.

## Selected State Statutes Governing Mediation in Virginia

Section 8.01-581.21 et. seq. is the original mediation statute in the Code of Virginia. (See Appendix C for the full text of the statute) This statute defines mediation, describes the confidentiality of mediation, and establishes civil immunity for mediators. In 1991, the Virginia State Bar-Virginia Bar Association Joint Committee on Dispute Resolution, with the assistance of the Department of Dispute Resolution Services of the Supreme Court of Virginia, began exploring the possibility of introducing legislation to enable the courts to refer matters to alternative dispute resolution proceedings and to provide dispute resolution mechanisms in court-connected settings. Overwhelmingly passed in 1993, Code of Virginia § 8.01-576.4 et seq. (See Appendix D) enables judges to order appropriate civil cases to a free dispute resolution evaluation session so that the parties may explore whether they wish to use an alternative dispute resolution proceeding in their case.

Section 8.01-576.5 authorizes courts to refer any contested civil matter or selected issues in a civil matter to a dispute resolution evaluation session. The dispute resolution evaluation session is a preliminary orientation meeting in which a neutral helps the parties assess the case and decide whether to pursue a dispute resolution option or continue with adjudication. Attorneys for any party may be present during the evaluation session.

The primary goals of the evaluation session are to provide the parties an opportunity to communicate openly about the issues in dispute and the possibility of resolving the matter through a non-adversarial method, as well as to educate them about the dispute resolution options available to them. With this information, the parties may choose voluntarily to proceed with a dispute resolution process such as mediation. The judge continues to set a date for the parties to return to court in accordance with its regular docket and procedure, irrespective of the referral to an evaluation session.

Section 8.01-576.9 describes certain ethical standards of neutrals, including that they may not coerce the parties into entering a settlement agreement and that they must remain neutral and free from conflicts of interest. Section 8.01-576.8 discusses the qualification of neutrals and Section 8.01-576.10 discusses the confidentiality of dispute resolution proceedings. Section 8.01-576.11 describes the effect of a written settlement agreement. If the parties reach a settlement and execute a written agreement disposing of the dispute, the agreement is enforceable in the same manner as any other

written contract. Upon request of all parties and consistent with law and public policy, the court shall incorporate the written agreement into the terms of its final decree disposing of the case. While this statute does not specifically state whether mediators are authorized to prepare settlement agreements on behalf of the parties, 'dispute resolution services' is defined in Section 8.01-576.4 as including drafting agreements.

Section 8.01-576.12 states that the court shall vacate a mediated agreement or an order incorporating or resulting from such agreement, where: (1) the agreement was procured by fraud or duress, or is unconscionable, (2) if property or financial matters are in dispute, the parties failed to provide substantial full disclosure of all relevant property and financial information, (3) there was evident partiality or misconduct by the neutral, prejudicing the rights of any party.

For purposes of this section, "misconduct" includes failure of the neutral to inform the parties in writing at the commencement of the mediation process that: (1) the neutral does not provide legal advice, (2) any mediated agreement will affect the legal rights of the parties, (3) each party to the mediation has the opportunity to consult with independent legal counsel at any time and is encouraged to do so, and (4) each party to the mediation should have any draft agreement reviewed by independent counsel prior to signing the agreement or should waive his opportunity to do so.

Prior to this legislation, judges in Virginia made referrals of cases to mediation on an ad hoc basis. Mediation services were offered primarily by a few court service units and community mediation centers. The establishment of the Department of Dispute Resolution Services,[42] coupled with new legislation that empowered judges to refer cases to dispute resolution evaluation sessions, marked a critical turning point in the development of consistent and integrated court-connected mediation.

## Mediator Standards of Ethics

In Virginia, mediators may choose to be certified by the Judicial Council of Virginia. If certified, they are eligible to receive case referrals from Virginia courts. In order to gain certification, potential mediators must meet the requirements adopted by the Judicial Council of Virginia, which are set forth in its Guidelines for the Training and Certification of Court-Referred Mediators. (See Appendix E) Certified mediators must also comply with the Standards of Ethics and Professional Responsibility for Certified Mediators adopted by the Judicial Council of Virginia. (See Appendix F) The Standards set out basic ethical and professional responsibilities for certified mediators.

On October 20, 1997, the Judicial Council adopted revisions to its original 1993 Standards of Ethics. While the original Standards provided important guidance on ethical principles, the need for more specific and comprehensive ethical rules became clear with recent concerns regarding mediator conduct. The revisions are the product of the research and efforts of the Dispute Resolution Services Ethics Committee. This subsection discusses the Standards that are most relevant to the issue of mediation and the unauthorized practice of law.

Prior to the commencement of the mediation, Section D(2)(a) of the Standards states that a mediator must inform the parties in writing that (1) the mediator does not provide legal advice, (2) any mediated agreement will affect their legal rights, (3) they are encouraged to seek legal counsel, and (4) they should have any draft agreement reviewed by independent counsel before signing it.

Section E of the Standards provides that mediators must encourage and respect the self-determination of the parties and may not coerce any party into an agreement or make decisions for any party. Section F states that mediators may only give information in areas in which they are qualified by training or experience and that information must be provided in a manner that does not affect the mediator's impartiality or the parties' self-determination. Section G again stresses impartiality and provides that mediators shall avoid any conduct that gives even the appearance of partiality toward one of the parties.

Section J of the Standards relates to settlement agreements. In general, it provides that mediators may offer suggestions to the parties but may not recommend particular solutions nor engage in any action that affects mediator impartiality or the self-determination of the parties. Specifically, this section requires mediators to determine that (1) the parties have considered all ramifications of their agreement, (2) the parties have considered the interests of other persons affected by the agreement who are not party to it, and (3) the parties have entered into the agreement voluntarily. Finally, this section states that if a mediator has concerns that any party does not fully understand the terms of the agreement or its ramifications, then the mediator should raise these concerns with the parties or withdraw from the mediation in the case of manifest injustice.

## Virginia Rules of Professional Conduct

On January 25, 1999 the Supreme Court of Virginia, following the recommendation of the Virginia State Bar, adopted a new set of ethical rules to govern attorney conduct in Virginia. The new Virginia Rules of Professional Conduct take effect on January 1, 2000 and will replace the existing Virginia Code of Professional Responsibility. (See Appendix G) Unlike the previous Code, the new Rules contain explicit provisions governing the professional conduct of attorneys acting as third party neutrals and as mediators.[43]

Rule 2.10 is the general rule governing alternative dispute resolution proceedings.[44] This rule provides, among other things, that a lawyer acting as a third party neutral does not represent either party,[45] and it prohibits a lawyer acting as a third party neutral from subsequently representing either of the parties in a matter related to the dispute resolution proceeding.[46] Comment 3 to this rule states that a third party neutral may not offer the parties legal advice but may offer a neutral evaluation if requested by the parties.

Rule 2.11 deals specifically with mediation as a type of alternative dispute resolution proceeding. It allows a lawyer-mediator to provide legal information to the parties[47] and to offer an evaluation of, for example, the strengths and weaknesses of positions, the value and costs of alternatives to settlement, or the barriers to settlement.[48] Comment 8 to this rule cautions lawyer-mediators to "restrict the use of evaluative techniques by the lawyer-mediator to situations where the parties have given their informed consent to the use of such techniques and where a neutral evaluation will assist, rather than interfere with the ability of the parties to reach a mutually agreeable solution to their dispute."

## Legal Ethics and UPL Opinions Relating to Mediation

The Virginia State Bar maintains two standing committees that issue opinions on mediation and UPL issues. The Standing Committee on Legal Ethics issues opinions that govern the conduct of attorneys licensed to practice law in Virginia, and the Standing Committee on the Unauthorized Practice of Law issues opinions regarding the practice of law by non-attorneys.

Several of the UPL Opinions promulgated by the Virginia State Bar's Standing Committee on the Unauthorized Practice of Law may be relevant to non-attorney mediators. For example, a number of UPL Opinions relate to the preparation of legal or quasi-legal documents by non-attorneys. In UPL Opinions 150 and 151 (1993), the Committee stated that the preparation by a collection agency's lay employees of a "form warrant in debt" that includes both a factual memorandum and the warrant itself constitutes the unauthorized practice of law. The Committee ruled that these "form warrants" are pleadings that may only be prepared by a licensed attorney. Pleadings are uniformly recognized as legal instruments and may not be drafted by lay persons.

The status of the lay person preparing the legal document also may be relevant to whether that person is illegally practicing law. For example in UPL Opinion 125 (1988), the Committee approved of lay employees of the Virginia Department of Transportation filling in "form deeds" prepared by the attorney general's office. The Committee apparently based its decision on the status of the employees as "regular" employees. The Committee quoted the provision from Supreme Court Rule Part 6, § I (B)(2), which allows "a regular employee acting for his employer" to prepare legal instruments. The Committee noted that whether a DOT consultant could prepare such deeds depended on whether the consultant was a "regular employee." By analogy, a mediator, who is typically contracted by the Office of the Executive Secretary on a per case basis to provide services to the courts, may not rely on the "regular employee" provision of this rule to permit the preparation by the mediator of legal instruments.

In another document opinion, the Committee ruled that an accountant does not illegally practice law when he or she fills in blank forms for a Commonwealth's Attorney that relate to the forfeiture of drug-related assets. In UPL Opinion 182 (1995), the accountant filled in the name and address of the defendant, the property seized, and the trial date. The documents then were reviewed and signed by the Commonwealth's Attorney. The Committee approved of this practice, perhaps because the information supplied by the accountant was factual (as opposed to legal) and the documents were always reviewed by a licensed attorney before they were filed with the court.

Whether the lay person preparing a legal instrument is subject to licensing requirements may determine whether he or she will be permitted to do so. In UPL Opinion 61 (1985), the Committee interpreted Commonwealth v. Jones & Robins, Inc.,[49] as not authorizing a business broker to prepare purchase agreements for businesses. The Committee noted that unlike real estate agents who are subject to licensing requirements (and who may prepare sale contracts), business brokers are not similarly regulated. Thus, the Committee opined that business brokers who prepare contracts of sale do so in violation of Commonwealth v. Jones & Robins, Inc. Likewise, in Virginia, mediators do not have to be licensed in order to mediate. Mediators may voluntarily seek certification by meeting the training and experience requirements adopted by the Judicial Council. Consequently, courts or the UPL Committee might view mediator document production activities as unregulated and without the protection of licensure requirements.

Finally, the UPL Committee has ruled that preparation of court orders by lay persons constitutes the unauthorized practice of law. According to the Committee in UPL Opinion 58

(1984), preparing court orders requires the exercise of legal skill and judgment and should not be undertaken by non-attorneys. This opinion is of particular relevance in those Virginia jurisdictions where court-referred mediators routinely prepare court orders at the court's request.

The UPL Committee, like the Legal Ethics Committee, has made a distinction in its opinions between legal advice and legal information. For example, in UPL Opinion 131 (1989), the Committee stated that non-attorneys may provide general information about legal matters (i.e. religious freedom) to members of the general public through seminars, publications, responses to letters, and telephone inquiries. In UPL Opinion 104 (1987), the Committee approved of an attorney licensed in a foreign jurisdiction publishing articles containing general legal information in a Virginia newspaper. The Committee stated that "general legal information is distinguished from specific legal advice to specific clients with regard to their respective problems."

In addition to the UPL Opinions just mentioned, the Legal Ethics Committee has addressed the issue of whether mediation by attorneys constitutes the practice of law and thus whether attorneys who engaged in mediation were subject to the former Virginia Code of Professional Responsibility. In Legal Ethics Opinion (LEO) 1368 (1990), the Committee ruled that a lawyer who mediated a dispute and who drafted a settlement agreement did not engage in the practice of law. (See Appendix H)

Nevertheless, the Committee stated that "providing legal information, albeit not legal advice, and assisting individuals to reach agreement on such issues as division of property, contractual obligations, liability and damages, by definition, entails the application of legal knowledge and training to the facts of the situation." Therefore, attorneys who engage in mediation are subject to the Code of Professional Responsibility (now the Virginia Rules of Professional Conduct) while carrying out their mediation activities.

Legal Ethics Opinion 1368 suggests that providing legal information and even drafting settlement agreements during a mediation session does not constitute the practice of law. In fact, the Ethics Committee noted that an attorney who acts as a mere scrivener for disputing parties by committing their oral agreement to writing does not engage in the practice of law. Like LEO 1368, the Guidelines that follow address the two types of mediator activities that most commonly implicate the potential practice of law - applying law to facts and drafting mediated agreements.

# Legal Information

## SECTION 1. INTRODUCTION

The purpose of this section is to provide mediators with guidance on how to avoid giving disputants legal advice and thereby engaging in unethical mediation practice, the unauthorized practice of law, or both. While adhering to these Guidelines should provide some measure of protection against charges of UPL or unethical practice, mediators should note that what constitutes legal advice is highly contextual and may vary according to the nature and type of the statements made by the mediator, the manner in which law-related information is provided to the parties, the purposes for which it is provided, and the expectations of the disputing parties. Furthermore, even when providing permissible legal information, mediators must be careful to give information only in those areas in which they are knowledgeable because of their training or experience.[50]

The Guidelines that follow are necessarily general in nature because the determination of what constitutes impermissible legal advice must, in most instances, be made on a case-by-case basis. Moreover, although the Guidelines are meant to be instructive, the determination of what constitutes UPL is made not by the Department of Dispute Resolution Services but by the Virginia State Bar's Standing Committee on the Unauthorized Practice of Law, the Attorney General's office, and ultimately by the courts. Mediators who are unsure of whether an anticipated course of conduct may be considered unethical practice or the unauthorized practice of law should proceed with caution and should seek advice from the Virginia State Bar.

## SECTION 2. LEGAL AND ETHICAL PROHIBITIONS AGAINST LEGAL ADVICE

Supreme Court of Virginia Rule Part 6, § I (B)(1) states that an attorney-client relationship exists and one is deemed to be practicing law whenever "one undertakes for compensation, direct or indirect, to advise another, not his regular employer, in any matter involving the application of legal

information to disputing parties, nor does it apply to mediators who are not being compensated (either directly or indirectly). While the UPL rules do not prohibit legal advice by uncompensated mediators, they must still comply with the ethical and statutory prohibitions against giving legal advice discussed below.

The crux of Supreme Court of Virginia Rule Part 6, § I(B)(1) is its prohibition against non-attorneys applying general legal principles to specific facts, purposes, or desires and then communicating legal advice to other persons. The term "legal advice" has not been precisely defined in Virginia. At a minimum, however, the following would appear to constitute legal advice in the mediation context:

At a minimum, a mediator provides legal advice whenever, in the mediation context, he or she applies legal principles to facts in a manner that (1) in effect predicts a specific resolution of a legal issue or (2) directs, counsels, urges, or recommends a course of action by a disputant or disputants as a means of resolving a legal issue.

Mediators should be aware that other conduct not included within this definition may also constitute the giving of legal advice and that the previous definition sets forth the minimum standard to which mediators should adhere.[51]

Like Supreme Court of Virginia Rule Part 6 §I(B)(1), the Virginia Standards of Ethics and Professional Responsibility for Certified Mediators ("mediator ethics") also prohibit mediators from giving legal advice. In fact, the ethical standards require mediators to inform the parties in writing, prior to the commencement of the mediation, that the mediator does not provide legal advice.[52] This provision reflects the requirements of Code of Virginia § 8.01-576.12 relating to court-referred cases, which states that a court shall set aside a mediated settlement agreement upon a showing of misconduct by the neutral. As defined in this code section, misconduct "includes the failure of the neutral to inform the parties in writing at the commencement of the mediation process that: (i) the neutral does not provide legal advice."

Although an attorney qualified to practice law in Virginia and serving as a mediator could not be charged with the unauthorized practice of law for giving legal advice during mediation, the attorney-mediator would violate mediator ethics if he or she gave legal advice, and any resulting settlement agreement could be challenged and set aside by a court on the ground of mediator misconduct. The attorney also would be subject to professional discipline by the Virginia State Bar for violating Rule 2.11 of the Virginia Rules of Professional Conduct ("Virginia Rules"), which prohibits a lawyer-mediator from giving legal advice during mediation.[53] Finally, a lawyer-mediator who gave legal advice to one or both of the parties during mediation may have engaged in dual representation in violation of Rule 1.7.[54]

Thus, neither lawyer nor non-lawyer mediators may give legal advice to the disputing parties during mediation. Non-lawyers who do so have engaged in unethical mediation practice, which may lead to decertification and are subject to criminal prosecution or civil action for UPL. Lawyer-mediators who provide legal advice have likewise engaged in unethical mediation practice which may lead to decertification and are subject to discipline by the Virginia State Bar.

### SECTION 3 THE RATIONALE FOR DEFINING LEGAL ADVICE AS PREDICTING THE RESOLUTION OF LEGAL ISSUES OR DIRECTING ACTION

The Committee on Mediation and UPL spent the better part of five months discussing the question of what constitutes legal advice in Virginia. The Guidelines that follow are the product of that debate and of the Committee's efforts to achieve a workable definition of legal advice. The Committee started with the premise that Supreme Court of Virginia Rule Part 6, § I (B)(1) requires, as one of its elements, the application of law to fact before a statement can be considered the practice of law in Virginia. This requirement is found in many court decisions defining the practice of law and is one of the more common "tests" for the practice of law used in other states. The Committee also recognized that Supreme Court of Virginia Rule Part 6, § I (B)(1) requires that to practice law one must "advise another" by applying general legal principles to specific facts. Because this language has not been interpreted by the appellate courts in Virginia, the Committee had no clear guidance on the meaning of the term "legal advice."

The definition of legal advice that emerged from the Committee was the product of much discussion and reflected an analysis of various considerations. The Committee considered and ultimately rejected a definition of legal advice that would have defined legal advice broadly to include the rendering of any legal opinion or conclusion.[55] The Committee also rejected a narrow definition that would have only included a formal attorney client relationship that resulted in urging, recommending or counseling a particular course of action. Ultimately, the Committee decided on a more practical approach that would allow all mediators some level of flexibility in techniques and style but also draw a line where activity would be unethical and/or illegal. As a starting point, the definition of legal advice outlined above includes the provision from Supreme Court of Virginia Rule Part 6, § I (B) (1) that requires the application of legal principles to facts. However, under the definition, the giving of "legal advice" also requires that one predict a specific resolution of a legal issue or direct the decision-making of a disputant. These components were included in the definition of legal advice for two reasons.

First, the Committee recognized that an important aspect of a lawyer's role is his or her ability to apply law to specific facts and predict how a court may rule on a particular legal question in order to influence a client's actions. Thus, in the mediation context, the practice of law consists of more than merely evaluating legal issues, assessing strengths and weaknesses of positions, or discussing barriers to settlement, all of which may be permissible under both mediator ethics and the Virginia Rules. Rather, the Committee believed that mediators should not predict the specific resolution of legal issues because such activity is part of a lawyer's function as adviser and counselor and could give rise to an implicit lawyer/client relationship. Moreover, predicting the specific resolution of legal issues may be incompatible with the role of a neutral and is generally not good mediation practice. Although the definition of legal advice adopted by the Committee prohibits mediators from predicting a specific resolution of a legal issue, providing a range of possible outcomes may be permissible under the definition.

Secondly, the Committee agreed that recommending a course of action to the parties would constitute unethical mediation practice because it would interfere with the self-determination of the parties and the impartiality of the mediator. Moreover, the Committee viewed the conduct of directing, urging, or recommending as activities typically performed by and expected of attorneys and thus embodied in the concept of giving legal advice that would be unauthorized practice of law and unethical mediation if performed by a mediator. With this background in mind, the following

sections attempt to define the boundary between providing permissible legal information and providing impermissible legal advice.

## SECTION 4. DISTINGUISHING LEGAL INFORMATION FROM LEGAL ADVICE

NOTE: The following sections include examples that are to be read in the context of the general Rule regarding what constitutes legal advice on page 13.

*A mediator may provide legal resource and procedural information to disputants.

Mediators sometimes need to provide disputants with copies of relevant Virginia statutes or court cases. Providing copies of statutes, such as § 20-124.3 dealing with child custody, is permissible and does not constitute legal advice. Likewise, providing disputants with reference information that will enable them to find a particular court case or statute in a library is also permissible. The Virginia State Bar, the American Bar Association, and other legal associations produce informational brochures or pamphlets on many areas of the law. Mediators are certainly free to provide disputants with copies of these documents without engaging in unethical mediation practice or the unauthorized practice of law. Providing relevant legal materials to the parties facilitates settlements by assisting the disputants in making fully-informed decisions.

Disputing parties are frequently uninformed about local court procedures regarding their cases. To the extent that mediators by training and experience are familiar with local procedures regarding scheduling, required fees, or the steps necessary to have a mediated agreement entered as a court order, they may provide this information to the parties without contravening the unauthorized practice rules or the ethical prohibitions against legal advice. Particularly in the court-referred or community mediation context, a mediator may serve as the primary informational resource available to the parties for this type of information.

### *A mediator may make statements declarative of the law.

Mediators may make statements that are declarative of the state of the law on a given legal topic and these statements are generally permissible. However, as noted previously, the manner in which law-related information is provided to the parties, the purposes for which it is provided, and the expectations of the disputing parties can transform an otherwise permissible statement into legal advice by essentially predicting the resolution of a legal issue relevant to the dispute at hand. Mediators may rely on their training, experience, or even their own analysis of statutes or case law when making these declarations. Like any private citizen, mediators are free to expound upon the law so long as their statements do not otherwise constitute the practice of law.[56] However, what may be a permissible statement declarative of the law in one context may constitute unethical mediation practice or legal advice in another. Mediators must carefully consider whether, under the totality of the circumstances, a law-related statement is likely to have the effect of predicting a specific resolution of a legal issue or of directing the actions of the parties. Under this totality of the circumstances analysis, statements made by a mediator in the presence of the disputants' attorneys are less likely to influence or direct their actions than if made outside of the attorneys' presence.[57]

Below are some examples of statements declarative of the law that probably would not be considered legal advice. Mediators are cautioned that these statements, while accurate, contain

exceptions and limitations. They are presented here for illustrative purposes only and should not be relied upon as definitive pronouncements concerning the state of the law for any legal subject area.

In the context of a divorce mediation:

- "Under the statutes, a person who is not seeking current spousal support but who wants the ability to get it in the future must expressly reserve the right to future spousal support in the settlement agreement and in the appropriate court order."[58]

- "In Virginia, custody involves two major components: with whom will the child primarily reside and who is responsible for making decisions concerning the upbringing of the child."[59]

- In the context of a personal injury dispute:

- "In Virginia, a plaintiff is usually barred from recovering damages in a negligence suit if the plaintiff was guilty of any negligence that contributed to his or her injuries."[60]

- "Generally, the statute of limitations in Virginia for personal injury claims is two years."[61]

- In the context of a commercial contract dispute:

"Generally speaking, a contract for the lease of goods that exceeds $1000 must be in writing to be enforceable."[62]

Although making general statements declarative of the law is a permissible activity, mediators may not have the training or expertise necessary to make the types of statements mentioned above. Mediators who make statements declarative of the law should do so only if they are competent to make such statements and are sure that they are accurate and complete. In addition, the mediator must be sure that any statement made does not interfere with either the self-determination of the parties or the impartiality of the mediator.

*A mediator may ask reality-testing questions that raise legal issues.

A helpful and often-used technique for assisting disputing parties in reaching a settlement is to ask the parties questions that are designed to cause them to reflect on the viability, fairness, or the strengths and weaknesses of their respective positions. Whether labeled as "raising issues" or "reality testing," this technique sometimes involves asking the parties to reflect on the legal ramifications of their case.

Reality testing questions do not, by themselves, constitute legal advice so long as they do not predict resolutions of legal issues or direct decision-making. With this caveat in mind, mediators are free to ask reality-testing questions of disputing parties even if those questions are designed to cause reflection by the parties on legal issues relevant to their dispute.

Below are two brief mediation scenarios where the use of reality-testing questions might be appropriate. Several possible questions are listed, and they are labeled as permissible or impermissible depending upon whether they may constitute legal advice. Impermissible questions are those that predict the specific resolution of a legal issue. They would probably constitute legal advice and therefore UPL and unethical mediation practice.

Bill and Mary are separated and intend to get a divorce. They have sought mediation to assist them in resolving some issues involving child custody and the distribution of assets. Mary states that she wants to relocate to Florida with the couple's two children. Bill objects to Mary's relocation and wants the children to remain in Virginia. Bill also claims one half ownership in some stock that Mary received as an inheritance last year from her grandfather. The stock is currently held in a joint brokerage account under both Mary and Bill's names.

| Permissible | Impermissible |
| --- | --- |
| "Have you both considered whether a court would allow Mary to take the children to Florida?" | "Mary, do you realize that the court that would hear this case would not allow you to take the children to Florida over Bill's objection?" |
| "How would the stock be appointed under the equitable distribution statute?" | "Bill, have you considered giving up on the stock issue since a court probably would view the asset as a separate property?" |

Three years ago, Ken and Nicole were involved in a traffic accident. Ken ran a stop sign and was hit by Nicole, who was exceeding the speed limit by about 10 miles per hour. Both vehicles received minor damage and Nicole incurred $750 in medical expenses. Ken was uninsured when the accident occurred and was forced to pay for the repairs of his vehicle. On the other hand, Nicole never received compensation from Ken for her medical bills. Because she does not want to file suit unless absolutely necessary, Nicole has persuaded Ken to enter into mediation at a local community mediation center. Both Ken and Nicole blame each other for the accident.

| Permissible | Impermissible |
|---|---|
| "What is the statute of limitations for your claims?" | "Mary, do you realize that the two year statute of limitations for personal injury claims has expired and that if the statute was raised by Ken as an affirmative defense, a court would dismiss your lawsuit?" |
| "Do either of you know what the Virginia rules are regarding negligence and contributory negligence?" | "Ken, have you considered that your own contributory negligence would prevent you from recovering damages from Nicole in court?" |

The key difference between the two sets of questions above is that the impermissible questions predict specific resolutions of legal issues, while the permissible questions are open-ended and do not suggest resolutions that are based on the application of law to specific facts. Again, the impermissible questions predict resolutions of legal issues by applying specialized knowledge of legal subjects to the unique facts of the disputants. These types of questions may constitute legal advice and should be avoided by mediators.

In this area, perhaps more than any other, the boundary between permissible questions and those that cross the line into legal advice is very narrow. The phrasing of the questions and the context are crucial. Open-ended questions that do not suggest an answer are almost always usually safe. On the other hand, leading questions that apply law to fact are problematic and may constitute legal advice since they are more likely to predict specific legal resolutions or direct or recommend a course of action.

*A mediator may inform the disputing parties about the mediator's experiences with a particular court or type of case.

Occasionally, mediators find it helpful to relate their experiences with case outcomes to disputants in an effort to assist them in reaching a settlement. For example, a mediator who has been involved in a great many landlord/tenant disputes in a particular jurisdiction and who possesses substantial experience may communicate her observations about the outcomes of such disputes to the parties in an effort to assist them in assessing the strengths and weaknesses of their positions. A mediator should be able to identify the basis for his or her observations, such as personal experience or empirical research.

Mediators are sometimes called upon to give disputants a sense for what the legal damages might be in their case. If through personal observation or empirical research a mediator is sufficiently familiar with jury awards in a given type of dispute and in a particular location, then the mediator may make those observations known to the parties without giving legal advice. These activities, by themselves, do not involve predictions of specific legal outcomes but rather may constitute the giving of empirical information.

Good mediation practice would suggest that mediators avoid making case outcome predictions when relating empirical observations or experiences to the parties. Parties should be told that courts reach decisions based on the facts and applicable law in each case and that no two cases are identical. Parties should also be told that the mediator is simply relating his or her experiences as a court observer and not predicting how the court will rule. The danger in making even experience-based predictions of case outcomes is that such predictions may interfere with the rights of the parties to self-determination and may create the perception that the mediator is biased.

**\*A mediator may inform the disputing parties about the enforceability of a mediated agreement.**

When contemplating the preparation of a written agreement during mediation, parties frequently ask mediators what legal effect such an agreement will have. Section 8.01-576.11 of the Code of Virginia states that mediated agreements are enforceable like any other contract. Mediators are free to refer the parties to this code section or to summarize it contents for them. However, whether a mediated agreement constitutes a valid and enforceable contract is matter of state contract law. Like any purported contract, a mediated agreement may not meet the requirements necessary to be enforceable. Thus, mediators should not advise the parties as to whether their particular agreement is enforceable as a valid contract. Advising the parties about the enforceability of a specific agreement is tantamount to predicting the resolution of a legal issue, and as the below Guideline makes clear, may be considered giving legal advice.

**\*A mediator may not make specific predictions about the resolution of legal issues or direct the decision-making of any party.**

In general, the line between legal information and legal advice is crossed whenever a mediator applies legal principles to facts in the mediation and predicts the specific resolution of a legal issue or otherwise makes statements that direct the actions of the parties. Using the permissible statements declarative of the law discussed previously on pages 16-17, the following italicized statements,

communicated to one or both of the parties following the otherwise permissible statements, would probably constitute legal advice if made by a mediator for compensation:

In the context of a divorce mediation:

- "Under the statutes, a person who is not seeking current spousal support but who wants the ability to get it in the future must expressly reserve the right to future spousal support in the settlement agreement and in the appropriate court order. *If you want to be able to get spousal support in the future, you should require a provision in the settlement agreement that permits such a possibility.*"

- "In Virginia, custody involves two major components: with whom will the child primarily reside and who is responsible for making decisions concerning the upbringing of the child. *You can resolve this dispute by simply calling your arrangement joint custody and stating that the child's primary residence will be with the mother.*"

In the context of a personal injury dispute:

- "In Virginia, a plaintiff is barred from recovering damages in a negligence suit if the plaintiff was guilty of any negligence that contributed to his or her injuries. *Because you were contributorily negligent, you would not be able to recover damages if this case were to proceed to trial.*"

- "The statute of limitations in Virginia for personal injury claims is two years. *As a result, your claim is barred and would not be heard by a Virginia court.*"

In the context of a commercial contract dispute:

- "Generally speaking, a contract for the lease of goods that exceeds $1000 must be in writing to be enforceable." *Since your agreement was in writing, you would have no problem getting a court to enforce it.*"

Each of the italicized statements listed above applies law to facts in the mediation and either predicts a specific legal resolution or suggests a course of action. Other examples of legal advice include predicting that a court would not award certain damages (e.g. punitive damages) because the plaintiff could not prove malice or predicting that a party would lose a lawsuit because he or she could not prove an essential element of the claim. Mediators can avoid giving legal advice by carefully limiting their law-related statements to general principles of law that do not predict the resolution of legal issues and that do not urge, direct, or influence the parties to the dispute.

### SECTION 5. CONCLUSION

Many of the potential problems with the unethical practice of mediation or the unauthorized practice of law addressed in this section rarely arise in everyday mediation. Mediators who adopt a facilitative approach to mediation will seldom find themselves in the position of questioning whether a particular statement may constitute legal advice. On the other hand, mediators whose style and practice tends more toward the evaluative end of the mediation spectrum may need to consider more carefully whether the questions that they raise or the statements that they make during mediation are permissible legal information or impermissible legal advice. Furthermore, if mediators choose to provide legal information to the disputants, they should do so only if they are confident that they-have the necessary training and experience and that the information is complete and will not be viewed as coercive, directive, or biased in favor of one of the parties.[63]

Whatever style of mediation they adopt, mediators must keep in mind that in order to avoid potential problems with unauthorized practice or with charges of misconduct, they should always inform the disputing parties in writing at the start of the mediation process that (1) mediators are prohibited from giving legal advice, (2) a settlement agreement may affect the legal rights of the parties, (3) the parties are encouraged to seek independent legal counsel, and (4) a mediated agreement should be reviewed by independent counsel before the parties sign the agreement.[64] Complying with these Guidelines should help protect mediators in Virginia from allegations that they engaged in UPL, unethical mediation practice, or a violation of the Virginia Rules of Professional Conduct.

## Preparing Mediated Agreements

### SECTION 1. INTRODUCTION

Once parties to a mediation have reached agreement on some or all of the issues in dispute, most desire to memorialize their agreement in the form of a written document.[65] Sometimes this document is entitled a "Memorandum of Understanding;" in other cases, it may be called a "Settlement Agreement" or a "Mediated Agreement." The purpose of this section of the Guidelines is to provide mediators with guidance on how to assist parties in committing their agreement to writing without contravening the Virginia UPL rules, mediator ethics, or in the case of attorney-mediators, the Virginia Rules of Professional Conduct. As with the previous chapter on legal advice, the Department of Dispute Resolution Services does not have the final say on what agreement preparation activities may constitute the practice of law. That determination is left to the Virginia State Bar, the Attorney General's office, or the courts.

### SECTION 2. THE LEGAL CONTEXT OF MEDIATED AGREEMENTS

Supreme Court of Virginia Rule Part 6, § I(B)(2) provides that a person is practicing law whenever "one, other than a regular employee acting for his employer, undertakes, with or without compensation, to prepare for another legal instruments of any character, other than notices or contracts incident to the regular course of conducting a licensed business." Unlike Part 6, § I(B)(1) discussed in the previous section on legal advice, the above subsection of the rule does not require that a person prepare the legal instrument for compensation. Thus, even volunteer mediators who are not being compensated for their services are subject to the rule on drafting legal instruments.[66] Furthermore, since most court-connected mediators are contracted by the Office of the Executive Secretary to provide services to the courts on a per case basis, they are not "regular employees" of the disputing parties and so cannot avoid the rule on that basis.

Finally, agreements prepared by mediators are probably not the "contracts incident to the regular course of conducting a licensed business" referred to in the rule. This particular provision was adopted by the Supreme Court of Virginia to address the preparation of sales contracts by real estate agents - a practice explicitly approved of by the court in Commonwealth v. Jones & Robins, Inc.[67] Unlike real estate agents, mediators in Virginia (even court-certified mediators) are not licensed. Mediators do not have to pass a licensure exam, nor is licensure mandatory to practice the mediation profession. Moreover, in the real estate profession, sales contracts, which include a provision for the agent's commission, are necessary to insure that the real estate agent receives compensation for his or her services. In the mediation context, it could be argued that written agreements resulting from the mediation are not required for mediator compensation.

However, in Jones & Robins, Inc., the Supreme Court of Virginia was concerned that prohibiting real estate agents from preparing sales contracts would run counter to their long-standing practice of providing this service, would be impractical, and would be detrimental to the real estate business. These same concerns would also be evident if mediators were denied the ability to prepare written agreements for disputing parties. Although it is possible that a court could construe a mediated agreement as a "contract incident to the regular course of conducting a licensed business," mediators would be prudent not to rely on this provision in order to claim an exemption from the UPL rule.

Despite the Supreme Court of Virginia rule prohibiting laypersons from preparing legal instruments, the Virginia mediation statutes refer to the preparation of written agreements by non-attorney mediators. In defining the various terms used in the dispute resolution chapter of the Code of Virginia § 8.01-576.4 states that "'dispute resolution services' includes screening and intake of disputants, conducting dispute resolution proceedings, drafting agreements, and providing information or referral services" (emphasis added). Furthermore, § 8.01-576.11 contemplates that written agreements would emerge from mediation sessions by providing that such agreements are "enforceable in the same manner as any other written contract." Finally, in defining misconduct by neutrals, § 8.01-576.12 states that upon the motion of a party, a court "shall vacate a mediated agreement reached in a dispute resolution proceeding" if the neutral fails to inform the disputants in writing of certain specified information (emphasis added).

Thus, while the Virginia mediation statutes appear to authorize the preparation by mediators of written agreements that may be enforceable as contracts, contracts are legal instruments, and the Unauthorized Practice of Law rules from the Supreme Court of Virginia prohibit non-attorneys from drafting legal instruments. To further complicate matters, the Virginia State Bar has authorized attorney-mediators to act as scriveners in committing mediated agreements to writing.[68] However, the State Bar's Legal Ethics Committee has cautioned attorney-mediators that if they provide agreement-writing services beyond those of a scrivener, then they have engaged in the practice of law.[69] Moreover, a conflict of interest would arise under the Virginia Rule of Professional Responsibility 2.10 (e), which states that "a lawyer who serves or has served as a third party neutral may not serve as a lawyer on behalf of any party to the dispute."

It appears that the Virginia mediation statutes, particularly § 8.01-576.4, authorize non-attorney mediators to prepare written agreements for disputing parties so long as they, like attorney-mediators, limit their drafting services to those of a scrivener. This harmonizing of the UPL rules and the mediation statutes gives mediators the flexibility to assist the parties in committing their mediated agreements to writing but stops short of allowing mediators to draft instruments in which they include legally operative terms not requested or contemplated by the parties during the mediation process. Allowing mediators to prepare written agreements for the parties facilitates the efficient resolution of disputes and minimizes the costs to the parties, who may not desire or be able to afford their own attorneys.

This approach is consistent with the conclusion of the State Bar's Legal Ethics Committee that "to the extent that the [lawyer]-mediator is engaged by the parties as a scrivener of the agreement reached during the mediation process, such tasks do not constitute the practice of law."[70] Likewise, when non-attorney mediators act as scriveners for the parties in committing their mediated agreements to writing, they have not engaged in the practice of law. However, like the Legal Ethics Committee, the Guidelines on Mediation and UPL Committee also believes that non-attorney mediators have engaged in the practice of law if their agreement preparation activities extend beyond acting as a scrivener for the parties.

A broad reading of § 8.01-576.4 would place no limits on the agre ement writing activities of mediators and would essentially allow them to practice law when drafting written agreements. However, such a construction of this statute would render inoperative the entire mechanism for regulating the practice of law in the context of mediated agreement preparation. Although § 8.01-576.4 has not been construed by Virginia's appellate courts, the Committee on Guidelines on Mediation and UPL does not believe that the Virginia legislature intended this broad interpretation of the statute. Therefore, these Guidelines take the approach that both attorney and non-attorney mediators may act only as scriveners of the agreement. The Guidelines that follow help define what is meant by that term of art.

### SECTION 3. ROLE OF THE MEDIATOR IN PREPARING WRITTEN AGREEMENTS

* Acting as a scrivener, a mediator may prepare settlement agreements and memoranda of understanding for the parties.

The Code of Virginia states that mediated agreements are legally enforceable as contracts.[71] Whether a contract is formed between disputing parties when they reach an agreement to settle their dispute is matter of state contract law. Generally speaking, however, a contract is formed whenever each party agrees to a settlement and promises that something will or will not be done for the benefit of another.[72] Thus, the particular form that a written agreement takes does not necessarily determine its enforceability as a contract. Documents entitled "Memoranda of Understanding," Settlement Agreements," or merely "Agreements" may all be enforceable if they meet the conditions for the formation of contracts under the laws of the Commonwealth of Virginia.

Regardless of the document's title, mediators in Virginia are permitted to assist the parties in committing their agreement to writing. A mediator may take an active role in preparing the agreement for the parties if they want the mediator to perform this function. The mediator may simply copy the agreement as dictated by the parties or may choose particular words or phrases to include in the agreement so long as the parties indicate that the language chosen by the mediator accurately reflects their desires. A mediator is also free to ask questions of the parties to clarify their agreement and may properly raise issues for their consideration. Likewise, a mediator may assist the parties in organizing their agreement by, for example, creating subsections in the document and placing the subsections in a logical order.

Mediators who prepare written agreements for disputing parties should strive to use the parties' own words whenever possible and in all cases should write agreements in a manner that comports with the wishes of the disputants. Mediators should not use language that one or both of the parties do not understand, and they should always allow the parties to review the written agreement carefully and make any changes that the parties believe are appropriate. As the Code of Virginia[73] and the Standards of Ethics and Professional Responsibility for Certified Mediators[74] require, mediators must always inform the parties in writing that mediated agreements should be reviewed by independent counsel before they are signed or that the parties should waive their opportunity for independent review.

* Unless required by law, a mediator should not add provisions to an agreement beyond those specified by the disputants.

Mediators are most likely to run afoul of UPL or ethical rules in drafting agreements when they attempt to include provisions in them that are not contemplated or requested by the parties themselves. In drafting settlement agreements for the parties, mediators should avoid the use of legal "boilerplate" and legal terms of art. These terms have legal consequences resulting from judicial interpretation and may favor one party over the other. The use of such terms may affect the parties in unintended ways and should be avoided.

Below are some examples of phrases or clauses that if included by a mediator in a written agreement may increase the likelihood that the Virginia State Bar, the Attorney General's office, or a court would view the preparation of the mediated agreement as the practice of law. Most of the examples are standard contractual terms used by attorneys for specific purposes and may be inappropriate for mediators to include in written agreements.

### Merger Clauses

- A and B agree that this Agreement contains the entire understanding between them and that no additional agreements regarding marital property rights have been made. They agree that this Agreement is a full and complete settlement of all property rights between them from the time of their marriage until the date of this Agreement.

- A and B agree that any and all previous agreements regarding marital property rights are hereby superseded by this Agreement and that this Agreement contains the entire understanding between them.

### Binding Effect Clauses

All provisions of this Agreement shall be binding upon the respective heirs, next of kin, executors, agents, assigns, and administrators of the parties.

### Choice of Law Clauses

This agreement is made under and shall be governed in all aspects by the laws of the Commonwealth of Virginia.

### Remedies Clauses

In the event that either of the parties to this Agreement commits a material breach of the Agreement, the party in breach agrees to pay the non-breaching party's attorney's fees and other reasonable costs associated with the breach.

### Severability Clauses

The parties agree that if any part of this Agreement shall be deemed legally defective, inoperative, or unenforceable, the remaining portions of the agreement shall continue to bind the parties and shall remain in full force and effect.

Although mediators should not ordinarily, on their accord, add the above terms to mediated agreements, they may include the concepts embodied in them if requested by the parties. Section E of the Standards of Ethics and Professional Responsibility for Certified Mediators states that consistent with the self-determination of the parties, a mediator may raise issues for the parties to consider. In the agreement context, § J of the Standards makes clear that a mediator may suggest options for the parties to consider when reaching an agreement. Thus, a mediator is not precluded from raising issues or suggesting options to the parties, but the mediator may not add provisions, particularly boilerplate provisions, to a written agreement that the parties themselves have not fully explored and requested. If the parties ask a mediator to include a provision in the written agreement like one of those listed above, the mediator should use plain language and should avoid legal terminology or terms of art with which he or she is not familiar.[75] Not only does legal boilerplate increase the likelihood that the preparation of the agreement will be considered an impermissible activity, but boilerplate may favor one of the parties over the other and thus may constitute a violation of mediator ethics.

In some cases, a statute or a court may require that a certain provision be included in a written agreement. For example, § 8.01-576.11 of the Code of Virginia states that a court order which incorporates a written agreement involving the support of a child must include the statutory child support guidelines worksheet and any written reasons for deviating from the guidelines. This particular provision contemplates that mediators may complete child support worksheets and mandates their attachment to a subsequent court order. Thus, mediators who complete these worksheets for the parties have not prepared a legal instrument and have not engaged in the practice of law.[76]

Similarly, § 20-124.5 provides that as a condition for granting any custody or visitation order, a court must require any party to the agreement to give 30 days written notice of an intention to relocate. This code section allows courts to dictate the form that such notice must take, and many courts require that the 30 day relocation notice provision be placed in the custody or visitation order itself. Consequently, in order to have a mediated custody agreement incorporated into a court order, a mediator may be required to include the 30-day relocation notice provision in the written agreement. A mediator who includes a standard relocation notice required by a local court in a mediated agreement has not engaged in the practice of law.

***Mediators may use a court-approved form when preparing a written agreement.***

A mediator probably would not be found to have engaged in the practice of law by utilizing a court-sponsored or approved form when preparing a written agreement for the parties. Generally speaking, the preparation of court orders is considered the practice of law.[77] However, it is standard practice for some courts in the Commonwealth to provide agreement forms to court-certified mediators that contain the appropriate language and signature lines to either order the dismissal of the court case pursuant to the agreement or, in some cases, to convert the agreement itself into a court order. Using such forms probably does not constitute the practice of law by mediators. Even if it does, the practice is authorized and supervised by the courts and presumably carries less risk to the public than normally associated with laypersons preparing court orders.[78]

### *A mediator may include standard provisions in written agreements relating to the mediation process itself.

If a mediator deems it appropriate, he or she may include provisions in a written agreement that are intended to provide information to the parties about the mediation process. For example, provisions stating that the mediator does not give legal, financial, or tax advice may be included. Provisions that explain confidentiality[79] or which state that the agreement may affect legal rights or that encourage the parties to have the agreement reviewed by independent counsel[80] are likewise permissible. In essence, provisions that are designed to inform the parties about the mediation process and which are not part of the substantive agreement between the parties may be included in a written agreement prepared by a mediator.

### SECTION 4. CONCLUSION

Mediators are neutrals whose function is to help parties resolve their disputes. If parties to a mediation agree to resolve their dispute, part of a mediator's role may be to help them put their agreement in written form. When parties are willing and able to write their own agreement, self-determination is maximized. However, some disputants may prefer that the mediator memorialize the terms of their agreement and others may view the preparation of a written agreement as a natural extension of the mediator's facilitative role.

The Guidelines in this chapter allow mediators in Virginia to take an active role in preparing written agreements for disputing parties if the parties so desire. Mediators may assist the parties in framing the terms of their agreement, they may help them choose appropriate words or phrases, and they may provide an organizational framework for the agreement. The Guidelines allow mediators flexibility and prohibit only the addition by them of terms that do not make up part of the agreement between the disputants or that may have unanticipated legal consequences. Following these Guidelines should help protect mediators from charges that they engaged in the practice of law or unethical mediation practice in preparing mediated agreements.

## Appendix E Notes

1.   See ABA Model Rules of Professional Conduct 2.2 (lawyers acting as intermediaries) and 5.7 (Responsibilities Regarding Law-Related Services).

2.   See e.g., VA State Bar Comm. on Legal Ethics, Op. 1368 (1990)(the practice of mediation closely resembles the practice of law and therefore attorney-mediators are subject to the Virginia Rules of Professional Conduct).

3.   American Bar Association, NonLawyer Activity in Law-Related Situations: A Report with Recommendations (1995).

4.   Barlow F. Christensen, The Unauthorized Practice of Law: Do Good Fences Really Make Good Neighbors - Or Even Good Sense?, 1980 American Bar Foundation Journal 159 (1980).

5.   Supra note 3, at 9.

6.   See generally Andrew S. Morrison, Is Divorce Mediation the Practice of Law? A Matter of Perspective, 75 California Law Review 1093 (1987).

7.   Id. at 1096.

8.   366 P.2d 1 (Ariz. 1961).

9.   Id. at 9.

10.   Morrison, supra note 6, at 1096.

11.   Opinion of the Justices, 194 N.E. 313 (Mass. 1935).

12.   Morrision, supra note 6, at 1097.

13.   41 S.E.2d 720 (Va. 1947).

14.   This decision was subsequently codified in Virginia Unauthorized Practice Rule Part 6-103(3), which authorizes real estate agents to prepare sales contracts.

15.   Morrison, supra note 6, at 1098; see Agran v. Shapiro, 273 P.2d 619 (Cal. App. 1954) (preparation of simple income tax returns was not the practice of law); Gardner v. Conway, 48 N.W.2d 788 (Minn. 1951)(resolution of complex tax questions was the practice of law). But see State Bar Ass'n v. Connecticut Bank & Trust Co., 140 A.2d 863, 871 (Conn. 1958)(rejecting the routine/complex dichotomy and holding that a trust officer who drafts certain instruments may be engaged in UPL even though no difficult legal questions are involved).

16.   273 P.2d 619 (Cal. App. 1954).

17.   Gardner v. Conway, 48 N.W.2d 788 (Minn. 1951).

18.   Morrison, supra note 6, at 1103.

19.   366 P.2d 1 (Ariz. 1961).

20.   Id. at 9.

21. Donald T. Weckstein, In Praise of Party Empowerment - And of Mediator Activism, 33 Willamette Law Review 501 (1997).

22. Id. at 543-44.

23. Morrison, supra note 6, at 1104.

24. See, e.g. Oregon State Bar v. Gilchrist, 538 P.2d 913 (Or. 1975).

25. See, e.g. Florida Bar v. Stupica, 300 So. 2d 683 (Fla. 1974).

26. Morrison, supra note 6, at 1105.

27. See Palmer v. Unauthorized Practice Committee, 438 S.W.2d 374 (Tex. Civ. App. 1969).

28. See Morrison, supra note 6, at 1106.

29. Morrison, supra note 6, at 1107.

30. See State Bar v. Cramer, 249 N.W.2d 1 (Mich. 1976).

31. Sup. Ct. of Va. R. Part 6, § I.

Professor Menkel-Meadow is a professor at Georgetown Law Center and is the co-director of the Center for Conflict Resolution at UCLA law school.

32. Carrie Menkel-Meadow, Ethics in Alternative Dispute Resolution: New Issues, No Answers from the Adversary Conception of Lawyers' Responsibilities, 38 South Texas Law Review 407, 424 (1997).

33. Carrie Menkel-Meadow, Is Mediation the Practice of Law?, Alternatives, May 1996, at 60, 61.

34. Supra note 33, at 451-53.

35. Professor Weckstein is a professor of law at the University of San Diego.

36. Donald T. Weckstein, In Praise of Party Empowerment - And of Mediator Activism, 33 Willamette Law Review 501, 543-44 (1997).

37. Id. at 543-44.

38. See Richmond Assoc. of Credit Men v. Bar Assoc. of Richmond, 167 Va. 327, 189 S.E. 153 (1937); Va. Sup. Ct. Rule Part 6, § I.

39. Commonwealth v. Jones & Robins, Inc., 186 Va. 30, 41 S.E.2d 720 (1947).

40. Richmond Assoc. of Credit Men v. Bar Assoc. of Richmond, 167 Va. 327, 189 S.E. 153 (1937).

41. The Department of Dispute Resolution Services is a department within the Supreme Court of Virginia's Office of the Executive Secretary. It is responsible for developing dispute resolution alternatives and for certifying court-referred mediators in Virginia.

42. See Rule 2.10 (Third Party Neutral) and Rule 2.11 (Mediator).

43. Comment 1 to Rule 2.10 states that "dispute resolution proceedings . . . include mediation, conciliation, early neutral evaluation, non-binding arbitration, and non-judicial settlement conferences."

44. Rule 2.10 (a)("The third party neutral does not represent any party.").

45. Rule 2.10 (e)("A lawyer who serves or has served as a third party neutral may not serve as a lawyer on behalf of any party to the dispute, nor represent one such party against the other in any legal proceeding related to the subject of the dispute resolution proceeding.").

46. Rule 2.11 (c)("A lawyer-mediator may offer legal information if all parties are present or separately to the parties if they consent.").

47. Rule 2.11 (d)(lawyer-mediator may offer evaluation "only if such evaluation is incidental to the facilitative role and does not interfere with the lawyer-mediator's impartiality or the self-determination of the parties.").

48. 186 Va. 30, 41 S.E.2d 720 (1947).

49. Subsection F of the Standards of Ethics and Professional Responsibility for Certified Mediators in Virginia states that "a mediator shall give information only in those areas where qualified by training or experience."

50. The conduct referred to in this section is consistent with existing Rules including the Standards of Ethics for Court-Certified Mediators, the Virginia Rules of Professional Conduct, and the Code of Virginia.

51. Virginia Standards of Ethics and Professional Responsibility for Certified Mediators, § D(2)(a)(1).

52. Comment 7 to Rule 2.11 (Mediator) provides that a lawyer-mediator may not give legal advice. Comment 3 to Rule 2.10(Third Party Neutral) states that a lawyer acting as a third party neutral also may not give legal advice.

53. Unless a lawyer obtains informed consent from both parties, Rule 1.7 of the Virginia Rules of Professional Conduct prohibits the lawyer from representing a client when such representation will be directly adverse to the interests of another client. While the Virginia Rules (2.2) permit dual representation under certain circumstances, Rule 2.10(e) prohibits a lawyer-mediator from representing either party to a mediation.

54. Cf. Virginia Rule of Professional Conduct 2.10, Comment 3 ("A lawyer serving as a third party neutral shall not offer any of the parties legal advice . . . [but] may, however, offer neutral evaluations, if requested by the parties."); Rule 2.11 (d)("A lawyer-mediator may offer evaluation of, for example, strengths and weaknesses of positions, assess the value and cost of alternatives to settlement or assess barriers to settlement.").

55. See New York County Lawyer's Ass'n v. Dacy, 234 N.E.2d 459 (N.Y. 1967); Oregon State Bar v. Gilchrist, 538 P.2d 913 (Or. 1975).

56. Cf. Virginia State Bar Comm. on the Unauthorized Practice of Law, Op. 107 (1987) (It is permissible for a non-Virginia attorney to advise a Virginia attorney who may then render the advice to a client if he deems it acceptable.).

57. Va. Code § 20-109(C).

58. Va. Code § 20-124.1.

59. Fein v. Wade, 210 S.E.2d 29 (Va. 1950).

60. Va. Code § 8.01-243(A).

61. Va. Code § 8.2A-201(1).

62. Virginia Standards of Ethics and Professional Responsibility for Certified Mediators, § E.

63. Va. Code § 8.01-576.12(3).

64. Good mediation practice suggests that parties who reach an agreement should commit their agreement to writing. Oral agreements may be difficult to prove if the need should arise. Although Virginia Code § 8.01-581.22 provides that "a mediated agreement" shall not be keptconfidential, § 8.01-576.10 states only that a "written settlement agreement" shall not be kept confidential. Although these statutes have not been construed by the courts, it is possible that a court could rely on § 8.01-576.10 and decide that an oral agreement must remain confidential. Parties can avoid proof and confidentiality problems by memorializing their agreement in writing.

65. See, e.g., Va. Comm. On Unauthorized Practice of Law, Op. 119 (1988) (activities which are otherwise the unauthorized practice of law remain such even if done on a pro bono basis).

66. 186 Va. 30, 41 S.E.2d 720 (1947).

67. Va. Comm. on Legal Ethics, Op. 1368 (1990).

68. See id.

69. Va. Comm. on Legal Ethics, Op. 1368 (1990).

70. Va. Code § 8.01-576.11.

71. See, e.g., Blake Co. v. Smith & Son, 147 Va. 960, 133 S.E. 685 (1926). Please note that the law governing the formation of contracts is complex and that the rule stated above is subject to exceptions and limitations. It provided only for illustrative purposes and should not be relied upon as a complete statement of the law of contracts in Virginia.

72. § 8.01-576.12.

73. § D(2)(a)(4).

74. If the parties and /or their attorneys request that specific boilerplate provisions be included in a mediated agreement, good practice would suggest that the mediator

request the parties to provide the exact language desired as well as attribute those provision(s) to the individual(s) requesting it in the agreement itself.

75. Providing information to the parties on how to calculate child support under the Guidelines or on the statutory reasons for deviating from them would not constitute the practice of law. Similarly, using a commercially available computer program to calculate child support does not constitute the practice of law.

76. See 1-A Interiors, Inc. v. Meer Street Investment Assoc., 10 Va. Cir. 93 (Va. Beach 1987). In that case, the Virginia Beach Circuit Court held that the preparation of a court order by a non-lawyer who was also a party to the case was the unauthorized practice of law. Without much explanation, the court stated that the preparation of a court decree necessarily involves the exercise of professional legal judgment and can only be undertaken by a licensed attorney.

77. The routine practice by many courts in Virginia is to allow mediators to prepare written agreements on forms that are entered as court orders in non-complex civil matters, e.g. those not involving equitable distribution.

78. For example, § I(c) of the Standards of Ethics and Professional Responsibility for Court- Certified Mediators provides that mediated agreements shall not be confidential unless otherwise agreed by the parties in writing.

79. This provision is one of several that mediators must inform the parties of in writing prior to the commencement of the mediation. Va. Code § 8.01-576.12.

# Summary Of Research Findings

At the outset of this project, a survey was designed to gather information from all 50 states on the subject of mediation and the unauthorized practice of law. The survey, which follows this summary, was mailed to approximately 180 bar associations and mediation groups across the country. Associations representing twenty-eight states (56 percent) responded to the survey.

| Responded | Did Not Respond |
|---|---|
| Alabama | Alaska |
| Arizona | Delaware |
| Arkansas | District of Columbia |
| California | Georgia |
| Colorado | Indiana |
| Florida | Iowa |
| Hawaii | Kentucky |
| Idaho | Louisiana |
| Illinois | Maine |
| Kansas | Massachusetts |
| Maryland | Nevada |
| Michigan | New Jersey |
| Minnesota | New Mexico |
| Missouri | New York |
| Montana | Oklahoma |
| Nebraska | Pennsylvania |
| New Hampshire | Rhode Island |
| North Carolina | South Carolina |
| North Dakota | Tennessee |
| Ohio | Washington |
| Oregon | West Virginia |
| South Dakota | Wyoming |
| Texas | |
| Utah | |
| Vermont | |
| Wisconsin | |

The vast majority of responding states indicated that they do not have any formal or informal rules regarding UPL and mediation and that they are unaware of any court cases or ethics opinions in their states that deal with this issue. Below is a summary of the responses from those few states that have addresses the issue of mediation and UPL, either through ethics or UPL opinions, court rules, or guidelines.

## Survey Results

### Alabama

The Alabama State Bar has issued two informal ethics opinions that relate to mediation and UPL. In the first opinion, an attorney for the state bar advised a non-lawyer mediator that completing Alabama's child support guidelines was probably the unauthorized practice of law. In the second opinion, an assistant general counsel for the Alabama State Bar opined that "early neutral evaluation" by a retired judge who held only special (inactive) membership in the state bar did not constitute the practice of law.

### Florida

Florida has established rules for court-appointed mediators and is in the process of drafting new rules. Rule 10.037(c) of the proposed rules states that "a mediator shall not offer a personal or professional opinion as to how the court in which the case has been filed will resolve the dispute." However, the rule goes on to state that "a mediator may point out possible outcomes of the case and discuss the merits of a claim or defense." Also, the comment to this rule allows mediators to assist the parties in drafting settlement agreements.

### Maryland

The Maryland Court of Appeals has provisionally approved a set of rules applicable to court-referred mediation. The rules distinguish between neutral case evaluation, which requires the services of a lawyer, and mediation, which can be practiced by non-lawyers. With regard to mediation, the rules simply state that mediators are not to give legal advice. No definition of legal advice is provided in the rules.

### North Carolina

The North Carolina Bar is the process of approving a set of guidelines governing mediation and UPL. Although these guidelines are finished, they have not yet been formally adopted. The guidelines were unavailable at the time this report was prepared.

### Oregon

In Formal Opinion No. 1991-101, the Oregon State Bar stated that the drafting of settlement agreements for others during mediation would constitute the practice of law.

### Texas

The State Bar of Texas' Ethical Guidelines for Mediators state that a mediator should not give legal advice (Rule 11). Again, no definition of legal advice is provided in the guidelines. The guidelines also state that a mediator should encourage the parties to reduce their agreements to writing (Rule 14).

### Reported Mediation/UPL Decisions

As these responses indicate, the unauthorized practice of law by non-attorney mediators has been formally or informally addressed by only seven (including Virginia) of the responding states. Of these, only Virginia and North Carolina have attempted to create rules or guidelines to assist non-attorney mediators in avoiding the unauthorized practice of law. If the unauthorized practice of law by mediators was a wide-spread problem, it seems likely that more of the responding states would have received complaints and would have acted to address the problem. Of course, the summaries reported above include only those states that responded to the survey. However, an exhaustive search of the relevant literature and of the electronic legal databases (LEXIS and WESTLAW) revealed only a single reported court decision on the alleged unauthorized practice of law by a non-attorney mediator.

In Werle v. Rhode Island Bar Association,[1] the Rhode Island Bar Association sent plaintiff Werle a cease and desist letter after determining that a brochure advertising his family mediation business contravened Rhode Island's unauthorized practice statutes. The brochure advertised that Werle, a psychologist, would offer mediation to divorcing couples and would assist them in reaching an agreement on property division, support, and child custody. Werle sued the Rhode Island Bar and the members of its UPL Committee under 42 U.S.C. § 1983, claiming that they had deprived him of his First and Fourteenth Amendment rights by ordering him not to advertise or to engage in his mediation practice.

The First Circuit Court of Appeals held that the defendants were entitled to immunity under section 1983. Either the defendants were entitled to the absolute immunity afforded to prosecutors exercising their discretionary function, or they were entitled to qualified immunity because a reasonable person could conclude that Dr. Werle's services constituted the unauthorized practice of law.

## Conclusion

Although the decision in Werle did not define what constitutes the unauthorized practice of law by a non-attorney mediator, it did afford immunity from suit to members of the Rhode Island Bar Association who concluded that a psychologist could not engage in divorce mediation under Rhode Island law without also practicing law illegally. The decision is now 14 years old, and divorce mediation by non-attorney mediators has become commonplace in almost all states. The mediation services that Dr. Werle advertised - property division, support, and child custody are now commonly undertaken by non-attorney mediators both in Virginia and elsewhere.

The challenge in regulating the unauthorized practice of law by non-attorney mediators is to craft rules that recognize the value of the services provided by these persons (both in divorce settings and otherwise) and that provide them the flexibility to engage in meaningful mediation practice. At the same time, the public must also be protected from inaccurate and potentially harmful legal services rendered by untrained and unqualified mediators. The Unauthorized Practice of Law Guidelines for Virginia Mediators developed during this project attempted to tread this very narrow path.

1. 755 F.2d 195 (1st Cir. 1985).

# Rules of the Supreme Court of Virginia

## Section I. Unauthorized Practice Rules and Considerations

### INTRODUCTION

The right of individuals to represent themselves is an inalienable right common to all natural persons. But no one has the right to represent another; it is a privilege to be granted and regulated by law for the protection of the public.

The Supreme Court of Virginia has the inherent power to make rules governing the practice of law in the Commonwealth of Virginia. The Court has promulgated the definition of the practice of law. See "PRACTICE OF LAW IN THE COMMONWEALTH OF VIRGINIA," infra.

The public is best served in legal matters by lawyers. A client is entitled to be served disinterestedly by a lawyer who is not motivated or influenced by any allegiance other than to the client and our system of justice.

The services of a lawyer are essential and in the public interest whenever the exercise of professional legal judgement is required. The essence of such judgement is the lawyer's educated ability to relate the general body and philosophy of law to a specific legal problem. The public is better served by those who have met rigorous educational requirements, have been certified of honest demeanor and good moral character, and are subject to high ethical standards and strict disciplinary rules in the conduct of their practice.

By statute, any person practicing law without being duly authorized or licensed is guilty of a misdemeanor. The Attorney General of Virginia may leave the prosecution to the local attorney for the Commonwealth, or he may in his discretion institute and conduct such proceedings.

The courts of the Commonwealth have the inherent power, apart from statute, to inquire into the conduct of any person to determine whether he is illegally engaged in the practice of law, and to enjoin such conduct. The State Corporation Commission of Virginia may order the dissolution of any corporation or revoke its certificate of authority to transact business in the Commonwealth upon a finding that any officer, member, agent or employee thereof has been engaged in the unauthorized practice of law.

Any fees charged by a person engaged in the unauthorized practice of law are not collectible in court.

Any lawyer who aids a non-lawyer in the unauthorized practice of law is subject to discipline and disbarment. A lawyer has an affirmative duty to report unprivileged knowledge of such misconduct by another lawyer to the appropriate District Committee, and to discontinue his representation of a client when he discovers that his employment furthers the unauthorized practice of law by the client. Advisory opinions on the unauthorized practice of law, therefore, are as much intended to assist lawyers in fulfilling their ethical responsibilities as to inform and deter those who are engaged, or would engage, in such practice in derogation of the public's interest in a trained and regulated legal profession.

With the increase in the complexity of our society and its laws, the independence and integrity of a strong legal profession, devoted disinterestedly to those requiring legal services, are crucial to a free and democratic society. Allegiance to this principle, rather than the preservation of economic benefits for lawyers, is the basis upon which the Virginia State Bar, as the Administrative agency of the Supreme Court of Virginia, carries forward the responsibility for the discipline of lawyers and the investigation of persons practicing law in the Commonwealth without proper authority.

## Practice of Law in The Commonwealth of Virginia

(A) No non-lawyer shall engage in the practice of law in the Commonwealth of Virginia or in any manner hold himself out as authorized or qualified to practice law in the Commonwealth of Virginia except as may be authorized by rule or statute.

(B) Definition of the Practice of Law. - The principles underlying a definition of the practice of law have been developed through the years in social needs and have received recognition by the courts. It has been found necessary to protect the relation of attorney and client against abuses. Therefore, it is from the relation of attorney and client that any practice of law must be derived.

The relation of attorney and client is direct and personnel, and a person, natural or artificial, who undertakes the duties and responsibilities of an attorney is nonetheless practicing law though such person may employ others to whom may be committed the actual performance of such duties.

The gravity of the consequences to society resulting from abuses of this relation demands that those assuming to advise or to represent others shall be properly trained and educated, and be subject to a peculiar discipline. That fact, and the necessity for protection of society in its affairs and in the ordered proceedings of its tribunals, have developed the principles which serve to define the practice of law.

Generally, the relation of attorney and client exists, and one is deemed to be practicing law whenever he furnishes to another advice or service under circumstances which imply his possession and use of legal knowledge or skill.

Specifically, the relation of attorney and client exists, and one is deemed to be practicing law whenever -

1. One undertakes for compensation, direct or indirect, to advise another, not his regular employer, in any matter involving the application of legal principles to facts or purposes or desires.

2. One, other than as a regular employee acting for his employer, undertakes, with or without compensation, to prepare for another legal instruments of any character, other than notices or contracts incident to the regular course of conducting a licensed business.

3. One undertakes, with or without compensation, to represent the interest of another before any tribunal - judicial, administrative, or executive - otherwise than in the presentation of facts, figures, or factual conclusions, as distinguished from legal conclusions, by an employee regularly and bona fide employed on a salary basis, or by one specially

employed as an expert in respect to such facts and figures when such representation by such employee or expert does not involve the examination of witnesses or preparation of pleadings.

(C) Definition of *'Non-Lawyer'*. - The term "non-lawyer" means any person, firm, association or corporation not duly licensed or authorized to practice law in the Commonwealth of Virginia.

However, the term "non-lawyer" shall not include foreign attorneys who provide legal advice or services in Virginia to clients under the following restrictions and qualifications:

1. Such foreign attorney must be admitted to practice and in good standing in any state in the United States; and

2. The services provided must be on an occasional basis only and incidental to representation of a client whom the attorney represents elsewhere; and

3. The client must be informed that the attorney is not admitted in Virginia.

A lawyer who provides services not authorized under this rule must associate with an attorney authorized to practice in Virginia.

Nothing herein shall be deemed to overrule or contradict the requirements of Rules of this Court regarding foreign attorneys admitted to practice in the courts of the Commonwealth of Virginia including the association of counsel admitted to practice before the courts of this Commonwealth.

A lawyer who provides services as authorized under this rule, or who is admitted pro hac vice under Rule 1A:4 shall, with regard to such services or admission, be bound by the disciplinary rules set forth in the Virginia Code of Professional Responsibility.

Failure of the foreign attorney to comply with the requirements of these provisions shall render the activity by the attorney in Virginia to be the unauthorized practice of law.

(D) The unauthorized Practice rules which follow represent a nonexclusive list of specific types of practice which would violate these rules.

Cross references. - For penalty provisions for the unauthorized practice of law, see § 54.1-3904. For authority of Attorney General to institute proceedings, see § 2.1-124. For unauthorized practice of law opinions, see the Legal Ethics and Unauthorized Practice Opinions Volume of the code of Virginia.

Editor's note. - The unauthorized practice considerations and rules which follow are derived from the Virginia Rules of Court, Part Six, § I; 171 Va. xvii (1938); 216 Va. 1062 (1976). Part Six, § IV, Paragraph 10 of the Rules of Court prescribes the procedures governing petitions for and promulgating and publication of advisory unauthorized practice of law opinions by the council of the Virginia State Bar. Section Ia (now Section I) of the Rules was originally published as an Appendix to Paragraph 10 of Section IV. See 221 Va. 381 (1980). The designation for each UPL advisory opinion as "Rule 6.1-1, Rule 6.1-2" etc., has been amended; they are now designated "unauthorized Practice Rule 1," etc. Unauthorized Practice Rules 8 and 9 were published at 221 Va. 1147 (1981). Unauthorized

Practice Rules 6 and 7 were adopted by the Supreme Court on Oct. 16, 1981, effective Jan. 1, 1982, but were not originally published in the Virginia Reports. The amendment, effective September 18, 1996, adopted September 18, 1996, in subdivision (C), added the last sentence of the introductory paragraph, added subdivisions (1) through (3), and added the concluding paragraphs.

Law review. - For article, "Virginia: the Unauthorized Practice of Law Experience," see 19 U.Rich. L. Rev. 499(1985).

Representation of client at bankruptcy proceeding. - Appearance on behalf of a client at a § 341 bankruptcy proceeding constitutes the practice of law in Virginia. Duncan v. Garrett (In re Tanksley), 174 Bankr. 434 (Bankr. W. D. Va. 1994).

Applied in Commonwealth Virginia State Bar v. Jones & Robins, Inc., 186 Va. 30, 41

S.E.2d 720 (1947); NLRB v. Harvey, 349 F.2d 900 (4th Cir. 1965).

# Code of Virginia: Chapter 21.2 Mediation

### § 8.01-581.21. Definitions. - As used in this chapter:

"Mediation" means the process by which a mediator assists and facilitates two or more parties to a controversy in reaching a mutually acceptable resolution of the controversy and includes all contacts between the mediator and any party or parties, until such time as a resolution is agreed to by the parties or the parties discharge the mediator.

"Mediation Program" means a program through which mediators or mediation is made available and includes the director, agents and employees of the program.

"Mediator" means an impartial third party selected by agreement of the parties to a controversy to assist them in mediation.

§ 8.01-581.22. Confidentiality; exceptions. - All memoranda, work products and other materials contained in the case files of a mediator or mediation program are confidential. Any communication made in or in connection with the mediation which relates to the controversy being mediated, whether made to the mediator or a party, or to any other person if made at a mediation session, is confidential. However, a mediated agreement shall not be confidential, unless the parties otherwise agree in writing.

Confidential materials and communications are not subject to disclosure in any judicial or administrative proceeding except (i) where all parties to the mediation agree, in writing, to waive the confidentiality, (ii) in a subsequent action between the mediator and a party to the mediation for damages arising out of the mediation, or (iii) statements, memoranda, materials and other tangible evidence, otherwise subject to discovery, which were not prepared specifically for use in and actually used in the mediation.

§ 8.01-581.23. Civil immunity. - Mediators and mediation programs shall be immune from civil liability for, or resulting from, any act or omission done or made while engaged in efforts to assist or facilitate a mediation, unless the act or omission was made or done in bad faith, with malicious intent or in a manner exhibiting a willful, wanton disregard of the rights, safety or property of another.

## Code of Virginia: Chapter 20.2 Dispute Resolution Proceedings

### § 8.01-576.4. Definitions. - As used in this chapter:

"Conciliation" means a process in which a neutral facilitates settlement by clarifying issues and serving as an intermediary for negotiations in a manner which is generally more informal and less structured than mediation.

"Court" means any juvenile and domestic relations district court, general district court, circuit court, or appellate court, and includes the judges and any intake specialist to whom the judge has delegated specific authority under this chapter.

"Dispute resolution proceeding" means any structured process in which a neutral assists disputants in reaching a voluntary settlement by means of dispute resolution techniques such as mediation, conciliation, early neutral evaluation, nonjudicial settlement conferences or any other proceeding leading to a voluntary settlement conducted consistent with the requirements of this chapter. The term includes the evaluation session.

"Dispute resolution program" means a program that offers dispute resolution services to the public which is run by the Commonwealth or any private for-profit or not-for-profit organization, political subdivision, or public corporation, or a combination of these.

"Dispute resolution services" includes screening and intake of disputants, conducting dispute resolution proceedings, drafting agreements and providing information or referral services.

"Evaluation session" means a preliminary meeting during which the parties and the neutral assess the case and decide whether to continue with a dispute resolution proceeding or with adjudication.

"Intake specialist" means an individual who is trained in analyzing and screening cases to assist in determining whether a case is appropriate for referral to a dispute resolution proceeding.

"Mediation" means a process in which a neutral facilitates communication between the parties and, without deciding the issues or imposing a solution on the parties, enables them to understand and resolve their dispute.

"Neutral" means an individual who is trained or experienced in conducting dispute resolution proceedings and in providing dispute resolution services.

§ 8.01-576.5. Referral of disputes to dispute resolution proceedings. - While protecting the right to trial by jury, a court, on its own motion or on motion of one of the parties, may refer any contested civil matter, or selected issues in a civil matter, to a dispute resolution evaluation session in order to encourage the early settlement of disputes through the use of procedures that facilitate (i) open communication between the parties about the issues in the dispute, (ii) full exploration of the range of options to resolve the dispute, (iii) improvement in the relationship between the parties, and (iv) control by the parties over the outcome of the dispute. The court shall set a date for the parties to return to court in accordance with its regular docket and procedure, irrespective of the referral to an evaluation session. The parties shall notify the court, in writing, if the dispute is resolved prior to the return date.

Upon such referral, the parties shall attend one evaluation session unless excused pursuant to §8.01-576.6. Further participation in a dispute resolution proceeding shall be by consent of all parties. Attorneys for any party may be present during a dispute resolution proceeding.

§ 8.01-576.6. Notice and opportunity to object. - When a court has determined that referral to a dispute resolution evaluation session is appropriate, an order of referral to a neutral or to a dispute resolution program shall be entered and the parties shall be so notified as expeditiously as possible. The court shall excuse the parties from participation in a dispute resolution evaluation session if, within fourteen days after entry of the order, a written statement signed by any party is filed with the court, stating that the dispute resolution process has been explained to the party and he objects to the referral.

§ 8.01-576.7. Costs. - The evaluation session shall be conducted at no cost to the parties. Unless otherwise provided by the statute or agreed to by the parties and the neutral, the court may set a reasonable fee for the services of any neutral to whom a case is referred by the court as provided in §8.01-576.8. Prior to setting the rate and method of payment pursuant to this chapter, the court shall determine whether any of the parties is indigent. If it is determined that one or more of the parties is indigent and no agreement as to payment is reached between the parties, the court shall refer the case to a dispute resolution program that offers services at no charge to the parties or to a neutral who has agreed to accept cases on a pro bono or volunteer basis. If it is determined that neither of the parties is indigent, and the parties have not selected a dispute resolution program that offers services at no cost nor agreed with the neutral as to another method of payment, the judge may assess the fees of the neutral as costs of suit.

§ 8.01-576.8. - Qualifications of neutrals; referral. - A neutral who provides dispute resolution services other than mediation pursuant to this chapter shall provide the court with a written statement of qualifications, describing the neutral's background and relevant training and experience in the field. A mediator who desires to receive referrals from the court shall be certified pursuant to guidelines promulgated by the Judicial Council of Virginia. A dispute resolution program may satisfy the requirements of this section on behalf of its neutrals by providing the court with a written statement of the background, training, experience and certification, as appropriate, of any neutral who participates in its program.

The court shall maintain a list of neutrals and dispute resolution programs which have met the requirements of this section. The list may be divided among the areas of specialization or expertise maintained by the neutrals. At the conclusion of the evaluation session, or no later than ten days thereafter, parties electing to continue with the dispute resolution proceeding may: (i) continue with the neutral who conducted the evaluation session, (ii) select any neutral or dispute resolution program from the list maintained by the court to conduct such proceedings, or (iii) pursue any other alternative for voluntarily resolving the dispute to which the parties agree. If the parties choose to proceed with the dispute resolution proceeding but are unable to agree on a neutral or dispute resolution program during that period, the court shall refer the case to a neutral or dispute resolution program on the list maintained by the court on the basis of a fair and equitable rotation, taking into account the subject matter of the dispute and the expertise of the neutral, as appropriate.

§ 8.01-576.9. Standards and duties of neutrals; confidentially; liability. - A neutral selected to conduct a dispute resolution proceeding under this chapter may encourage and assist the parties in reaching a resolution of their dispute, but may not compel or coerce the parties into entering into a settlement agreement. A neutral has an obligation to remain impartial and free from conflict of interests in each case, and to decline to participate further in a case should such partiality or conflict arise. Unless expressly authorized by the disclosing party, the neutral may not disclose to either party information relating to the subject matter of the dispute resolution proceeding provided to him in confidence by the other. In reporting on the outcome of the dispute resolution proceeding to the referring court, the neutral shall indicate only the terms of any agreement reached or the fact that no agreement was reached. The neutral shall not disclose information exchanged or observations regarding the conduct and demeanor of the parties and their counsel during the dispute resolution proceeding, unless the parties otherwise agree.

However, where the dispute involves the support of minor children of the parties, the parties shall disclose between themselves and to the neutral the information to be used in completing the child support guidelines worksheet required by §20-108.2. The guidelines computations and any reasons for deviation shall be incorporated in any written agreement between the parties.

With respect to liability, the provisions of §8.01-581.23 shall apply in claims arising out of services rendered by any neutral.

§ 8.01-576.11. **Effect of written settlement agreement.** - If the parties reach a settlement and execute a written agreement disposing of the dispute, the agreement is enforceable in the same manner as any other written contract. Upon request of all parties and consistent with law and public policy, the court shall incorporate the written agreement into the terms of its final decree disposing of a case. In cases in which the dispute involves support for the minor children of the parties, an order incorporating a written agreement shall also include the child support guidelines worksheet and, if applicable, the written reasons for any deviation from the guidelines. The child support guidelines worksheet shall be attached to the order.

§ 8.01-576.12. **Vacating orders and agreements.** - Upon the filing of an independent action by a party, the court shall vacate a mediated agreement reached in a dispute resolution proceeding pursuant to this chapter, or vacate an order incorporating or resulting from such agreement, where:

1. The agreement was procured by fraud or duress, or is unconscionable;

2. If the property or financial matters are in dispute, the parties failed to provide substantial full disclosure of all relevant property and financial information; or

3. There was evident partiality or misconduct by the neutral, prejudicing the rights of any party

For purposes of this section, "misconduct" includes failure of the neutral to inform the parties in writing at the commencement of the mediation process that: (i) the neutral does not provide legal advice, (ii) any mediated agreement will affect the legal rights of the parties, (iii) each party to the mediation has the opportunity to consult with independent legal counsel at any time and is encouraged to do so, and (iv) each party to the mediation should have any draft agreement reviewed by independent counsel prior to signing the agreement or should waive his opportunity to do so.

        a. The fact that any provisions of a mediated agreement were such that they could not or would not be granted by a court of law or equity is not, in and of itself, grounds for vacating an agreement. A motion to vacate under this section shall be made within two years after the mediated agreement is entered into, except that, if predicated upon fraud, it shall be made within two years after these grounds are discovered or reasonably should have been discovered.

## Guidelines for the Training and Certification of Court-Referred Mediators

    See http://www.courts.state.va.us/courtadmin/aoc/djs/programs/drs/mediation/training/tom.pdf

## Standards of Ethics and Professional Responsibility for Certified Mediators

    See http://www.courts.state.va.us/courtadmin/aoc/djs/programs/drs/mediation/soe.pdf

# Virginia Rules of Professional Conduct

The Virginia Rules of Professional Conduct were adopted by the Supreme Court of Virginia on January 25, 1999, to become effective January 1, 2000.

## RULE 2.10. - Third Party Neutral

- A third party neutral assists parties in reaching a voluntary settlement of a dispute through a structured process known as a dispute resolution proceeding. The third party neutral does not represent any party.

- A lawyer who serves as a third party neutral:
    - shall inform the parties of the difference between the lawyer's role as third party neutral and the lawyer's role as one who represents a client;
    - shall encourage unrepresented parties to seek legal counsel before an agreement is executed; and
    - may encourage and assist the parties in reaching a resolution of their dispute; but
    - may not compel or coerce the parties to make an agreement.

- A lawyer may serve as a third party neutral only if the lawyer has not previously represented and is not currently representing one of the parties in connection with the subject matter of the dispute resolution proceeding.

- A lawyer may serve as a third party neutral in a dispute resolution proceeding involving a client whom the lawyer has represented or is representing in a matter unrelated to the mediation, provided

- there is full disclosure of the prior or present representation;

- in light of the disclosure, the third party neutral obtains the parties' informed consent; and

- the third party neutral reasonably believes that a prior or present representation will not compromise or adversely affect the ability to act as a third party neutral; and

- there is no unauthorized disclosure of information in violation of Rule 1.6.

- A lawyer who serves or has served as a third party neutral may not serve as a lawyer on behalf of any party to the dispute, nor represent one such party against the other in any legal proceeding related to the subject of the dispute resolution proceeding.

- A lawyer shall withdraw as third party neutral if any of the requirements stated in this Rule is no longer satisfied or if any of the parties in the dispute resolution proceeding so requests. If the parties are participating pursuant to a court referral, the third party neutral shall report the withdrawal to the authority issuing the referral.

- A lawyer who serves as a third party neutral shall not charge a fee contingent on the outcome of the resolution proceeding.

- This Rule does not apply to intermediation, which is covered by Rule 2.2.

## Comment

This Rule sets forth conflicts of interest and other ethical guidelines for a lawyer who serves as a third party neutral. Dispute resolution proceedings that are conducted by a third party

neutral include mediation, conciliation, early neutral evaluation, non-binding arbitration and non-judicial settlement conferences.

A lawyer who serves as a third party neutral under this Rule or as a mediator under Rule 2.11 is engaged in the provision of a law-related service that may involve the application of a lawyer's particular legal expertise and skills. The standards set forth in this Rule, however, do not amount to a determination that a lawyer who serves as a third party neutral pursuant to this Rule or as a mediator pursuant to Rule 2.11 is engaged in the practice of law. The determination of whether a particular activity constitutes the practice of law is beyond the scope and purpose of these Rules.

A lawyer serving as third party neutral shall not offer any of the parties legal advice, which is a function of the lawyer who is representing a client (See Preamble: A Lawyer's Responsibilities). A third party neutral may, however, offer neutral evaluations, if requested by the parties. Special provisions under which a lawyer-mediator can offer certain neutral evaluations are contained in Rule 2.11.

Confidentiality of information revealed in the dispute resolution process is governed by Code of Virginia Sections 8.01-576.9 and 8.01-576.10.

A third party neutral as defined in these Rules does not include a lawyer providing binding arbitration services (See Code of Virginia Section 8.01-577 et. seq.).

Committee Commentary

The Committee adopted this Rule, not part of the ABA Model Rules, to provide guidelines for lawyers who serve as neutrals and who do not represent a party to a dispute or transaction.

## RULE 2.11. - Mediator

- A lawyer-mediator is a third party neutral (See Rule 2.10) who facilitates communication between the parties and, without deciding the issues or imposing a solution on the parties, enables them to understand and resolve their dispute.

- Prior to agreeing to mediate and throughout the mediation process a lawyer-mediator should reasonably determine that:

  - mediation is an appropriate process for the parties;

- each party is able to participate effectively within the context of the mediation process; and

- each party is willing to enter and participate in the process in good faith.

- A lawyer-mediator may offer legal information if all parties are present or separately to the parties if they consent. The lawyer-mediator shall inform unrepresented parties or those parties who are not accompanied by legal counsel about the importance of reviewing the lawyer- mediator's legal information with legal counsel.

- A lawyer-mediator may offer evaluation of, for example, strengths and weaknesses of positions, assess the value and cost of alternatives to settlement or assess the barriers to settlement (collectively referred to as evaluation) only if such evaluation is incidental to the facilitative role and does not interfere with the lawyer http://www.patientsafetyinstitute.ca/en/Topic/Pages/Surgical-Care-Safety.aspx?k=Surgical%20Care%20Safety-mediator's impartiality or the self-determination of the parties.

- Prior to the mediation session a lawyer-mediator shall:

  a. Consult with prospective parties about

    - the nature of the mediation process;

    - the limitations on the use of evaluation, as set forth in subparagraph (d) above;

    - the lawyer-mediator's approach, style and subject matter expertise; and

    - the parties' expectations regarding the mediation process; and

- enter into agreement to mediate which references the choice and expectations of the parties, including whether the parties have chosen, permit or expect the use of neutral evaluation or evaluative techniques during the course of the mediation.

A lawyer-mediator shall conduct the mediation in a manner that is consistent with the parties' choice and expectations.

## Comment

- Offering assessments, evaluations, and advice are traditional lawyering functions for the lawyer who represents a client. A lawyer-mediator, who does not represent any of the parties to the mediation, should not assume that these functions are appropriate. Although these functions are not specifically prohibited in the statutory definition of mediation which is set forth as subparagraph (a) of this Rule, an evaluative approach which interferes with the parties' self-determination and the mediator's impartiality would be inconsistent with this definition of mediation.

- Defining mediation to exclude an evaluative approach is difficult not only because practice varies widely but because no consensus exists as to what constitutes an evaluation. Also, the effects of an evaluation on the mediation process depend upon the attitude and style of the mediator and the context in which it is offered. Thus, a question by a lawyer-mediator to a party that might be considered by some as "reality testing" and facilitative, might be viewed by others as evaluation. On the other hand, an evaluation by a facilitative mediator could help free the parties from the narrowing effects of the law and help empower them to resolve their dispute.

### Informed Consent to Mediator's Approach

- The Rule focuses on the informed consent of the prospective mediation clients to the particular approach, style and subject matter expertise of the lawyer-mediation. This begins with consultation about the nature of the mediation process, the limitations on evaluation, the lawyer-mediator's approach, style and subject matter expertise and the parties' expectations regarding the mediation process. If the parties request an evaluative approach, the lawyer-mediator shall explain the risk that evaluation might interfere with mediator impartiality and party self-determination. Following this consultation the lawyer-mediator and the parties shall sign a written agreement to mediate which reflects the choice and expectation of the parties. The lawyer-mediator shall then conduct the mediation in a manner that is consistent with the parties' choice and expectations. This is similar to the lawyer-client consultation about the means to be used in pursuing a client's objectives in Rule 1.2.

### Continuing Responsibility to Examine Potential Impact of Evaluation

- If the parties choose a lawyer-mediator who is willing and able to offer evaluation during the mediation process and has met the requirements of subparagraph (e), a lawyer-mediator has a continuing responsibility under subparagraphs (b) and (d) to assess the situation and consult with the parties before offering or responding to a request for an evaluation. Consideration shall be given again to whether mediator impartiality and party self-determination are at risk. Consideration should also be given as to whether an evaluation could detract from the willingness of the parties to work at understanding their own and each other's situation and at considering a broader range of interests, issues and options. Also, with an evaluation the parties may miss out on opportunities to maintain or improve relationships or to create a higher quality and more satisfying result.

- On the other hand, the parties may expect the lawyer-mediator to offer an evaluation in helping the parties reach agreement, especially when the most important issues are the strengths or weaknesses of legal positions, or the significance of commercial or financial risks. This is particularly useful after parties have worked at possible solutions and have built up confidence in the mediator's impartiality or where widely divergent party evaluations are major barriers to settlement.

- The presence of attorneys for the parties offers additional protection in minimizing the risk of a poor quality evaluation and of too strong an influence on the parties' self-determination. An evaluation, coupled with a reminder to the parties that the evaluation is but one of the factors to be considered as they deliberate on the outcome, may in certain cases be the most appropriate way to assure that the parties are making fully informed decisions.

## Legal Advice, Legal Information and Neutral Evaluation

- A lawyer-mediator shall not offer any of the parties legal advice which is a function of the lawyer who is representing a client. However, a lawyer-mediator may offer legal information under the conditions outlined in subsection (c). Offering legal information is an educational function which aids the parties in making informed decisions. Neutral evaluations in the mediation process consist of, for example, opining as to the strengths and weaknesses of positions, assessing the value and costs of alternatives to settlement or assessing the barriers to settlement.

- The lawyer-mediator shall not, however, make decisions for any party to the mediation process nor shall the lawyer-mediator use a neutral evaluation to coerce or influence the parties to settle their dispute or to accept a particular solution to their dispute. Subparagraphs (d), (e), and (f) restrict the use of evaluative techniques by the lawyer-mediator to situations where the parties have given their informed consent to the use of such techniques and where a neutral evaluation will assist, rather than interfere with the ability of the parties to reach a mutually agreeable solution to their dispute.

## Mediation and Intermediation

- While a lawyer is cautioned in the Comment to Rule 2.2 not to act as intermediary between clients where contentious litigation or negotiation is expected, this should not deter a lawyer-mediator from accepting clients for mediation. Unlike intermediation, where the lawyer represents all parties, a lawyer-mediator represents none of the parties and should be trained to deal with strong emotions. In fact mediation can be especially useful in a case where communication and relational breakdown have made negotiation or litigation of legal issues more difficult.

## Confidentiality and Professional Responsibility Standards

- Confidentiality of information revealed in the mediation process is governed by Code of Virginia Sections 8.01-576.09 and 8.01-576.10 and section 8.01-581.22.

## Committee Commentary

- The committee adopted this Rule, not part of the ABA Model Rules, to give further guidance to lawyers who serve as mediators. Although Legal Ethics Opinions (such as LEO 590 (May 17, 1985)

- have approved of lawyers serving as mediators, different approaches to and styles of mediation ranging from pure facilitation to evaluation of positions are being offered. This Rule requires lawyer-mediators to consult with prospective parties about the lawyer-mediators' approach and style and to honor the parties' choice and expectations.

# Legal Ethics Opinion No. 1368

Mediation-Arbitration: Attorneys Forming Lay Corporation to Provide Mediation/Arbitration Services to Corporation's Customers

You have indicated that Attorneys A and B are the sole shareholders of Virginia Corporation X which was formed for the purpose of providing mediation and arbitration services, in all fields except domestic relations, to the general public. Mediation and arbitration services will be provided by A and B, as well as by other attorneys, on an independent contractual basis with Corporation X. Each mediator or arbitrator will disclose to the parties at the outset that although he/she is a licensed attorney, he/she will not be serving as an attorney and will not provide legal advice at any time to any person during or in connection with the mediation or arbitration process.

Further, you advise that Corporation X will charge an administrative fee, to be totally retained by the Corporation, and an hourly fee for the services of the mediator or arbitrator, a portion of which will be paid to the mediator or arbitrator and the remainder of which will be retained by the Corporation. With specific regard to mediation, you indicate that the lawyer/mediators would agree in advance that they (1) will clearly inform the parties of the lawyer's role and will obtain the parties' consent to this arrangement; (2) will draft settlement agreements but only after advising and encouraging the parties to seek independent legal advice before executing it; (3) will not act on behalf of any party in court nor representing one party against the other in any related legal proceeding; and (4) will withdraw as mediator if any party so requests or if any of the conditions (1) through (3) above are no longer satisfied, following which withdrawal the lawyer/mediator will not continue to act on behalf of any of the parties in the matter that was the subject of the mediation. Finally, you indicate that potential arbitrators and mediators who have prior relationships with parties will not be appointed to serve in a dispute involving such parties.

You have inquired if the scenario you present violates any disciplinary rules. In addition, you have asked the committee to consider specifically the propriety of (1) Attorneys A and B, who will serve as mediators or arbitrators, soliciting business for Corporation X from other attorneys, insurance carriers and the general public; and (2) attorneys entering into contractual arrangements with Corporation X in which the hourly fee charges for the mediator's or arbitrator's services is split between the corporation and the mediator.

Based on the descriptions you have provided as to the activities involved in the proposed mediation/arbitration endeavor, and upon Virginia Code § 8.01-581.21 which defined a mediator as "an impartial third party" without regard to that individual's status as an attorney, the committee is of the view that such activities do not constitute the per se practice of law. Therefore, the committee opines that the Code of Professional Responsibility has only limited application to the circumstances you describe. Although the facts, as you have presented them, indicate that the attorney/mediators will not be serving as attorneys and will not be providing legal advice to the parties, the committee is of the view that the activities involved in mediation and the subject matter to which the mediation is addressed closely resemble the practice of law. The committee believes that providing legal information, albeit not legal advice, and assisting individuals to reach agreement on such issues as division of property, contractual obligations, liability and damages, by definition, entails the application of legal knowledge and training to the facts of the situation, See

LEO #511, 513, 516, 519. Therefore, under the rationale of LEO #1325 and ABA Opinion 336, the committee believes that such activities subject the attorney/mediator to the provisions of the Code of Professional Responsibility while carrying out the tasks involved in mediation.

The committee has consistently recognized the permissibility of lawyers engaged simultaneously in the practice of law and related entrepreneurial endeavors. Thus, the committee is of the opinion that the solicitation of business for Corporation X, as you describe, would not be improper. The committee cautions, however, that the attorneys' ownership interest in the mediation/arbitration enterprise, Corporation X, may constitute the type of financial, business, property or personnel interest envisioned by DR 5-101(A). Thus, before referring a client to Corporation X, or before accepting representation of a client who was theretofore served by Corporation X, albeit by another mediator or arbitrator, Attorneys A and B must obtain the consent of the client after full and adequate disclosure of the attorney's personal interest. See LEOs #1345, 1254, 1198, 1131, 939, 512, 187. In addition, Ethical Consideration 5-20 provides specific direction regarding the provision of mediation services by attorneys and their subsequent professional relationships with the parties involved. See LEOs #849, 590, 544, 519, 516, 513, 511.

With regard to your question (2), related to the splitting of fees between the mediator and Corporation X, the committee is of the opinion that, since the business of Corporation X does not constitute the practice of law, the prohibitions of the Code of Professional Responsibility against sharing fees with non-lawyers are inapplicable in the usual course of the business of Corporation X. To the extent that the mediator is engaged by the parties as a scrivener of the agreement reached during the mediation process, such tasks do not constitute the practice of law and, therefore, fees paid for that service are not deemed to be legal fees. Should, however, the mediator/lawyer provide any services beyond those of a scrivener, the mediator/lawyer must meet the requirements of DR 3-102, which prohibit the sharing of legal fees with a nonlawyer, and DR 5-107, relative to settling similar claims of clients. See Kansas Opinion 84-8 (10/4/84), ABA/BNA Law. Man. on Prof. Conduct 801:3818; Association of the Bar of the City of New York Opinion 1987-1(2/23/87),

ABA/BNA Law. Man. on Prof. Conduct 901:6404; Tennessee Ethics Opinion 83-F-39 (1/25/83), ABA/BNA Law. Man. on Prof. Conduct 801:8107.

Finally, the committee cautions that, as in any other activities engaged in by members of the Bar, any criminal or deliberately wrongful act, or any conduct involving dishonesty, fraud, deceit, or misrepresentation which reflects adversely on a lawyer's fitness to practice law would be improper and violative of DR 1-102(A)(3 and 4) and would subject the attorney to disciplinary action. See ABA Formal Opinion 336; LEO #1325 at 3.

Committee Opinion December 12, 1990

# Legal Ethics Opinion No. 107

### Foreign Attorneys-Scope of Permissible Practice

It is not the unauthorized practice of law for a non-Virginia licensed attorney to do "client intakes" - providing that this involves nothing more than the gathering of factual data. [UPR Definition (A)]

It is the unauthorized practice of law for a non-Virginia licensed attorney to render legal advice in Virginia - either on Virginia law or the law of his home jurisdiction. However, it is permissible for this

non-Virginia attorney to advice a Virginia attorney who may then render advice to a client if he deems this advice acceptable. [UPR definition (A)(1), (B)]

A non-Virginia licensed attorney may render advice and execute cases in Virginia involving federal law.[UPL Op.No.55,;UPR 9-102(A)(2)]

An attorney licensed in a foreign country should be referred to and identified as a lawyer licensed to practice in that foreign country only.{DR 3-104(E); UPR Definition B]

Committee Opinion August 14, 1987

## Issues for Future Study

During the course of development of these Guidelines, a number of issues were raised that are beyond the scope of this project and are referred for future study by the appropriate entities.

1. Licensure or certification for all mediators

2. Supreme Court Rule revisions

3. Review of the mediation and dispute resolution proceedings statutes including the statutory immunity provision

4. Professional liability insurance for mediators

# Appendix F: Certification Forms

## F1. Mediator Certification Form

### OFFICE OF THE EXECUTIVE SECRETARY

### INSTRUCTIONS FOR COMPLETION OF FORM ADR-1000A

### APPLICATION FOR MEDIATOR CERTIFICATION

General Note: Please check the application to ensure all necessary areas are completed. Many applications are put on hold because forms are missing signatures or some other bit of information is missing.

### Section I. General Information

1.    Fill in your name, your business name (if different), and your address. You are free to use either business or home address here, as long as it is the address to which you want mail sent.

2.    Please complete the last four digits of your Social Security number, telephone and fax numbers, e-mail address and website.

3.    Fill in the colleges and/or graduate schools you have attended and note any degrees you have received.

4.    Check "Yes" or "No" to verify whether you are already currently certified as a mediator at a different level from the one for which you are applying at this time. If you answered, "Yes," you may disregard answering question #5 even if you do not have a bachelor's degree.

5.    If you have not received a bachelor's degree, complete this section by attaching a letter relating relevant experiences. The letter must be accompanied by a resume and two letters of recommendation that address your oral and written communication skills. Additional information may be requested. Owning or operating a business, work as a paralegal, or time spent as a volunteer at a community dispute resolution center might provide the experience needed, depending on other circumstances. Applicants must demonstrate an ability to read, write, communicate, and analyze information.

6.    Fill in the memberships you hold in professional organizations relevant to this application, i.e.: Association for Conflict Resolution; Virginia Mediation Network; American Bar Association; National Association of Social Workers; and others.

7.    Note whether you are applying for certification to do General District Court (GDC), Juvenile and Domestic Relations District Court (JDRC), Circuit Court-Civil (CCC), or Circuit Court-Family (CCF) mediation. You may apply for more than one certification at the same time, if you desire to do so.

## Section II. Certified Training

1. If you are seeking General District Court certification, fill in the information requested regarding basic mediation training. Use of Form ADR-1006 (Trainee Evaluation Form) is required.

2. If you are seeking Juvenile and Domestic Relations District Court certification, fill in the information requested regarding both basic and family mediation training. Use of Form ADR-1006 (Trainee Evaluation Form) is required.

3. If you are seeking Circuit Court-Civil certification, please fill in the information regarding the advanced mediation training received. Use of Form ADR-1006 (Trainee Evaluation Form) is required. Please note that certification in Circuit Court-Civil requires 20 hours of basic mediation training and 20 hours of advanced mediation training.

4. If you are seeking Circuit Court-Family certification, please fill in the information regarding the advanced family mediation training received. Use of Form ADR-1006 (Trainee Evaluation Form) is required. Please note that certification in Circuit Court-Family requires 20 hours of basic mediation training, 20 hours of family mediation training, and 12 hours of advanced family mediation training.

## Section III. Training in Domestic Abuse

1. If you are seeking Juvenile and Domestic Relations District Court certification or Circuit Court-Family certification, fill in the information regarding your training or experience in screening for and dealing with domestic abuse in the mediation context. A minimum of eight hours of formal training is required. Use of Form ADR-1006 (Trainee Evaluation Form) is required.

## Section IV. Training in Virginia's Judicial System

1. All certification types require four hours of training in Virginia's Judicial System. Fill in the information regarding your training or experience in Virginia's judicial system. Use of Form ADR-1006 (Trainee Evaluation Form) is required.

## Section V. Observations and Co-Mediations

(Please note that a "qualified mentor" is one who has been granted Mentor Status by the Office of the Executive Secretary. A mediator without such status may not serve as a mentor.)

1. Fill in the information requested either in 1.a. or 1.b.regarding observations of mediations. Use of Form ADR-1007 (Verification of Observation Form) is required for observations and use of Form ADR-1006 (Trainee Evaluation

Form) is required if an observation course is used to meet this requirement. See Section C.3. of the Guidelines for the Training and Certification of Court-Referred Mediators (effective 7/1/2011) for type and number of observations required.

2. Complete the information requested regarding co-mediations completed. Please reference Section C.3. of the Guidelines for the Training and Certification of Court-Referred Mediators (effective 7/1/2011) for type and number of co-mediations required. Use of Form ADR-1001 (Mentee Evaluation Form) completed by a qualified mentor is required for each co-mediation. A Form ADR-1008 (Mentee Portfolio Form) completed by each of your mentors and by you as mentee must be submitted with your application. Please ensure all forms are complete, including Section IV of the Mentee Evaluation Form, Mentee Feedback.

3. & 4. Attach requested documentation (a Memorandum of Agreement/Understanding written by you as the primary scrivener, for each type of certification sought, and a Child Support Worksheet completed by you, by hand, using a calculator and statute) from your co-mediations.

**Section VI. Reciprocity**

(NOTE: This section need only be completed if you are currently practicing mediation in another state. Please see the Guidelines for the Training and Certification of Court-Referred Mediators, Section C.4. for more information on Reciprocity.)

1. Fill in the mediation training you have received and attach required documentation.

2. Document completion of training in Virginia's judicial system and attach ADR-1006 (Trainee Evaluation Form).

3. Document completion of training in Virginia's Standards of Ethics and attach

ADR-1006 (Trainee Evaluation Form).

4. If seeking JDR or Circuit Court Family, document required training in domestic abuse. You must also document training in family law, specifically addressing Virginia child and spousal support. Attach ADR-1006 (Trainee Evaluation Form).

5. Document the mediations you have conducted with suggested attachments.

6. List two personal references, including name, address and telephone number.

### Section VII. Background

1. Fill in the information requested about convictions for violations of the law.

See <u>Guidelines</u>, Section E.1. and E.2.

2. Answer question and, if the answer is yes, provide a description.

3. If the answer to number 1 or number 2 above is yes, please describe any impact this event could have on your ability to provide mediation services.

### Section VIII. Evaluation and Certification

Part of the work of mediation in the Commonwealth of Virginia will include provision of orientation sessions at no cost to the parties to educate and inform them about the availability of dispute resolution services and the propriety of using mediation in a particular case. Your signature on this page indicates your agreement to provide these orientation sessions at no cost to the parties when you accept a referral in those jurisdictions that do not offer these sessions to the parties through the court system itself. Your application will not be processed without this agreement.

Your signature on this page also certifies that the information in the application is correct and indicates your understanding that all information contained in the application is subject to verification.

### Section IX. Statement of Adherence to Ethical Standards

Read the Standards of Ethics and Professional Responsibility for Certified Mediators. Sign and date the statement indicating that you agree to abide by these standards. The application will not be processed without your signature in this Section.

***A check payable to the Treasurer of Virginia in the amount of $25.00 must accompany Form ADR-1000A in order for it to be processed. Do not send cash.***

Please forward Form ADR-1000A, its attachments, and your application fee to the address located on the bottom of application page 6. For questions or comments, you may call (804) 786-6455.

(Commonwealth of Virginia, 2011a)

# OFFICE OF THE EXECUTIVE SECRETARY
## OF THE Supreme Court of Virginia

## APPLICATION FOR MEDIATOR CERTIFICATION

*Please use black ink so this document will be legible when scanned.*

*This application will be considered pursuant to certification criteria established by the Judicial Council of Virginia and without regard to race, color, political affiliation, national origin, disability, sex or age.*

*SECTION I*      *GENERAL INFORMATION*      *Please type or print.*

1. Name:

   _____
   Last               First               Middle

   Business Name (if different from above):
   _____

   Primary Address:
   _____
   Street and/or Post Office Box

   _____
   City           State           Zip Code          County

2. Last 4 Digits Social Security Number: _____ Office Phone: _____

   Home Phone: _____ Fax: _____

   E-mail: _____ Website: _____

3. Colleges, Universities, and Graduate Schools Attended:

| Name | City/State | Dates Attended From | To | Degree(s) Attained | Major |
|---|---|---|---|---|---|
| | | | | | |
| | | | | | |
| | | | | | |

4. Are you already currently certified as a mediator for a different category of cases?
   Yes_____ No_____
   If yes, in what category?_____
   If yes, you do not need to fill in #5 below if you have no bachelor's degree.

5. If you have not received a bachelor's degree, please attach a letter describing your relevant work and life experience and qualifications sufficient to support certification, such as specific business or military experience or experience in the field of dispute

resolution. The letter must be accompanied by a resume and two letters of recommendation that address your oral and written communication skills. Additional information may be requested. (*You should seek a waiver prior to beginning mediation training.*)

I have a bachelor's degree.    Yes _____
                                No _____
                    (Letter, resume & letters of recommendation must be attached)

6.     Please list all professional affiliations that you consider relevant to your certification.

_____
_____
_____
_____

7.     Please check the type(s) of certification for which you are applying:

_____ General District Court                  _____ Circuit Court-Civil
_____ Juvenile and Domestic Relations District Court   _____ Circuit Court-Family

SECTION II         CERTIFIED TRAINING

(If you have taken a mediation training out of state, you may request a waiver for the analogous Virginia certified training from Dispute Resolution Services. You should request a waiver prior to beginning any other training. If you have received a waiver, please attach documentation of the waiver to this application.)

1.     General District Court Mediation (Minimum 20 hours: 20-hr basic)

List the certified mediation training you have received. Form ADR-1006 (Trainee Evaluation Form) is required from the trainer.

| Course/Hours | Trainer | Location | Date |
| --- | --- | --- | --- |
| | | | |

2.     Juvenile and Domestic Relations District Court Mediation (Minimum 40 hours: 20-hr basic and 20-hr family)

List the certified mediation training you have received. Form ADR-1006 (Trainee Evaluation Form) is required from the trainer.

| Course/Hours | Trainer | Location | Date |
| --- | --- | --- | --- |
| | | | |

3.     Circuit Court-Civil Mediation Training (Minimum 40 hours: 20-hr basic and 20-hr circuit court civil)

List the certified mediation training you have received. Form ADR-1006 (Trainee Evaluation Form) is required from the trainer.

| Course/Hours | Trainer | Location | Date |
|---|---|---|---|
| | | | |
| | | | |
| | | | |

4. Circuit Court-Family Mediation Training (Minimum 52 hours: 20-hr basic, 20-hr family, and 12-hour circuit court family)

List the certified mediation training you have received. Form ADR-1006 (Trainee Evaluation Form) is required from the trainer.

| Course/Hours | Trainer | Location | Date |
|---|---|---|---|
| | | | |
| | | | |
| | | | |

SECTION III      TRAINING IN SCREENING FOR DOMESTIC ABUSE (required for Juvenile and Domestic Relations District Court and Circuit Court-Family Mediators) (Minimum 8 hours)

1. Describe the certified training you have received in screening for and dealing with domestic abuse in the mediation context. Form ADR-1006 (Trainee Evaluation Form) is required from the trainer.

| Course/Hours | Trainer | Location | Date |
|---|---|---|---|
| | | | |

SECTION IV      TRAINING IN VIRGINIA'S JUDICIAL SYSTEM

1. Describe the certified training or experience you have received in Virginia's judicial system. (Minimum 4 hours) Form ADR-1006 (Trainee Evaluation Form) is required from the trainer. If you are a member in good standing of the Virginia State Bar, please provide your bar number.

| Course/Hours | Trainer | Location | Date |
|---|---|---|---|
| | | | |

SECTION V      OBSERVATIONS AND CO-MEDIATIONS

1. a. Observations: Attach Forms ADR-1007 (Verification of Observation) from qualified Mentors attesting to your observations. Please see Section C.3. of the Guidelines for number of observations required.

| Case Type: General District, J&DR, Circuit-Civil or Circuit-Family | Date(s) of Observation | Name of Mentor |
|---|---|---|
| | | |
| | | |
| | | |

_or_

b. Certified Observation Course:  Form ADR-1006 (Trainee Evaluation Form) is required from the trainer.

| Course/Hours | Trainer | Location | Date |
|---|---|---|---|
| | | | |
| | | | |

2. Co-Mediations:  Attach Forms ADR-1001 (Mentee Evaluation Form) which must be completed by qualified Mentors and Form ADR-1008 (Mentee Portfolio Form) completed by both Mentors and Mentee.  Please see Section C.3.of the Guidelines for type and number of co-mediations required.

| Case Type:  General District, J&DR, Circuit-Civil or Circuit-Family | Dates of Co-mediations | Hours of Mediation | Name of Mentor |
|---|---|---|---|
| | | | |
| | | | |
| | | | |
| | | | |
| | | | |
| | | | |
| | | | |
| | | | |
| | | | |

3. Please enclose a written Memorandum of Agreement/Understanding written by you (for which you served as primary scrivener) for each level of certification you are seeking.

Date of Mediation: _____  Mentor: _____

Date of Mediation:_____  Mentor:_____

4. If you are seeking Juvenile and Domestic Relations District Court or Circuit Court-Family certification, please enclose a child support worksheet completed by you, by hand, using a calculator and the statute.

Date of Mediation: _____  Mentor: _____

SECTION VI       RECIPROCITY  (If you are currently practicing mediation in another state, please complete this Section.)

1.    Please provide evidence of mediation training.  Attach copies of outlines, agendas, and letters or certificates of successful completion.

| Course/Hours | Trainer | Location | Date |
|---|---|---|---|
| | | | |
| | | | |
| | | | |
| | | | |

2.    Please provide evidence of successful completion of four hours of training in Virginia's judicial system.
Form ADR-1006 (Trainee Evaluation Form) completed by the trainer is required.

| Course/Hours | Trainer | Location | Date |
|---|---|---|---|
| | | | |
| | | | |

3.    Please provide evidence of at least two hours of education on Virginia's Standards of Ethics for certified mediators.  Form ADR-1006 (Trainee Evaluation Form) completed by the trainer is required.

| Course/Hours | Trainer | Location | Date |
|---|---|---|---|
| | | | |
| | | | |

4.    If you are seeking Juvenile and Domestic Relations District Court or Circuit Court-Family certification, please provide evidence of eight hours of training in screening for and dealing with domestic abuse in the mediation context and also evidence of training in family law, specifically addressing Virginia child and spousal support.  Forms ADR-1006 (Trainee Evaluation Form) completed by the trainer are required.

| Course/Hours | Trainer | Location | Date |
|---|---|---|---|
| | | | |
| | | | |

5.    Please provide evidence of number of mediation cases/hours and case types.  You may submit letters from clients, court personnel or mediation programs.

6.    Please list two references (name, address, and telephone number):

SECTION VII        BACKGROUND

1.     Have you ever been convicted of, or plead guilty or nolo contendere to violations of the law, including traffic violations resulting in suspension or revocation of a driver's license and DUI offenses?   Yes \_\_\_\_\_   No \_\_\_\_\_   If Yes, list (please include the specific code section(s) violated).  Please see Section E.1. and E.2. of the Guidelines.

2.     Have you ever 1) had a disciplinary action related to a profession, including mediation (for example, a professional license suspended or revoked); 2) had any professional privileges curtailed; and/or 3) relinquished a professional privilege or license while under investigation? Yes \_\_\_\_\_   No \_\_\_\_\_
If Yes, describe on the lines provided below.

_____

_____

3.     If you answered "Yes" to question #1 or #2 above, please describe the impact, if any, this could have on your ability to provide mediation services.

_____

_____

SECTION VIII       EVALUATION AND CERTIFICATION

I understand that, in court-referred cases, if there is no orientation session provided for the parties by the court, **I will provide an initial orientation session for the parties, and their lawyers if they choose to attend, at no cost to the parties.**

I also understand that I am obligated as a condition of my certification to ensure that Forms ADR-1002 (Evaluation of Mediation Session(s) and Mediator(s)) are provided to all parties referred from the courts.

I also hereby certify that the information provided in this application is true to the best of

my knowledge and accurately reflects my qualifications to provide mediation services in

cases referred through the court system of the Commonwealth of Virginia. I understand

that all information herein is subject to verification.

_____      _____

     Signature of Applicant                          Date

SECTION IX          STATEMENT OF ADHERENCE TO ETHICAL STANDARDS

I hereby certify that I have read the <u>Standards of Ethics and Professional Responsibility for Certified Mediators</u> adopted by the Judicial Council of Virginia effective July 1, 2011 and do swear or affirm that I will abide by those standards.

_____       _____
         Signature of Applicant                                     Date

---

A $25.00 check or money order must accompany this application. Please make the check payable to the **Treasurer of Virginia**. Do not send cash.

---

Please forward this application and your check to:

Dispute Resolution Services
Office of the Executive Secretary
Supreme Court of Virginia

100 N. Ninth Street, Third Floor
Richmond, VA 23219

**If you have any questions or comments, please contact
Dispute Resolution Services, 804-786-6455.**

# F2. Observation Form

OFFICE OF THE EXECUTIVE SECRETARY

SUPREME COURT OF VIRGINIA

INSTRUCTIONS FOR COMPLETING THE

*VERIFICATION OF OBSERVATION* FORM (ADR-1007)

## I. INSTRUCTIONS FOR MENTEES

**Save and submit** all *Verification of Observation* forms (regardless of the nature of the feedback) with the application for certification. An observation form must be completed for each observation that will be counted for certification purposes.

## II. INSTRUCTIONS FOR MENTORS

**Complete** Sections I and II of the Verification of Observation form. Describe how the mentee participated in the de-briefing at the conclusion of the mediation. Provide additional comments as necessary.

(Commonwealth of Virginia, 2011a)

**OFFICE OF THE EXECUTIVE SECRETARY**
**SUPREME COURT OF VIRGINIA**

---

## VERIFICATION OF OBSERVATION FORM

---

*Please use black ink so this document will be legible when scanned.*
**(To be completed by Mentor and returned to Mentee within ten days following case completion.)**

Please type or print.

**SECTION I.    BACKGROUND INFORMATION**

1.   Name of Mentee:

_____

2.   Name of Mentor:

_____

   (Are you currently certified as a Mentor for this court level? ____ Yes ____ No)

3.   Certification Number:

**SECTION II.    OBSERVATION INFORMATION**

1.   Date(s) of Observation:

_____

2.   Nature of Case:   _____ GDC   _____ J&DR   _____ CCC   _____ CCF

3.   Length of Mediation:

_____

4.   Describe the Mentee's participation in the de-briefing session.

_____
_____
_____
_____

**OFFICE OF THE EXECUTIVE SECRETARY**
**SUPREME COURT OF VIRGINIA**

## VERIFICATION OF OBSERVATION FORM

*Please use black ink so this document will be legible when scanned.*
**(To be completed by Mentor and returned to Mentee within ten days following
case completion.)**

Please type or print.

**SECTION I.    BACKGROUND INFORMATION**

1.  Name of Mentee:

    _____

2.  Name of Mentor:

    _____

    (Are you currently certified as a Mentor for this court level? ____ Yes ____ No)

3.  Certification Number:

**SECTION II.    OBSERVATION INFORMATION**

1.  Date(s) of Observation:

    _____

2.  Nature of Case:  _____ GDC  _____ J&DR  _____ CCC  _____ CCF

3.  Length of Mediation:

    _____

4.  Describe the Mentee's participation in the de-briefing session.

    _____
    _____
    _____
    _____

5. Additional comments:

_____
_____
_____
_____
_____

_____     _____
Signature of Mentor Mediator                    Date

**FORM ADR-1007 (1/09)**
(Commonwealth of Virginia, 2011a)

248

# F3. Mentee Portfolio Form

OFFICE OF THE EXECUTIVE SECRETARY

**SUPREME COURT OF VIRGINIA**

(Commonwealth of Virginia, 2011a)

## INSTRUCTIONS FOR COMPLETING

## THE *MENTEE PORTFOLIO* FORM (ADR-1008)

### INSTRUCTIONS FOR MENTEES

1) **Complete** "Section I: Skill Development Goals" of the *Mentee Portfolio* with the assistance and input of the Mentor.

### INSTRUCTIONS FOR MENTORS

1) **Indicate** the number for the current co-mediation at the top of the document.

2) **Review** earlier *Mentee Portfolio* form(s) prior to beginning the pre-mediation discussion at the second and all subsequent co-mediations.

3) **Discuss** with the mentee his or her progress towards the skill development or goals previously identified and the nature of the current mediation case.

4) **Identify** goals for the mentee's skill development during the current mediation case.

5) **Observe** the mentee during the mediation session, noting specifically the areas previously identified.

6) **Complete** the *Mentee Portfolio* form, noting both the mentee's self-identified goals and the Mentor's identified goals (if different). Include any recommendations for additional training (courses, readings, co-mediations, or other developmental activities).

7) **Sign and date** the *Mentee Portfolio* form and give to the mentee before concluding the de-briefing.

8) If the case has multiple sessions, the *Mentee Portfolio* should be completed at the end of each session and reviewed prior to the beginning of the next session. The comments at the end of each session of a multi-session mediation should be initialed and dated by the Mentor. A single *Mentee Portfolio* form can be used for a multi-session mediation. (Commonwealth of Virginia, 2011a)

## MENTEE PORTFOLIO FORM

*Please use black ink so this document will be legible when scanned.*
(To be completed by Mentor and mentee at the end of each co-mediation session.)

Co-Mediation Case # (Circle)   1   2   3   4   5   6   7   8

Case Type: ____GDC   ____JDR   ____CCC   ____CCF

Mentee Mediator: _____

Mentor Mediator: _____   Certification Number: _____

        (Are you currently certified as a Mentor for this court level? ____Yes   ____No)

Date(s) of Mediation: _____

**Section I: Skill Development Goals**
Complete prior to mediation.

   I.  MENTOR & MENTEE:  (Review previous co-mediation case portfolio pages.)  The mentee and Mentor identified the following goals for the mentee's skill development during the case.

_____
_____
_____
_____
_____
_____
_____
_____
_____
_____
_____
_____
_____
_____
_____
_____

**Section II: Skill Development Progress**
Complete after the co-mediation session.

   II.  MENTOR:  Describe the mentee's progress toward the skill development goals identified in Section I.

_____
_____
_____

_____
_____
_____
_____
_____
_____
_____
_____
_____
_____
_____
_____
_____

**Section III: Skill Development Priorities**
Complete after the co-mediation session or at the conclusion of the case.

III. MENTOR: Based on your post-mediation discussions with the mentee and your observations during the case, identify the skill development priorities you recommend for the mentee in subsequent mediations. Include any recommendations you may have for additional training, reading, or other developmental activity.

_____
_____
_____
_____
_____
_____
_____
_____
_____
_____
_____
_____
_____
_____
_____
_____

Signature of Mentor _____     Date_____

Signature of Mentee _____     Date_____

(Commonwealth of Virginia, 2011a)

252

# F4. Mentee Evaluation Form

**OFFICE OF THE EXECUTIVE SECRETARY**

**SUPREME COURT OF VIRGINIA**

**INSTRUCTIONS FOR COMPLETING**

**THE *MENTEE EVALUATION* FORM (ADR-1001)**

## I. INSTRUCTIONS FOR MENTEES

1) **Save and submit** all evaluations (regardless of the nature of the feedback) with the application for certification. An evaluation form must be completed for each co-mediation that will be counted for certification purposes. An evaluation form is not necessary, however, if the case will not count for certification purposes.

2) **Complete** "Section IV: Mentee Feedback" of the *Mentee Evaluation* form upon receipt from the Mentor. The mentee should reflect on the case and the mentoring experience: Was the pre- and post- mediation de-briefing helpful? Does your self-evaluation differ from the Mentor's assessment of your mediation skills?

3) The mentee can choose to share "Section IV: Mentee Feedback" with the Mentor but is not obligated to do so.

4) An evaluation form should not be completed if the case is not a complete case. A complete case consists of one or more mediation sessions that included enough stages of the mediation process to allow the mentee to demonstrate competence in mediation skills.

## INSTRUCTIONS FOR MENTORS

1. **Complete** the Mentee Evaluation form and return it to the mentee **within ten days** from the date of the last co-mediation session for the case.

1. **Describe** the case in Section I of the Mentee Evaluation form, noting both the nature of the case and the major issues involved (e.g., multi-party, presence of counsel, custody/visitation/support, truancy, General/JDR/Circuit: Civil or Family). Additional information should be included if the case was complex or difficult.

1. **Rate** the mentee's skills in Section II of the Mentee Evaluation form using the rating scale. A rating of "1 - Unacceptable" or "2 - Needs Improvement" requires further explanation in Section III of the form.

1. **Provide** an overall assessment of the mentee's performance in Section III of the Mentee Evaluation form. The Mentor should consider the mentee's acquisition of basic mediation skills to date: Does the mentee understand the mediation process? Does the mentee need additional co-mediations or training? Is the mentee prepared to mediate independently?

1. **Suggest** verbally (during the post-mediation de-briefing) and in writing (on the form) that the mentee take additional co-mediations or training, if necessary, to improve mediator skill level.

1. **Provide** additional feedback upon request of the Dispute Resolution Services' office.

(Commonwealth of Virginia, 2011a)

# Appendix G: Agreement to Mediate

## G1. Agreement to Mediate

AGREEMENT TO MEDIATE

We the undersigned parties agree to voluntarily enter the mediation process and understand and consent to the following:

1. **Definition of Mediation:** Mediation is a process in which a mediator facilitates communication between the parties and, without deciding the issues or imposing a solution on the parties, enables them to understand and to reach a mutually agreeable resolution to their dispute.

1. **Role of the Mediator:** The mediator acts as a facilitator, not an advocate, judge, jury, counselor, or therapist. The mediator assists the parties in identifying issues, reducing obstacles to communication, maximizing the exploration of alternatives, and helping parties reach voluntary agreements.

1. **Mediator's Style/Approach:** (for example) The mediator uses a facilitative approach. A facilitative mediator guides the parties' conversation and discussion of issues that are important to them, without providing an opinion or judgement regarding the merit of the claims or the likely judicial outcome. The mediator can assist the parties in assessing the strengths and weaknesses of their case. The mediator will not tell the parties what to do or suggest a particular outcome.

1. **The Mediation Process:** The process will include at a minimum, an opportunity for all parties to be heard, the identification of issues to be resolved, the generation of alternatives for resolution, and if the parties so desire, the development of a Memorandum of Understanding or Agreement.

1. **Other procedures to be used during the mediation include:** (for example) caucus; the ability of any party or the mediator to terminate the mediation.

1. **Confidentiality:** All memoranda, work products and other materials contained in the case files of a mediator or mediation program are confidential. Any communication made in or in connection with the mediation, which relates to the controversy being mediated, including screening, intake, and scheduling a mediation, whether made to the mediator, mediation program staff, to a party, or to any other person, is confidential. However, a written mediated agreement signed by the parties shall not be confidential, unless the parties otherwise agree in writing.

Confidential materials and communications are not subject to disclosure in discovery or in any judicial or administrative proceeding except:

i. where all parties to the mediation agree, in writing, to waive the confidentiality,

ii. in a subsequent action between the mediator or mediation program and a party to the mediation for damages arising out of the mediation,

iii. statements, memoranda, materials and other tangible evidence, otherwise subject to discovery, which were not prepared specifically for use in and actually used in the mediation,

iv. where a threat to inflict bodily injury is made,

v. where communications are intentionally used to plan, attempt to commit, or commit a crime or conceal an ongoing crime,

vi. where an ethics complaint is made against the mediator by a party to the mediation to the extent necessary for the complainant to prove misconduct and the mediator to defend against such complaint,

vii. where communications are sought or offered to prove or disprove a claim or complaint of misconduct or malpractice filed against a party's legal representative based on conduct occurring during a mediation,

viii. where communications are sought or offered to prove or disprove any of the grounds listed in § 8.01-581.26 in a proceeding to vacate a mediated agreement, or

ix. as provided by law or rule.

1. **Mandatory Reporting:** According to Virginia Code §63.2-1509, if mediators have reason to suspect that a child is abused or neglected, they must report the suspected abuse immediately. Therefore, the information about the abuse is not confidential.

1. **Complaints Against Mediators:** If someone who is not a party to the mediation files an ethics complaint against the mediator, confidentiality will be waived to the extent necessary for the complainant to prove misconduct and the mediator to defend against the complaint.

1. **Full Disclosure of Assets:** In domestic relations cases involving divorce, property, support or the welfare of a child, each party agrees to provide substantial full disclosure of all relevant property and financial information.

1. **Legal Counsel / Effect of Agreement:** The mediator(s) does not provide legal advice. Parties are encouraged to seek the advice of independent counsel at any time. Any mediated agreement may affect the legal rights of the parties. Each party to the mediation should have any draft agreement reviewed by independent counsel prior to signing the agreement.

1. **Fees:** (if applicable) The fee arrangement is as follows:

| | |
|---|---|
| _____ | _____ |
| Plaintiff/Petitioner | Date |
| _____ | _____ |
| Plaintiff/Petitioner Attorney | Date |
| _____ | _____ |
| Respondent | Date |
| _____ | _____ |
| Respondent Attorney | Date |
| _____ | _____ |
| Mediator | Mediator |

# G2. Evaluation of Mediation Session

## Supreme Court of Virginia
### Office of the Executive Secretary

---

### Evaluation of Mediation Session(s) and Mediator(s)

This information will be used to inform the court system and the Mediator(s) about your experience with mediation. With your help, we can ensure that quality mediation services continue to be available to the citizens of the Commonwealth. This information may be shared with the Mediator(s).

**I.     Session Evaluation**

Name: _____     Date: _____

Address: _____
                                                          Street

_____
          City                            State              Zip

Phone Number:  (Day) _____  (Evening) _____

1. I am (check one):  ☐ a party to the mediation  ☐ an attorney representing a party

2. For this case, mediation was (check one):

     ☐ very appropriate          ☐ somewhat appropriate   ☐ not at all appropriate

Comments:

_____

_____

3. Total hours spent in the mediation session(s): _____  Number of Sessions: _____

4. The mediation process was:

     ☐ very helpful          ☐ somewhat helpful          ☐ not at all helpful

5. Mediation ended with an agreement on:

     ☐ all of the issues      ☐ some of the issues       ☐ none of the issues

6. Would you use mediation again?            ☐ yes       ☐ no

7. Would you recommend mediation to others?    ☐ yes       ☐ no

## II.    Mediator Evaluation

Mediator A: _____     Mediator B: _____
　　　　　　　 Print First & Last Name 　　　　　　　　　　　　　 Print First & Last Name

_____     _____
　 Mediator's Certification Number 　　　　　　　 Mediator's Certification Number

Please rate your Mediator(s) on the following.  Circle the appropriate number.

**5 = Very Good   4 = Good   3 = Adequate   2 = Unsatisfactory   1 = Poor   0 = Does not apply**

| The Mediator . . . | Mediator A | Mediator B |
|---|---|---|
| 1. explained the mediation process and procedures | 5 4 3 2 1 0 | 5 4 3 2 1 0 |
| 2. provided useful information | 5 4 3 2 1 0 | 5 4 3 2 1 0 |
| 3. was a good listener | 5 4 3 2 1 0 | 5 4 3 2 1 0 |
| 4. allowed me to talk about issues that were important to me | 5 4 3 2 1 0 | 5 4 3 2 1 0 |
| 5. was respectful | 5 4 3 2 1 0 | 5 4 3 2 1 0 |
| 6. helped clarify issues | 5 4 3 2 1 0 | 5 4 3 2 1 0 |
| 7. encouraged us to come up with our own solutions | 5 4 3 2 1 0 | 5 4 3 2 1 0 |

8. informed me that I could consult an attorney     ☐ yes     ☐ no

9. was neutral     ☐ yes     ☐ no

10. wrote our agreement clearly and accurately   ☐ yes     ☐ no   ☐ doesn't apply

11. Share any comments on the mediation process and/or the Mediator(s):

_____

_____

_____

Please return this Form to the Mediator or Program Director, or mail directly to:

Dispute Resolution Services
Office of the Executive Secretary
Supreme Court of Virginia
100 North Ninth Street
Richmond, VA  23219

| **FOR MEDIATOR USE ONLY** |
|---|
| Court: ☐ JDR  ☐ GD/SC  ☐ Circuit |
| Type of Dispute: _____ |
| Source of Referral:  Alexandria Court |

259

# Appendix H. Logs

## H1. MEDIATED CASES LOG

| LOG DATE | REFER-RAL # | REFER-RAL SOURCE | MEDI-ATION DATES | # PAR-TIES | LENGTH OF ME-DIATION TIME | CASE TYPE | MEDIATOR & CO- ME-DIATOR | OUTCOME OF MEDIA-TION | DOCUMENTA-TION LOCA-TION |
|---|---|---|---|---|---|---|---|---|---|
| Recertification Period | | Court Name, Pri-vate Name | | | | GDC, JDR, CCC, CCF, Other | | SM=Successful Mediation, PSM=Partially successful Mediation UM=Unsuccessful Media-tion, NM=Not Mediated | |
| | 1 | | | | | | | | |
| | 2 | | | | | | | | |
| | 3 | | | | | | | | |
| | 4 | | | | | | | | |
| | 5 | | | | | | | | |
| | 6 | | | | | | | | |
| | 7 | | | | | | | | |
| | 8 | | | | | | | | |
| | 9 | | | | | | | | |
| | 10 | | | | | | | | |
| | 11 | | | | | | | | |
| | 12 | | | | | | | | |
| | 13 | | | | | | | | |
| | 14 | | | | | | | | |
| | 15 | | | | | | | | |
| | 16 | | | | | | | | |
| | 17 | | | | | | | | |
| | 18 | | | | | | | | |
| | 19 | | | | | | | | |
| | 20 | | | | | | | | |

## H2. MEDIATION TRAINING LOG

| TRAINING DATE | TRAINING | TRAINER | G CME'S | F CME'S | ETHICS | DRS APPROVAL? | LOCATION OF PAPER RECORDS |
|---|---|---|---|---|---|---|---|
| MONTH/DAY/CAL-ENDAR | TITLE | NAME | # HRS | # HRS | # HRS | YES OR NO | |
| | | | | | | | |
| | | | | | | | |
| | | | | | | | |
| | | | | | | | |
| | | | | | | | |
| | | | | | | | |

# Appendix I: Complaint against Mediator Procedure

## OFFICE OF THE EXECUTIVE SECRETARY
## OF THE SUPREME COURT OF VIRGINIA

---

**PROCEDURES FOR COMPLAINTS AGAINST CERTIFIED MEDIATORS, MEDIATION TRAINERS, AND MEDIATOR MENTORS**

**Adopted by the Judicial Council of Virginia April 5, 2011**

**Effective Date: July 1, 2011**

### 1. GENERAL

a. The purpose of these Procedures is to provide a means of enforcing the Standards of Ethics and Professional Responsibility for Certified Mediators (hereinafter the "Standards"), the Guidelines for the Training and Certification of Court-Referred Mediators, the Guidelines for the Certification of Mediation Training Programs, and the Mentor Guidelines (hereinafter the "Guidelines").

b. These rules apply to all proceedings involving complaints filed on or after July 1, 2011 against certified mediators in their capacities as mediators, trainers, and/or mentors.

c. If a mediator's certification is suspended or revoked under these Procedures, the mediator's privileges to serve as a mentor or trainer shall also be suspended or revoked. If the mediator's privileges to serve as a mentor or trainer are suspended or revoked, his or her certification as a mediator may also be suspended or revoked.

d. If the complaint involves the conduct of a certified mediator in a mediation, the complaint will not be considered until the mediation is concluded.

e. If the complaint involves a procedure that is a combination of mediation with another dispute resolution process, such as arbitration, the scope of review under these Procedures is limited to the mediation portion of the proceeding.

f. The role of the mediator differs substantially from other professional roles. These Complaint Procedures do not apply to a certified mediator providing services in another professional role, unless it can be shown that the mediator was also clearly conducting mediation services, mediation mentoring services, mediation training services or the business of one of these services.

g. See the "Initiation of a Complaint" section below for the time frame for filing a complaint.

### 2. DEFINITIONS

a. Complainant — the initiator of a complaint

b. Complaint — a written communication to DRS on the Mediation Complaint Form (OES Form ADR-1004) alleging misconduct or a violation of or failure to comply with the Standards and/or the Guidelines.

c. Complaint Hearing Committee — The Complaint Hearing Committee is composed of five members: four certified mediators, at least one of whom is a mentor, at least one of whom is a mediation trainer, and at least one of whom is an attorney, and one active or retired judge. The five members shall be designated by the Executive Secretary and serve for two-year staggered terms. Members may be appointed for successive terms. If a member resigns, the Executive Secretary shall appoint a member to fill the unexpired term. If a member is temporarily unable to serve, the Executive Secretary shall appoint a member pro tempore.

d. Complaint Review Panel — The Complaint Review Panel is composed of three members: two certified mediators, one of whom may be the intake attorney, and one active or retired judge. The three members shall be designated by the Executive Secretary and serve for two-year staggered terms. Members may be appointed for successive terms. If a member resigns, the Executive Secretary shall appoint a member to fill the unexpired term. If a member is temporarily unable to serve, the Executive Secretary shall appoint a member pro tempore.

e. Decertification/Revocation — Removal of mediator, trainer or mentor privileges and functions for a defined period of time and/or until specified conditions are met. At the end of the decertification or revocation period, the respondent remains uncertified. If the respondent seeks certification after decertification or revocation, he or she must go through the certification application process.

f. Disciplinary Record — any tangible or electronic record of:

- any proceeding in which the respondent has been found in violation of the Guidelines and/or the Standards, and
- any proceeding in which a complaint has been resolved by agreed terms and conditions as described in Sections 4.i and 4.j, and
- any actions taken under the Guidelines including (1) curtailment, modification, suspension or revocation of certification or status or (2) any course for improvement. g. DRS — The Division of Dispute Resolution Services of the Office of the Executive Secretary (OES) of the Supreme Court of Virginia (or any subsequently authorized entity) is responsible for the oversight and certification of mediators providing services in court-referred cases, in mediation training programs, and as mentors.

g. Executive Secretary - Executive Secretary of the Supreme Court of Virginia

h. Guidelines — Guidelines is defined as the Guidelines for the Training and Certification of Court-Referred Mediators, the Guidelines for the Certification of Mediation Training Programs, and/or the Mentor Guidelines.

i. Intake attorney — An attorney, familiar with mediation, employed by OES or DRS, whose duties shall include an initial review of complaints against certified mediators, mentors and certified mediation trainers.

j. Party — The complainant or the respondent.

k. Respondent — The mediator, trainer or mentor against whom a complaint is lodged.

l. Standards — Standards is defined as the Standards of Ethics and Professional Responsibility for Certified Mediators.

m. Suspension — Temporary removal of mediator, trainer and/or mentor privileges and functions for a defined period of time and/or until specified conditions are met. At the end of suspension, privileges and functions are automatically restored.

## 3. INITIATION OF A COMPLAINT

a. The complaint procedure may be initiated by anyone with knowledge of the actions or behaviors raising concern, including any employee of OES. A complaint must be in writing on the Mediation Complaint Form (OES Form ADR-1004). The complaint must clearly identify: 1) the mediator, mentor or mediation trainer who is the subject of the complaint; 2) the person making the complaint; 3) the nature of any alleged misconduct or violation; 4) the date(s) the alleged misconduct or violation occurred; and 5) the complainant's contact information.

b. Any complaint must be received by DRS within two years of the alleged misconduct, except in unusual cases, where 1) the basis for the complaint was discovered after the two-year period and could not reasonably have been discovered before and 2) the complaint alleges a serious ethical breach. If a complaint is dismissed for lack of facial sufficiency, the complainant may initiate a new revised complaint if the time limit has not elapsed. The time limitation for filing may also be tolled as set forth in paragraph 3.e. below.

c. DRS will provide individuals who allege misconduct, violations or failure to comply with a Mediation Complaint Form (OES Form ADR-1004), and a copy of these Procedures, or direct them to the documents on the Virginia Judicial System website. Where a comment on an evaluation form raises ethics issue(s), DRS may provide the commenting individual with the same form and document.

d. DRS will notify the mediator, trainer or mentor of the complaint and will send him or her a copy of the complaint.

- If the respondent resigns his or her certification or allows it to lapse while he or she is the subject of a complaint or the complaint proceeding, that decision, and the circumstances surrounding the complaint, will be taken into consideration if and when the respondent reapplies for certification. If and when the respondent becomes certified, DRS may reactivate the complaint proceeding.

- If a complaint is filed after the respondent resigns his or her certification or allows it to lapse, regarding an incident prior to the resignation or lapse, that decision to resign or allow certification to lapse, and the circumstances surrounding the complaint, will be taken into consideration if and when the respondent reapplies for certification. The time limitation for filing set forth in paragraph 3.b. above is tolled from the date of resignation or lapse to the date the respondent becomes certified.

e. A complaint may be dismissed upon a request by a complainant to withdraw his or her complaint only with the agreement of DRS.

## 4. REVIEW OF COMPLAINTS

a. Once DRS receives a complaint, it shall first determine whether it has jurisdiction to consider the complaint. If DRS does not have jurisdiction, the complaint will be dismissed for lack of jurisdiction and no further action will be taken. DRS will notify the complainant and respondent of the dismissal in writing.

b. Once jurisdiction is established, an intake attorney will review the complaint to determine whether, assuming the allegations were true, the complaint as written is facially sufficient to state a claim that the respondent has violated or failed to comply with the Guidelines and/or the Standards.

c. The intake attorney may in his or her discretion refer the complaint to the Complaint Review Panel to make the determination of facial sufficiency and carry out all the functions of DRS described in this Section. Two (2) out of three (3) members of the Complaint Review Panel shall constitute a quorum. Decisions of the Panel shall be made by a majority of those present.

d. If the complaint would not constitute a violation of or failure to comply with the Guidelines and/or the Standards, assuming the allegations were found to be true, the complaint will be dismissed, and no further action will be taken. DRS will notify the complainant and the respondent of the decision in writing. If DRS dismisses the complaint, but believes remedial action or training may be beneficial, DRS may suggest that the respondent voluntarily participate in appropriate training or mentorship.

e. If the complaint asserts facts that would, if true, constitute a violation of or failure to comply with the Guidelines or the Standards, DRS will send a letter indicating the nature of the concerns to the respondent with a copy to the complainant. The respondent has twenty (20) calendar days from the date of the DRS letter to send a written response to DRS with a copy to the complainant.

f. If DRS receives no written response from the respondent within five (5) calendar days after expiration of the twenty (20)-day time period, DRS may immediately suspend the respondent's mediator and/or trainer certification and/or mentor status pending resolution of the complaint.

g. If the written response addresses the concerns to DRS's satisfaction, DRS may dismiss the complaint. DRS will notify the complainant and the respondent of the decision in writing. If DRS dismisses the complaint but believes remedial action or training may be beneficial, DRS may suggest that the respondent voluntarily participate in appropriate training or mentorship.

h. If DRS receives no written response from the respondent within the allotted time period, or if the response does not adequately address the concerns of DRS, DRS shall decide whether further information is necessary to determine how to proceed. If so, DRS staff will investigate the facts stated in the complaint. The investigation may include, but need not be limited to, review of any relevant documents and interviews of parties and witnesses.

i. If after investigation, DRS determines the complaint is unfounded, DRS may dismiss the complaint and notify the parties in writing of the dismissal.

   - If DRS determines no further information is necessary, or if the investigation does not find the complaint to be unfounded, DRS may

   - refer the complaint to the Complaint Hearing Committee, or

     - elect an option from subsections i. and j. below.

     - Upon agreement of the complainant and the respondent, DRS may refer the complaint matter to a third party neutral for a facilitated meeting.

j. If the meeting results in resolution of the complaint to the satisfaction of the parties and DRS, DRS shall not refer the matter to the Complaint Hearing Committee, unless and until it determines the respondent is not complying with the requirements, if any, of the facilitated resolution. Once the respondent has complied fully with the requirements, if any, the facilitated resolution shall become the final disposition of the complaint, and DRS shall so notify the parties in writing.

k. If the meeting with a third party neutral does not result in resolution of the complaint to the satisfaction of the parties and DRS, DRS shall refer the complaint to the Complaint Hearing Committee and so notify the parties in writing.

l. If DRS determines that the complaint is best addressed by remedial action, training or mentorship, then DRS may send a letter notifying the respondent that, based on the facts asserted in the complaint and the respondent's response, DRS proposes that the respondent agree in writing to specific terms and conditions, which may include, but are not limited to, any combination of sanctions listed in Section 8, to be completed within a specified period of time. The respondent must send a written response to DRS's proposal within ten (10) calendar days from the date thereof, indicating whether he or she accepts or rejects the proposed terms and conditions. The written response must be received by DRS within five (5) calendar days after expiration of the ten (10)-day time period.

m. If the respondent agrees in writing to the specified terms and conditions, DRS shall not refer the complaint to the Complaint Hearing Committee, unless and until it determines that the respondent is not complying with the agreed terms and conditions. Once the respondent has complied fully, the specified terms and conditions shall become the final disposition of the complaint, and DRS shall so notify the parties in writing.

n. If the respondent does not accept the proposed terms and conditions, DRS shall refer the matter to the Complaint Hearing Committee and so notify the parties in writing.

## 5. COMPLAINT HEARING COMMITTEE

a. The Complaint Hearing Committee shall hear and address any complaints referred by DRS. The Complaint Hearing Committee shall consider DRS's concerns, the respondent's response to those concerns, if any, and the results of any investigation. The Complaint Hearing Committee shall then conduct an informal proceeding within sixty (60) calendar days after referral from DRS unless the Committee and respondent agree to a longer time frame.

b. The Complaint Hearing Committee shall be convened as necessary to hear complaints. DRS may provide staff support for the Complaint Hearing Committee.

c. Each time the Complaint Hearing Committee is called together to consider a complaint, it will select a Chair to handle the convening of meetings or conference calls and to run the informal proceeding.

d. Decisions of the Complaint Hearing Committee shall be made by a majority of those present. Four (4) out of five (5) members of the Committee shall constitute a quorum.

## 6. CONFIDENTIALITY AND RECORDS RETENTION

a. DRS, the Complaint Review Panel and the Complaint Hearing Committee may not disclose to the public any complaints or the disposition thereof, or any reports, information or records received and maintained relating thereto, except:

• to the extent necessary to investigate and dispose of any matter arising under these Complaint Procedures;

- to the extent necessary to implement and monitor the disposition of, or sanctions resulting from, any matter arising under these Complaint Procedures;

- in any subsequent trial or appeal of any disposition of, or sanctions resulting from, any matter arising under these Complaint Procedures;

- DRS may disclose to the public, and may publish in its newsletter, that the certification of a mediator, mentor or trainer has been suspended or revoked under these Complaint Procedures;

- DRS may disclose to the complaining party the disposition of the complaint; or

- upon written and notarized authorization by the respondent, or by a certified mediator, trainer and/or mentor, DRS may disclose:

  b. whether complaints have been lodged against that respondent or that mediator, trainer and/or mentor and

  c. what was the disposition of such complaints.

  d. Such complaints, dispositions, reports, information or records shall be considered personnel records and shall not be available for discovery or as evidence in any civil action, except by order of a court that has taken into consideration the confidentiality of the mediation process.

  e. For educational or research purposes, DRS may disclose a general description of the nature of the complaint and its resolution so long as the disclosures protect the anonymity of the respondent and any mediation participants.

  f. DRS will retain indefinitely the Disciplinary Records of any certified mediators, trainers or mentors. DRS may retain records regarding dismissed complaints.

## 7. THE HEARING

a. The Complaint Hearing Committee shall conduct a proceeding that is private and is not open to the public. The parties may present witnesses, documents and other information that would be supportive of their position and helpful to the Hearing Committee in making its decision. Both the respondent and the complainant may bring counsel or a support person to the hearing. The Complaint Hearing Committee may elect to take testimony by telephone when appropriate, taking into consideration the cost and inconvenience of the witness appearing, and any cost, inconvenience and prejudice to the respondent. The Complaint Hearing Committee may elect to sequester witnesses. If any party fails to appear or to participate in good faith, the Complaint Hearing Committee may proceed on the evidence before it. If the complainant fails to appear, the Committee may dismiss the complaint for want of prosecution.

b. DRS, the respondent, or the Complaint Hearing Committee may record the hearing electronically or by transcription. The entity seeking the recording will bear the cost of and the responsibility for the recording. Such record and/or transcript shall be made available to DRS, the respondent, the Complaint

Hearing Committee, and to the Executive Secretary in the event of an appeal. Any recording and/or transcript shall be governed by the confidentiality requirements in Section 6 above.

c. The rules of civil procedure and rules of evidence do not apply, but may serve as a guide for the Complaint Hearing Committee.

d. If, after the hearing, the majority of the Complaint Hearing Committee finds that clear and convincing evidence establishes a violation of or failure to comply with the Guidelines and/or the Standards, the Complaint Hearing Committee may impose any of the sanctions included in Section 8 below as it deems appropriate. If the respondent against whom a violation or failure to comply has been found has a Disciplinary Record, the facts and circumstances giving rise to such Disciplinary Record may be disclosed (1) to the Complaint Hearing Committee upon its request and (2) by the Complaint Hearing Committee in its letter decision. If the Complaint Hearing Committee does not find that clear and convincing evidence establishes a violation or failure to comply, it shall dismiss the complaint.

## 8. DECISION AND SANCTIONS

a. The Complaint Hearing Committee shall make its decision and file a copy of its written decision with DRS within thirty (30) calendar days after the close of the hearing. DRS shall promptly mail to the respondent and complainant notice of such filing and a copy of the decision. If no request for reconsideration by the Executive Secretary of the Committee's decision is received from the respondent by the expiration of the time period allotted for such requests, the decision of the Complaint Hearing Committee shall become the final disposition of the complaint.

b. If the Complaint Hearing Committee determines that sanctions are warranted, it may impose sanctions to be completed within a specified period of time, including, but not limited to, any one or more of the following:

- sending a formal letter identifying the corrective action necessary;

- notwithstanding the confidentiality requirements of Section 6 above, notifying the dispute resolution center, court, or other entity with which the respondent is affiliated, of sanction of suspended certification or decertification;

- requiring one or more consultations or co-mediations with a mentor selected from the list maintained by DRS;

- requiring group or individual training;

- restriction of certification by curtailment or modification of the type of cases to be mediated, mentored, or of the courses to be taught in the future;

- suspension of certification or mentor status for a specified term;

- revocation of certification or mentor status;

- reimbursement of fees or expenses received by the respondent for court-referred mediations, training, mentorship or related work as agreed upon by the respondent and the Complaint Hearing Committee; or

- reimbursement of any out-of-pocket expenses of the Complaint Hearing Committee members related to the Complaint Hearing Committee hearing.

c. In those instances in which a sanction less than decertification has been imposed by the Complaint Hearing Committee and DRS determines that the respondent has not complied with the sanction, DRS may suspend the respondent's certification until compliance has been achieved. If the respondent objects to this suspension, he or she may, within ten (10) days of notice of his or her suspension, request a hearing before the Complaint Hearing Committee on the limited issue of whether he or she has complied with the sanctions. The Complaint Hearing Committee shall convene within sixty (60) days and deliver a written decision within thirty (30) days thereafter. A decision by the Complaint Hearing Committee is final.

## 9. RECONSIDERATION

a. If sanctions are imposed by the Complaint Hearing Committee, the respondent may within fifteen (15) calendar days of the date of the notice of filing request reconsideration by the Executive Secretary. The written request must be received by the Executive Secretary within five (5) calendar days after expiration of the fifteen (15)-day time period.

b. Upon receipt of a request for reconsideration, the Executive Secretary shall review all documents and other information that was considered by the Complaint Hearing Committee. Review shall be limited to the issues raised before the Complaint Hearing Committee. The Executive Secretary may return the complaint to the Complaint Hearing Committee, affirm the imposition of sanctions, or dismiss the complaint. The factual findings of the Complaint Hearing Committee shall be accepted unless clearly erroneous and the conclusions of law, including the sanctions, shall be reviewed de novo. This decision of the Executive Secretary is final and shall be set forth in a letter to the respondent, complainant and the Complaint Hearing Committee.

c. Any decision of the Complaint Hearing Committee is stayed pending reconsideration by the Executive Secretary, or where the Executive Secretary returns the complaint to the Complaint Hearing Committee, pending reconsideration by the Complaint Hearing Committee.

# Appendix J. Alexandria Mediation Court Forms

*Alexandria Mediation Service*
**Agreement to Mediate**

Case Number: GV1 _____          Date: _____

We, the undersigned, understand and consent to the following:

1.  Confidentiality: All memoranda, work products, and other materials contained in the case files of a Mediator or mediation program are confidential. Any communications made in or in connection with the mediation, whether made to the Mediator, mediation program staff, to a party, or to any other persons, are confidential. However, a written mediated agreement signed by the parties shall not be confidential, unless the parties otherwise agree in writing.

    Confidential materials and communications are not subject to disclosure in discovery or in any judicial or administrative proceeding except:
    a.  where all parties to the mediation agree, in writing, to waive the confidentiality;
    b.  in a subsequent action between the Mediator or mediation program and a party to the mediation for damages arising out of the mediation;
    c.  statements, memoranda, materials, and other tangible evidence, otherwise subject to discovery, which were not prepared specifically for use in—and actually used in—the mediation;
    d.  where a threat to inflict bodily injury is made;
    e.  where communications are intentionally used to plan, attempt to commit, or commit a crime or conceal an ongoing crime;
    f.  where an ethics complaint is made against the Mediator by a party to the mediation to the extent necessary for the complainant to prove misconduct and the Mediator to defend against such complaint;
    g.  where communications are sought or offered to prove or disprove any of the grounds listed in §8.01-581.26 in a proceeding to vacate a mediated agreement, or
    h.  as provided by law or rule.

2.  All participants in the mediation (and the Mediator) retain the right to terminate the mediation at any time.

3.  The parties pledge to participate in good faith, and will not withhold any information or documents relevant to the issues being discussed, with the understanding that all information and documents produced during the mediation remain confidential.

4.  The Mediator does not give legal advice. Participants are encouraged to seek such advice. Each participant has the opportunity to have counsel present during mediation or to consult with independent legal counsel at any time during the mediation.

5.  Any mediated settlement the participants reach will affect their legal rights.

6.  Each participant in the mediation should have any draft settlement reviewed by independent legal counsel prior to signing the settlement or the opportunity to do so is waived.

7.  AMS does not charge fees for mediation services performed for the General District and Small Claims Courts of Alexandria. Mediation services performed in other contexts are charged at the rate of $125.00 per hour, beginning with the signing of this document. Fees are for mediation services, regardless of whether any settlement is reached.

_____          _____
                                                                                    Date

_____          _____
                                                                                    Date

_____          _____
Mediator: _____                              Date
Certification # _____

---

[10] All forms are available from Virginia's Judicial System web pages. See Office of the Executive Secretary, Supreme Court of Virginia (2009a).

EXAMPLE

**George Mason University Practice Forms**
**Conflict and Dispute Mediation Resources**
**Agreement to Mediate**

Case Number: GV _17  0219_                          Date: _3/23/2017_

We, the undersigned, understand and consent to the following:

1.  Confidentiality:  All memoranda, work products, and other materials contained in the case files of a Mediator or mediation program are confidential.  Any communications made in or in connection with the mediation, whether made to the Mediator, mediation program staff, to a party, or to any other persons, is confidential.  However, a written mediated agreement signed by the parties shall not be confidential, unless the parties otherwise agree in writing.

    Confidential materials and communications are not subject to disclosure in discovery or in any judicial or administrative proceeding except:
    a.  where all parties to the mediation agree, in writing, to waive the confidentiality;
    b.  in a subsequent action between the Mediator or mediation program and a party to the mediation for damages arising out of the mediation;
    c.  statements, memoranda, materials, and other tangible evidence, otherwise subject to discovery, which were not prepared specifically for use in—and actually used in—the mediation;
    d.  where a threat to inflict bodily injury is made;
    e.  where communications are intentionally used to plan, attempt to commit, or commit a crime or conceal an ongoing crime;
    f.  where an ethics complaint is made against the Mediator by a party to the mediation to the extent necessary for the complainant to prove misconduct and the Mediator to defend against such complaint;
    g.  where communications are sought or offered to prove or disprove any of the grounds listed in §8.01-581.26 in a proceeding to vacate a mediated agreement, or
    h.  as provided by law or rule.

2.  All participants in the mediation (and the Mediator) retain the right to terminate the mediation at any time.

3.  The parties pledge to participate in good faith, and will not withhold any information or documents relevant to the issues being discussed, with the understanding that all information and documents produced during the mediation remain confidential.

4.  The Mediator does not give legal advice.  Participants are encouraged to seek such advice.  Each participant has the opportunity to have counsel present during mediation or to consult with independent legal counsel at any time during the mediation.

5.  Any mediated settlement the participants reach will affect their legal rights.

6.  Each participant in the mediation should have any draft settlement reviewed by independent legal counsel prior to signing the settlement or the opportunity to do so is waived.

7.  Fees are for mediation services, regardless of whether any settlement is reached.

_Louis Rice_                                    3/23/2017
                                                Date
_Jessica Nixon_                                 3/23/2017
                                                Date
                                                3/23/2017
Mediator  Pamela K Struss, PhD                  Date
Certification #  2651

_Susan Mitchell #4100_        3/23/2017

271

## Alexandria Mediation Service
## Mediation Memorandum of Agreement

In the Alexandria General District Court:

Case Number: GV1 _____ Mediation Date: _____

Plaintiff: _____ Defendant: _____

We, the undersigned, having resolved our dispute in the above-numbered case, hereby agree that our settlement, outlined in the "Terms and Conditions" below, is an accurate reflection of our resolution.

We agree that the Terms and Conditions set forth here are the result of substantial full disclosure of all relevant property and financial information. We understand that we have had the opportunity to have the Memorandum of Agreement reviewed by independent legal counsel prior to signing and have either had this agreement so reviewed prior to signing or have chosen to waive our opportunity to do so.

We further agree to abide by all of the Terms and Conditions set forth herein.

### Terms and Conditions

Plaintiff agrees to accept the following, in full satisfaction of a dispute involving

A)  If a check is returned unpaid by the bank for any reason, Defendant will replace the full amount, plus $50.00, plus any bounced check fee incurred by Plaintiff, pursuant to Va. Code § 8.01-27.1, in certified funds (money order, cashier's check, certified check, or cash), within ten calendar days;

B)  If the above Terms and Conditions are not fully satisfied, Plaintiff may, after giving at least ten days advance written notice to Respondent, return to Court to request JUDGMENT in the amount of
$ _____ (the mediated amount or equivalent value), less any amounts already received, plus any additional court costs;

C)  If the above Terms and Conditions are fully satisfied, Plaintiff will send written notice to the Court, using the provided Letter of Satisfaction, within 15 calendar days of the completion of the Terms.

_____        _____
Plaintiff            Date                        Defendant
Date

_____
Mediator:
Certification # _____              *Updated June 2012*

272

# EXAMPLE

**George Mason University Practice Forms**
**Conflict and Dispute Resolution Mediation Resources**
**Mediation Memorandum of Agreement**

In the Alexandria General District Court:

Case Number: GV *17 0219*          Mediation Date: *3/23/2017*

Plaintiff: *Monument Apartumhoues*  Defendant(s) *Mike + Jessica Mixon*
*Louis Rice - Representative*

We, the undersigned, having resolved our dispute in the above-numbered case, hereby agree that our settlement, outlined in the "Terms and Conditions" below, is an accurate reflection of our resolution.

We agree that the Terms and Conditions set forth here are the result of substantial full disclosure of all relevant property and financial information. We understand that we have had the opportunity to have the Memorandum of Agreement reviewed by independent legal counsel prior to signing and have either had this agreement so reviewed prior to signing or have chosen to waive our opportunity to do so.

We further agree to abide by all of the Terms and Conditions set forth herein.

### Terms and Conditions

Plaintiff agrees to accept the following, in full satisfaction of a dispute involving *past Due rent.*

1) Plaintiff agrees to accept security deposit less $700 that will be refunded to Defendant.
2) Defendants agree to remove negative comments about Monument Apthomes from all social media account where the posted.
3) Plaintiff will mail a business check by April 10th in the amount of $700 via USPS to 321 hoving Ln #251, Arlington VA 22101
4) Defendants apologize for leaving apartment a mess. They verbally apologized at the table today.

A)   If a check is returned unpaid by the bank for any reason, Defendant will replace the full amount, plus $50.00, plus any bounced check fee incurred by Plaintiff, pursuant to Va. Code § 8.01-27.1, in certified funds (money order, cashier's check, certified check, or cash), within ten calendar days;

B)   If the above Terms and Conditions are not fully satisfied, Plaintiff may, after giving at least ten days advance written notice to Respondent, return to Court to request JUDGMENT in the amount of $ *700*      (the mediated amount or equivalent value), less any amounts already received, plus any additional court costs;

C)   If the above Terms and Conditions are fully satisfied, Plaintiff will send written notice to the Court, using the provided Letter of Satisfaction, within 15 calendar days of the completion of the Terms.

D)   The Plaintiff and Defendant will notify the Court and each other of any change of address and other contact information within 15 calendar days of such change.

*Louis Rice* 3/23/2017          *Mike Mixon* 3-23-2017
Plaintiff        Date                  Defendant        Date

                                   *Jessica Mixon* 3-23-2017
Plaintiff        Date                  Defendant        Date

*[signature]*        3-23-2017
Mediator: Pamela K Struss, PhD        Date
VA Certification # 2651

*Susan Mitchell* ‡ 3/23/2017
   4/100

273

## *Alexandria Mediation Service*
### Intake Form and Case Report
### Alexandria General District Court    Alexandria Small Claims Court

Intake Date: _____ Judge: _____ AMS # [_____]

Court Case #: GV1 _____ Filing Date: _____ Trial Date: _____

**Plaintiff:**                                    **Defendant:**

Name: _____    Name: _____

Address: _____    Address: _____

Home Phone: _____    Home Phone: _____

Other Phone: _____    Other Phone: _____

**Type of Case:**
( ) landlord/tenant     ( ) consumer/merchant     ( ) neighborhood     ( ) contract
( ) auto accident       ( ) auto repair           ( ) employer/employee  ( ) fee
( ) personal loan       ( ) home improvement      ( ) personal property  ( ) services
( ) other: _____

**Amount of claim: $** _____        **Counterclaim filed:  yes  no**

**Summary of Initial Positions:**
**Plaintiff:**                                    **Defendant:**

_____        _____

_____        _____

_____        _____

_____        _____

_____                          _____

_____        _____

_____        _____

**Mediator:** _____     Certification # 

**Mediator:** _____     Certification # 

**Apprentice:** _____ _____         (observer or co-mediator)

**Number of Sessions:** _____     **Total Number of Hours:** _____

**Date Mediation Completed:** _____

**Outcome:**
( ) Agreement          ( ) No Agreement          ( ) Partial Agreement

| MIS | monthly | quarterly |
|-----|---------|-----------|
|     |         |           |

# EXAMPLE

**George Mason University Practice Forms**
Intake Form and Case Report
Alexandria General District Court

Intake Date: 3/23/2017    Judge: Hancock

Court Case #: GV 17-0219    Filing Date: 2/28/2017    Trial Date: 3/23/2017

**Plaintiff:** Louis Rice
Name: Monument Apt. Homes
Email Address: lrice@monument.org
Address: 12361 Granite Lane
Fairfax, VA 22030
Home Phone: 703-690-1000
Other Phone:

**Defendant:**
Name: Mike & Jessica Mixon
Email Address: mmixon@yahoo.com
Address: 321 Loving Ln. #251
Arlington, VA 22101
Home Phone: 571-218-6216
Other Phone:

**Type of Case:**
(x) landlord/tenant    ( ) consumer/merchant    ( ) neighborhood    ( ) contract
( ) auto accident    ( ) auto repair    ( ) employer/employee    ( ) fee
( ) personal loan    ( ) home improvement    ( ) personal property    ( ) services
( ) other:

Amount of claim: $ 1500    Counterclaim filed: yes (no)

**Summary of Initial Positions:**

Plaintiff:
We received the move out notice from the Mixon's on 12/15/16 that they would be out on 1/15/17. They moved out and left some trash. Cost $300 to remove Still had $1500 sec. deposit

Defendant:
We submited moveout notice in a timely manner. We had initially paid $2000 in a security deposit. We knew we owed half on months rent of $1000 and hoped to receive $1000 back from security deposit.

Mediator: Pamela Struss    VA Certification # 2651

Mediator: Susan Mitchell    Certification # 4100

Apprentice: _____    (observer or co-mediator)

Number of Sessions: 1

Date Mediation Completed: 3/23/2017

Total Number of Hours: 2.25
#1 2.25  #2 ____  #3 ____  #4 ____

**Outcome:**
(✓) Agreement    ( ) No Agreement    ( ) Partial Agreement

Mediation Info Email Date: P ✓  D ✓
Foreign Language Interpreter Request Date: NA

275

*Alexandria Mediation Service*
**Commonwealth Mediation Associates**

Alexandria General District Court
Civil Division, 2nd floor
520 King Street
Alexandria, VA 22314

## Post-Mediation
## Letter of Satisfaction

Case Number: GV1 _____    Mediation Date: _____

Plaintiff: _____    Defendant: _____

To the Clerk:

    Please be advised that the Terms and Conditions contained in a
Mediated Agreement in the above case were fully satisfied on
(date). Total amount received (if applicable): $ _____ .

Signed: _____    Date: _____
         Plaintiff

*Updated June 2012*

EXAMPLE

**George Mason University Practice Forms**
**Conflict and Dispute Mediation Service**

**Post-Mediation**
**Letter of Satisfaction**

Case Number: _GV 17 0219_    Mediation Date: _3/23/2017_
Plaintiff: _Monument Apt. Homes_    Defendant: _Mike & Jessica Mixon_

To the Clerk:

Please be advised that the Terms and Conditions contained in a Mediated Agreement
in the above case were fully satisfied on _____ (date). Total amount received
(if applicable): $ _____.

Signed: _____    Date: _____
                    Plaintiff

Mail to:
Alexandria General District Court Clerk
520 S. King St., Room 203
Alexandria, VA 22314

*Alexandria Mediation Service*
**Mediation Report**

**Alexandria Small Claims Court**

Case #: _GV1_____

Plaintiff: _____Defendant: _____

The undersigned Mediator reports to the Court that a mediation orientation and discussion session was scheduled for the participants listed above on _____.

[ ]     Mediation is not recommended.

[ ]     The plaintiff did not appear.

[ ]     The defendant did not appear.

[ ]     Both appeared and completed orientation; mediation is refused.

[ ]     (1) Both appeared and participated in mediation, but were unable to reach a mediated agreement, and the process has been terminated.  The Parties are ready to proceed to **TRIAL**.  (Both parties must sign below.)

[ ]     (2) Both appeared and participated in mediation, but were unable to reach a mediated agreement, and the process has been terminated.  Please continue the case by agreement to _Thursday_____ at 11am for **TRIAL**. (Both parties must sign below.)

[ ]     (3) Both participated in mediation, and the attached agreement was reached. Please continue the case by agreement to _Thursday_____ at 11am for _either_:
                         A) request for **JUDGMENT** to enforce the mediated agreement,
          _or_
                         B) notice of satisfaction of the agreement.     (Both parties must sign below.)

[ ]     (4) Both appeared and participated in mediation, and further discussion has been scheduled.  Please continue the case by agreement to _Thursday_ at 11am for **TRIAL** if agreement is not reached.   (Both parties must sign below.)

[ ]     Next mediation appointment place and time: _____
        _____

[ ]     Other: _____
        _____
        _____

Respectfully submitted,                     Plaintiff: _____

                                            Defendant: _____

Mediator: _____
Certification # _____

EXAMPLE

## George Mason University Practice Forms
## Conflict and Dispute Mediation Services
## Mediation Report

Court _Fairfax General District Court_

Case #: GV _17-0219_

Plaintiff: _Louis Rice for Monument Apartmenthomes_    Defendant: _Mike + Jessica Mixon_

The undersigned Mediator reports to the Court that a mediation orientation and discussion session was scheduled for the participants listed above on _3/23/2017_ .

[ ]    Mediation is not recommended.

[ ]    The plaintiff did not appear.

[ ]    The defendant did not appear.

[ ]    Both appeared and completed orientation; mediation is refused.

[ ]    (1) Both appeared and participated in mediation, but were unable to reach a mediated agreement, and the process has been terminated. The Parties are ready to proceed to **TRIAL**. (Both parties must sign below.)

[ ]    (2) Both appeared and participated in mediation, but were unable to reach a mediated agreement, and the process has been terminated. Please continue the case by agreement to Friday _____ at 9:30am for **TRIAL**. (Both parties must sign below.)

[X]    (3) Both participated in mediation, and the attached agreement was reached. Please continue the case by agreement to Thursday _April 27_ at 11:00am for either:
   A) request for **JUDGMENT** to enforce the mediated agreement, or
   B) notice of satisfaction of the agreement.    (Both parties must sign below.)

[ ]    (4) Both appeared and participated in mediation, and further discussion has been scheduled. Please continue the case by agreement toThursday _____ at11:00am for **TRIAL** if agreement is not reached. (Both parties must sign below.)

[ ]    Next mediation appointment place and time: _____

[ ]    Other: _____

Respectfully submitted,

_____
Mediator
VA Certification # _2651_

_Susan Mitchell_
_#4100_

Plaintiff: _Louie Rice_

Defendant: _Mike_   _Jessica Mixon_

279

Sample

WARRANT IN DEBT — SMALL CLAIMS DIVISION
Commonwealth of Virginia    VA. CODE § 16.1-79; 16.1-122.3

VOID

........ ALEXANDRIA ........................................ General District Court
CITY OR COUNTY

COURTHOUSE, 520 KING STREET, SECOND FLOOR, ALEXANDRIA, VA 22314  703-838-4021
STREET ADDRESS OF COURT

TO ANY AUTHORIZED OFFICER: You are hereby commanded to summon the Defendant(s).
TO THE DEFENDANT(S): You are summoned to appear before this Court at the above address on

11:00 A.M. .......... to answer the Plaintiff(s)' civil claim (see below)
RETURN DATE AND TIME

DATE ISSUED              [ ] CLERK      [ ] DEPUTY CLERK    [ ] MAGISTRATE

CLAIM: Plaintiff(s) claim that Defendant(s) owe Plaintiff(s) a debt in the sum of

$ ........ net of any credits, with interest at .......... % from .......... until paid.
                                           INTEREST RATE    DATE FROM WHICH IS DUE

$ .......... costs with the basis of this claim being ..................................
     COSTS

[ ] Open Account  [ ] Contract  [ ] Note  [ ] Other (EXPLAIN) ..................

HOMESTEAD EXEMPTION WAIVED? [ ] YES    [ ] NO    [ ] cannot be demanded

..........................     ..........................     ..........................
      DATE                           PLAINTIFF                  PLAINTIFF'S EMPLOYEE

CASE DISPOSITION
[ ] JUDGMENT that the Plaintiff(s) recover against [ ] named Defendant(s) [ ] ..........

$ ........ net of any credits, with interest at .......... % from .......... until paid.
                                           INTEREST RATE    DATE FROM WHICH IS DUE

$ .......... costs
     COSTS

HOMESTEAD EXEMPTION WAIVED? [ ] YES    [ ] NO    [ ] CANNOT BE DEMANDED
[ ] JUDGMENT FOR [ ] NAMED DEFENDANT(S) [ ] ..................
[ ] NON-SUIT  [ ] DISMISSED
Defendant(s) Present?    [ ] YES
                         [ ] NO
[ ] Indemnifying bond of $ .......... [ ]secured [ ] unsecured required for lost instrument
                                                           (Va. Code § 8.01-32)

..........................     ..........................
        DATE                           JUDGE

FORM DC-402 (FRONT) 10/07    (A122741 3/12)

RETURN DATE                          CASE NO.

PLAINTIFF(S) (LAST NAME, FIRST NAME, MIDDLE INITIAL)

v.

DEFENDANT(S) (LAST NAME, FIRST NAME, MIDDLE INITIAL)

WARRANT IN DEBT —
SMALL CLAIMS DIVISION

* * *

VOID

TO DEFENDANT: You are not required to appear;
however, if you fail to appear, judgment may be entered
against you. By law, this case must be tried on the
return date above unless all parties agree upon a
different date for trial. Other continuances shall be
granted by the court only for good cause shown.

* * *

Grounds of Defense: .......... ORDERED .......... DATE

NEXT HEARING
DATE AND TIME

JUDGMENT PAID OR
SATISFIED PURSUANT
TO ATTACHED NOTICE
OF
SATISFACTION

.......... DATE
.......... CLERK

DISABILITY ACCOMMODATIONS for loss of
hearing, vision, mobility, etc., contact the court
ahead of time.

280

Front

# WARRANT IN DEBT (Civil Claim for Money)

Commonwealth of Virginia ............ VA. CODE § 16.1-79

COURTHOUSE OF: NO STREET ADDRESS OF COURT AVAILABLE ...... General District Court

................................................................
CITY OR COUNTY

STREET ADDRESS OF COURT

CASE NO. GV 17-0219

PLAINTIFF(S) NAME AND ADDRESS (EACH PLAINTIFF)

Monument Apartment Homes
Roberta Rivas, Representative
15361 Granite Lane
Fair Fax, VA 22030
703-698-1000

HEARING DATE AND TIME
1:30 P.M.

DEFENDANT(S) NAME AND ADDRESS (EACH DEFENDANT)

Mike and Jessica Mixon
321 Loving Ln #251
Arlington, VA 22101
571-318-6216

## WARRANT IN DEBT

TO ANY AUTHORIZED OFFICER: You are hereby commanded to summon the Defendant(s).

TO THE DEFENDANT(S): You are summoned to appear before this Court to answer the Plaintiff(s)' civil claim (see below).

March 23, 2017 ..... 11:00 P.M. .... to answer the Plaintiff(s)' civil claim (see below)

TO DEFENDANT: You are not required to appear; however, if you fail to appear, judgment may be entered against you. See the important notice on the reverse about requesting a change.

Feb. 28, 2017 .......................
DATE ISSUED

[ ] CLERK [X] DEPUTY CLERK [ ] MAGISTRATE

JUDGMENT PAID OR SATISFIED PURSUANT TO ATTACHED NOTICE OF SATISFACTION.

CLAIM: Plaintiff(s) claim that Defendant(s) owe Plaintiff(s) a debt in the sum of

$ 1500 ........ net of any credits, with interest at ... 6 .... % from date of 3/23/17 until paid

$ 56 ........ costs and $ ...............

[ ] To dispute this claim, you must appear on the return date to try this case.
[ ] To dispute this claim, you must appear on the return date for the judge to set another date for trial.

[ ] Open Account [ ] Contract [ ] Note [X] Other (EXPLAIN) Past due rent.

Grounds of Defense .......................

Bill of Particulars .......................

2/28/2017 .......................
DATE

[X] PLAINTIFF [ ] PLAINTIFF'S ATTORNEY [X] PLAINTIFF'S EMPLOYEE/AGENT

HOMESTEAD EXEMPTION WAIVED? [ ] YES [X] NO

cannot be demanded

ATTORNEY FOR PLAINTIFF(S) .......................
ORDERED                          DATE

ATTORNEY FOR DEFENDANT(S) .......................
ORDERED                          DATE

## CASE DISPOSITION

JUDGMENT against [ ] named Defendant(s) [ ]

for $ .......... net of any credits, with interest at ........ % from date

of .......... until paid, $ .......... costs and $ .......... attorney's fees

HOMESTEAD EXEMPTION WAIVED? [ ] YES [ ] NO [ ] CANNOT BE DEMANDED
[ ] JUDGMENT FOR [ ] NAMED DEFENDANT(S) [ ]
[ ] NON-SUIT [ ] DISMISSED

Defendant(s) Present? { } YES
                      { } NO

LIABILITY ACCOMMODATIONS for loss of hearing, vision, mobility, etc., contact the court ahead of time.

....................... .......................
DATE                    JUDGE

FORM DC-412 (FRONT) REVISED 07/14  (14) 16.1-79(2)

RETURNS: Each defendant was served according to law, as indicated below, unless not found.

NAME ................................

ADDRESS ................................

[ ] PERSONAL SERVICE  Tel.
No.

[ ] Being unable to make personal service, a copy was delivered in the following manner:

[ ] Delivered to family member (not temporary sojourner or guest) age 16 or older at usual place of abode of party named above after giving information of its purport. List name, age of recipient, and relation of recipient to party named above.

[ ] Posted on front door or such other door as appears to be the main entrance of usual place of abode, address listed above. (Other authorized recipient not found.)

[ ] Served on Secretary of the Commonwealth

[ ] NOT FOUND
                    SERVING OFFICER

DATE _____ for _____

---

NAME ................................

ADDRESS ................................

[ ] PERSONAL SERVICE  Tel.
No.

[ ] Being unable to make personal service, a copy was delivered in the following manner:

[ ] Delivered to family member (not temporary sojourner or guest) age 16 or older at usual place of abode of party named above after giving information of its purport. List name, age of recipient, and relation of recipient to party named above.

[ ] Posted on front door or such other door as appears to be the main entrance of usual place of abode, address listed above. (Other authorized recipient not found.)

[ ] Served on Secretary of the Commonwealth

[ ] NOT FOUND
                    SERVING OFFICER

DATE _____ for _____

---

NAME  Jessica Nixon

ADDRESS  321 Spring Ln #251  Tel.
Arlington

[✓] PERSONAL SERVICE  No.

[ ] Being unable to make personal service, a copy was delivered in the following manner:

[✓] Delivered to family member (not temporary sojourner or guest) age 16 or older at usual place of abode of party named above after giving information of its purport. List name, age of recipient, and relation of recipient to party named above.

[ ] Posted on front door or such other door as appears to be the main entrance of usual place of abode, address listed above. (Other authorized recipient not found.)

[ ] Served on Secretary of the Commonwealth

[ ] NOT FOUND

7-3-11  Officer Smart
DATE         for  Fax City Sheriff

I certify that I mailed a copy of this summons to the defendant named herein at the address shown above.

[ ] P₁. issued or
[ ] P₁. Plaintiff issued
Interrogatories issued on

DATE
[ ] Plaintiff
[ ] Plaintiff's Agent

**OBJECTION TO VENUE:**
To the Defendant(s): If you believe that Plaintiff(s) should have filed this suit in a different city or county, you may file a written request to have the case moved for trial to the general district court of that city or county. To do so, you must do the following:

1. Prepare a written request which contains (a) this case's number, (b) the case number and the "return date" as shown on the other side of this form in the right corner, (c) Plaintiff(s)' name(s) and Defendant(s)' name(s), (d) the phrase "I move to object to venue of this case in this court because" and state the reasons for your objection, and also state in which city or county the case should be tried, and (e) your signature and mailing address.

2. File the written request in the clerk's office before the trial date (use the mail at your own risk) or give it to the judge when your case is called on the return date. Also send (or deliver) a copy to plaintiff.

3. If you mail this request to the court, you will be notified of the judge's decision.

FORM DC-421 (back of Warrant in Debt)

**Transfer to Another Locality:** If the Defendant believes that Plaintiff(s) should have filed this suit in a different city or county, you may file a written request to have the case moved for trial to the general district court of that city or county. To do so, you must do the following:

1. Prepare a written request which contains (a) this court's name, (b) the case number and the "return date" as shown on the other side of this form in the top right corner, (c) Plaintiff(s)' name(s) and Defendant(s)' name(s), (d) "I move to object to venue of this case in this court because" and state the reasons for your objection and also state in which city or county the case should be tried, and (e) your signature and mailing address.

2. File the written request in the clerk's office before the trial date (use the mail at your own risk) or give it to the judge when your case is called on the return date. Also send or deliver a copy to plaintiff.

3. If mailed to the court, you will be notified of the judge's decision.

## REMOVAL TO GENERAL DISTRICT COURT

I, the undersigned defendant, am exercising my right to remove this case to the general district court of this jurisdiction by signing and giving this notice to this court before the case is decided.

_____    [ ] DEFENDANT    [ ] ATTORNEY FOR DEFENDANT
DATE

[ ] oral   [ ] written notice of removal has been received this day in this small claims division.

_____    [ ] CLERK    [ ] JUDGE
DATE

FORM DC-402 (REVERSE) 3/21

---

NAME .....................................

ADDRESS .................................

Tel. No. ...........

[ ] PERSONAL SERVICE

[ ] Being unable to make personal service, a copy was delivered in the following manner:

[ ] Delivered to family member (not temporary sojourner or guest) age 16 or older at usual place of abode of party named above after giving information of its purport. List name, age of recipient, and relation of recipient to party named above.

[ ] Posted on front door or such other door as appears to be the main entrance of usual place of abode, address listed above. (Other authorized recipient not found.)

[ ] Served on Secretary of the Commonwealth

[ ] Served on Clerk of the State Corporation Commission.

[ ] NOT FOUND

DATE _____    SERVING OFFICER _____ for _____

---

NAME .....................................

ADDRESS .................................

Tel. No. ...........

[ ] PERSONAL SERVICE

[ ] Being unable to make personal service, a copy was delivered in the following manner:

[ ] Delivered to family member (not temporary sojourner or guest) age 16 or older at usual place of abode of party named above after giving information of its purport. List name, age of recipient, and relation of recipient to party named above.

[ ] Posted on front door or such other door as appears to be the main entrance of usual place of abode, address listed above. (Other authorized recipient not found.)

[ ] Served on Secretary of the Commonwealth

[ ] Served on Clerk of the State Corporation Commission.

[ ] NOT FOUND

DATE _____    SERVING OFFICER _____

---

I certify that I mailed a copy of this document to the defendants named therein at the address shown therein on

_____
DATE

[ ] Plaintiff
[ ] Plaintiff's Employee

VOID

EXAMPLE

II.   **Mediator Evaluation**

Mediator A: __Pamela Struss__          Mediator B: _Susan Mitchell_
      Print First & Last Name                    Print First & Last Name

__2651__                                      _4100_
Mediator's Certification Number        Mediator's Certification Number

Please rate your Mediator(s) on the following.  Circle the appropriate number.

**5 = Very Good   4 = Good   3 = Adequate   2 = Unsatisfactory   1 = Poor   0 = Does not apply**

| The Mediator . . . | | Mediator A | Mediator B |
|---|---|---|---|
| 1. | explained the mediation process and procedures | 5 4 3 2 1 0 | 5 4 3 2 1 0 |
| 2. | provided useful information | 5 4 3 2 1 0 | 5 4 3 2 1 0 |
| 3. | was a good listener | 5 4 3 2 1 0 | 5 4 3 2 1 0 |
| 4. | allowed me to talk about issues that were important to me | 5 4 3 2 1 0 | 5 4 3 2 1 0 |
| 5. | was respectful | 5 4 3 2 1 0 | 5 4 3 2 1 0 |
| 6. | helped clarify issues | 5 4 3 2 1 0 | 5 4 3 2 1 0 |
| 7. | encouraged us to come up with our own solutions | 5 4 3 2 1 0 | 5 4 3 2 1 0 |

8.   informed me that I could consult an attorney   ☑ yes   ☐ no

9.   was neutral   ☑ yes   ☐ no

10. wrote our agreement clearly and accurately   ☑ yes   ☐ no   ☐ doesn't apply

11. Share any comments on the mediation process and/or the Mediator(s):

_Very fair process & will use again_

Please return this Form to the Mediator or Program Director, or mail directly to:
Dispute Resolution Services
Office of the Executive Secretary
Supreme Court of Virginia
100 North Ninth Street
Richmond, VA  23219

| FOR MEDIATOR USE ONLY |
|---|
| Court: ☐ JDR  ☐ GD/SC  ☐ Circuit |
| Type of Dispute: _____ |
| Source of Referral:  Alexandria Court |

**FORM ADR-1002**  revised December 2011

284

**EXAMPLE**

**SUPREME COURT OF VIRGINIA**
Office of the Executive Secretary

### Evaluation of Mediation Session(s) and Mediator(s)

This information will be used to inform the court system and the Mediator(s) about your experience with mediation. With your help, we can ensure that quality mediation services continue to be available to the citizens of the Commonwealth. This information may be shared with the Mediator(s).

I. **Session Evaluation**

Name: _Louis Rice_ Date: _8-23-2017_

Address: _12361 Granite Lane_
_____ Street
_Fairfax_ _VA_ _22030_
City State Zip

Phone Number: (Day) _703-690-100__(Evening) _____

1. I am (check one): ☑ a party to the mediation ☐ an attorney representing a party

2. For this case, mediation was (check one):
☑ very appropriate ☐ somewhat appropriate ☐ not at all appropriate

Comments: _Very helpful process_
_____

3. Total hours spent in the mediation session(s): _2.25_ Number of Sessions: _1_

4. The mediation process was:
☑ very helpful ☐ somewhat helpful ☐ not at all helpful

5. Mediation ended with an agreement on:
☑ all of the issues ☐ some of the issues ☐ none of the issues

6. Would you use mediation again? ☑ yes ☐ no

7. Would you recommend mediation to others? ☑ yes ☐ no

FORM ADR-1002 revised December 2011 (OVER)

EXAMPLE

## II. Mediator Evaluation

Mediator A: __Pamela Struss__
Print First & Last Name

Mediator B: _Susan Mitchell_
Print First & Last Name

__2651__
Mediator's Certification Number

_4100_
Mediator's Certification Number

Please rate your Mediator(s) on the following. Circle the appropriate number.

**5 = Very Good   4 = Good   3 = Adequate   2 = Unsatisfactory   1 = Poor   0 = Does not apply**

The Mediator . . .                                              Mediator A      Mediator B

1.  explained the mediation process and procedures      5 4 3 2 1 0     5 4 3 2 1 0
2.  provided useful information                          5 4 3 2 1 0     5 4 3 2 1 0
3.  was a good listener                                  5 4 3 2 1 0     5 4 3 2 1 0
4.  allowed me to talk about issues that were important to me   5 4 3 2 1 0     5 4 3 2 1 0
5.  was respectful                                       5 4 3 2 1 0     5 4 3 2 1 0
6.  helped clarify issues                                5 4 3 2 1 0     5 4 3 2 1 0
7.  encouraged us to come up with our own solutions      5 4 3 2 1 0     5 4 3 2 1 0

8.  informed me that I could consult an attorney     ☑ yes   ☐ no

9.  was neutral                                       ☑ yes   ☐ no

10. wrote our agreement clearly and accurately        ☑ yes   ☐ no   ☐ doesn't apply

11. Share any comments on the mediation process and/or the Mediator(s):

_Very fair process + will use again_

Please return this Form to the Mediator or Program Director, or mail directly to:
Dispute Resolution Services
Office of the Executive Secretary
Supreme Court of Virginia
100 North Ninth Street
Richmond, VA  23219

| FOR MEDIATOR USE ONLY |
| --- |
| Court: ☐ JDR  ☐ GD/SC  ☐ Circuit |
| Type of Dispute: _____ |
| Source of Referral:  Alexandria Court |

**FORM ADR-1002** revised December 2011

286

**SUPREME COURT OF VIRGINIA**
Office of the Executive Secretary

## Evaluation of Mediation Session(s) and Mediator(s)

This information will be used to inform the court system and the Mediator(s) about your experience with mediation. With your help, we can ensure that quality mediation services continue to be available to the citizens of the Commonwealth. This information may be shared with the Mediator(s).

**I.   Session Evaluation**

Name: _Mike + Jessica Mixon_   Date: _3-23-17_

Address: _321 Loving Ln #251_
_____
                                Street
_Arlington_        _VA_      _22101_
City                              State                    Zip

Phone Number: (Day) _571-218-6216_ (Evening) _____

1. I am (check one):   ☑ a party to the mediation   ☐ an attorney representing a party

2. For this case, mediation was (check one):
   ☑ very appropriate   ☐ somewhat appropriate   ☐ not at all appropriate

Comments: _Gave us a chance to tell our side_
_____

3. Total hours spent in the mediation session(s): _2 hrs_   Number of Sessions: _____

4. The mediation process was:
   ☑ very helpful   ☐ somewhat helpful   ☐ not at all helpful

5. Mediation ended with an agreement on:
   ☑ all of the issues   ☐ some of the issues   ☐ none of the issues

6. Would you use mediation again?   ☑ yes   ☐ no

7. Would you recommend mediation to others?   ☑ yes   ☐ no

FORM ADR-1002  revised December 2011                                      (OVER)

287

CPSIA information can be obtained
at www.ICGtesting.com
Printed in the USA
BVHW052012230920
589463BV00005B/338